Gender and Motivation

Volume 45 of
the Nebraska Symposium
on Motivation

University of Nebraska Press
Lincoln and London 1998

Volume 45 of the Nebraska Symposium on Motivation

Gender and Motivation

Richard A. Dienstbier
Dan Bernstein

Series Editor
Volume Editor

Presenters
Carol Tavris

Los Angeles, California

Reed Larson

Professor of Human Development and Family Studies, Department of Human and Community Development, University of Illinois at Urbana-Champaign

Joseph Pleck

Professor of Human Development and Family Studies, Department of Human and Community Development, University of Illinois at Urbana-Champaign

Nicki R. Crick

Associate Professor, Institute of Child Development, University of Minnesota–Twin Cities

Nicole E. Werner

Doctoral Student, Institute of Child Development, University of Minnesota–Twin Cities

Juan F. Casas

Doctoral Student, Institute of Child Development, University of Minnesota–Twin Cities

Kathryn M. O'Brien

Doctoral Student, Institute of Child Development, University of Minnesota–Twin Cities

David A. Nelson

Doctoral Student, Institute of Child Development, University of Minnesota–Twin Cities

Jennifer K. Grotpeter

Research Associate, University of Colorado at Boulder

Kristian Markon

Doctoral Student, Institute of Child Development, University of Minnesota–Twin Cities

Leonore Tiefer

Clinical Associate Professor of Psychiatry, Albert Einstein College of Medicine and New York University School of Medicine

Diane L. Gill

Professor and Department Head, Department of Exercise and Sport Science, University of North Carolina at Greensboro

Portions of Leonore Tiefer's chapter were previously
published in *Sex Is Not a Natural Act and Other Essays*
(Boulder co: Westview, 1995).
Gender and Motivation is Volume 45 in the series
CURRENT THEORY AND RESEARCH
IN MOTIVATION

∞

"The Library of Congress has cataloged
this serial publication as follows:"
Nebraska Symposium on Motivation.
Nebraska Symposium on Motivation.
[Papers] v. [1]–1953–
Lincoln, University of Nebraska Press.
v. illus., diagrs. 22cm. annual.
Vol. 1 issued by the symposium under
its earlier name: Current Theory and
Research in Motivation.
Symposia sponsored by the Dept. of
Psychology of the University of Nebraska.
1. Motivation (Psychology)
BF683.N4   159.4082   53-11655
Library of Congress

Contents

vii   Dan Bernstein   *Introduction*

1   Carol Tavris   *The Science and Politics of Gender Research: The Meanings of Difference*

25   Reed Larson and Joseph Pleck   *Hidden Feelings: Emotionality in Boys and Men*

75   Nicki R. Crick, Nicole E. Werner, Juan F. Casas, Kathryn M. O'Brien, David A. Nelson, Jennifer K. Grotpeter, and Kristian Markon   *Childhood Aggression and Gender: A New Look at an Old Problem*

143   Leonore Tiefer   *Challenging Sexual Naturalism, the Shibboleth of Sex Research and Popular Sexology*

173   Diane L. Gill   *Gender and Competitive Motivation: From the Recreation Center to the Olympic Arena*

209   *Subject Index*

217   *Author Index*

Introduction

Dan Bernstein
University of Nebraska–Lincoln

This volume is about motivation and gender. The chapters outline recent research and conceptual analysis related to four important motivational constructs—sexuality, emotion, competition, and aggression. In each case the author has examined the relation between the motivational construct and gender; the chapters describe those relations and analyze their origins and implications. There are two primary ideas that connect these accounts of gender and motivation: the authors generally report great diversity within gender groups in the degree to which these motivational characteristics are found, and they note that there is much to be considered in exactly how these motivational constructs are defined and measured. One could easily conclude that there is tremendous overlap in the amount of aggression, sexuality, emotion, and competition shown by males and females, even given conventional conceptions of the measurement of those constructs. When an alternative and thoughtful reconstruction of the motivational variables is added to the analysis, the overlap becomes even greater, and differences disappear or even reverse their order. Faced with data showing substantial overlap in characteristics, one is left to ponder why human perception of gender differences is so richly caricatured and so firmly held. This is an emergent theme of the volume, a question that is not always directly asked but is suggested by the chapters taken as a whole.

Attribution of Essential Difference

It seems to be a fundamental feature of human perception that complex and changing patterns of sensation are transformed into stable and manageable entities. Shape and size constancy, for example, make it possible for people to navigate sensibly despite the constantly variable patterns of stimulation made by the physical features of the environment on the sense organs. There are parallel phenomena in the perception of people, as the contextually embedded actions of people are formed into coherent and stable accounts of individual difference through the attribution of dispositional traits or personality types. Sometimes these abstracted characteristics leave out so much contextual detail and individual variability that we call them stereotypes, but much of the time our dispositional map allows for successful navigation through the social world with a minimum of damage to self or other.

Sometimes psychological scholarship can inadvertently contribute to the development of generalizations about people, especially to generalizations about groups of people. Our professional task often seems to be the identification of common elements (which we call main effects) among the varied specific individual cases that make up different samples of humanity that are observed. Success in that task can be a function of finding a measurement procedure powerful enough or a sample large enough to reveal an existing main effect (in this case a difference between the groups) despite the wide variability within the groups being compared. Skill in accomplishing this goal is described by the terms *statistical* or *experimental power*, as it may require a high degree of such power to identify an important but small effect in the noisy behavioral contexts in which we work.

It is clear that skilled researchers recognize the limits of what can be said about individuals given such measurement procedures, and there are regular pronouncements warning consumers of the research not to overgeneralize the findings. These warnings are not new to psychology, however, and their long standing is evidence of the resilience of this form of human perception. In 1910 Robert S. Woodworth published an essay on racial differences in mental traits in the journal *Science*; he made this point extraordinarily clear with regard to both culture and race in two sections. First, while considering the notion of cultural or national "types" (such as the typical German or the typical southerner), Woodworth wrote:

> If we would scientifically determine the facts regarding a group of men, we should, no doubt, proceed to examine all the individuals in the group, or at least a fair and honest representation of them. The first fact that meets us when we proceed in this way is that the individuals differ from each other, so that no one can really be selected as representing the whole number. We do find, indeed, when we measure the stature or any other bodily fact, or when we test any native mental capacity, that the members of a natural group are disposed about an average, many of them lying near the average, and few lying far above or far below it; and we thus have the average as a scientific fact regarding the group. But the average does not generally coincide with the type, as previously conceived, nor do the averages of different groups differ so much as the so-called types differ. Moreover, the average is itself very inadequate, since it does not indicate the amount of variation that exists within the group—and this is one of the most important facts to be borne in mind in understanding any collection of individuals. It is specially important in comparing different groups of men, since the range of variation within either group is usually much greater than the difference between the averages of the groups. The groups overlap to such an extent that the majority of the individuals composing either group might perfectly well belong to the other. (pp. 171–172)

Woodworth then claims that human perception seems naturally to include a tendency to make those erroneous generalizations, in spite of the nature of the actual data. When suggesting that this form of thinking can be misapplied to questions of race he wrote:

> Our inveterate love for types and sharp distinctions is apt to stay with us even after we have become scientific, and vitiate our use of statistics to such an extent that the average becomes a stumbling-block rather than an aid to knowledge. We desire,

for example, to compare the brain weights of whites and of ne-
groes. We weigh the brains of a sufficient number of each
race—or let us at least assume the number to be sufficient.
When our measurements are all obtained and spread before
us, they convey to the unaided eye no clear idea of a racial difference, so much do they overlap. If they should become
jumbled together, we should never be able to separate the ne-
groes from the whites by aid of brain weight. But now we cast
up the average of each group, and find them to differ; and
though the difference is small, we straightway seize on it as the
important result, and announce that the negro has a smaller
brain than the white. We go a step further, and class the white
as a large-brained race, the negro as a small-brained. Such
transforming of difference of degree into differences of kind,
and making antitheses between overlapping groups, partakes
not a little of the ludicrous. (p. 172)

It seems clear that there are many group average differences to be
identified among subpopulations; no one disputes that observation.
Woodworth's point has more to do with how people use the data
than is it a complaint about the data themselves.

Despite Woodworth's warnings and many others since, reason-
able people who are repeatedly exposed to findings reported as significant mean differences or nonchance factors in a multivariate representation sometimes begin to think and talk as if those differences
were actually true in most individual cases. Readers begin to use
constructs such as culture, personality, gender, clinical diagnosis,
and race as if they indicated the existence of distinct categories of
people. Perhaps for the same reasons of efficiency that human perception produces constancy of size and shape, the frequent use of
culture as a researchable variable results in the production of cultural stereotypes dressed up in statistical significance. Similarly
there are many caricatures of gender that arise as an unwanted byproduct of a useful reconsideration of the role of gender as a variable
in psychological research.

My own interest in this phenomenon was piqued while teaching a course in cross-cultural psychology to advanced undergraduate psychology students. After reading two leading texts in cross-
cultural psychology, the students became very fluent in cultural regularities; for example, they were happy to state that "collectivist"

cultures would of course show one pattern of behavior while in an "individualist" culture one would find a different (and implicitly distinct) pattern of action. All of these constructions were in fact drawn from the material presented in the texts, as the authors reviewed study after study that reported statistically significant differences in the behavior of varying cultures. In many cases these differences correlated with abstract dimensions like individualism/collectivism, leading to the students' articulate statements about what the data meant. Ultimately I was distressed because it seemed that students were trafficking in cultural stereotypes, even though the stereotypes were dressed up in academically respectable terms. The fundamental error was being made; a small average difference was being interpreted to imply the existence of truly distinct populations.

The overall theme of this volume is to suggest that data reported in studies examining group variables such as culture, gender, personality, or race should be presented in a complete way that might reduce the tendency of readers to form unwarranted and unwanted caricatures of categories of people. In particular, the presentations in this volume refer to data and inferences based on the variable of gender; this is a crucial variable in human life, because even people who live in homogeneous communities with little cultural diversity generally encounter members of both genders. The importance of gender stereotyping cannot be overemphasized as a phenomenon in human perception, and it is hoped that some of the data presented in this volume will help readers remember that there is great diversity among the members of each gender. Further, it can be useful to compare the literal magnitude of the variability within a group to the mean difference between groups.

Visual and Verbal Representations of Differences

Graphical distributions of the raw data from any compared groups might provide some modest inoculation against unwarranted stereotyping. As an example of how this might be done, consider the following data from a very interesting, competent, and professional cross-cultural study. Gibbons, Richter, Wiley, and Stiles (1996) collected self-report data from adolescents in four different countries. The respondents rank-ordered the importance of ten factors in the selection of an opposite-sex ideal person, and the authors reported differences among the four countries in the average rankings of seven of the ten characteristics of an opposite-sex ideal. Among the many intriguing findings from the complete study, it was found that American adolescents ranked "being sexy" as very important and "liking children" as less important, whereas Guatemalan adolescents gave those two characteristics the opposite rankings. Gibbons et al. make a coherent argument that the pattern of data is congruent with the notion of collectivist and individualist cultures.

Professor Judith Gibbons of St. Louis University, expressing interest in the results of an additional examination of the data, has graciously provided access to the original data set. The new analysis was very simple; subgroups of the whole data set that might be interestingly compared were identified, and histograms that show the frequency of selection of each rank for two of the ten items in the Gibbons et al. (1996) set of characteristics were produced. Some of these comparisons are of major cultural groups as reported in the original article, but the data set was also divided by gender of the respondent. The graphical representations of the distributions were used to complement the analysis based on differences among means.

Gibbons et al. (1996) reported a significant difference between adolescents in the United States and in Guatemala in the ranked importance of liking children by an opposite-sex ideal person. Figure 1 shows the data represented as a histogram for each country. The difference reported is well represented in the figure, with the modal importance ranking being higher (3rd most important) for Guatemalan adolescents than for U.S. adolescents (10th most important). Visual inspection of the figure also reveals that the range of rankings for both countries was the same; all ten rankings were selected. Knowing an adolescent's home country would not allow one to rule out any of the possible rankings. Within the Guatemalan sample there were only small variations in the percent of participants using each rank, varying from about 5% to 15%. Within the U.S. sample the variation was greater, ranging from around 2% to slightly over 20%. There was, however, substantial overlap in category use; the middle categories of the ranking scale (ranks 3–8) were used by about 60% of the Guatemalan adolescents and by about 55% of the U.S. sample. Knowing only the country of origin for an ado-

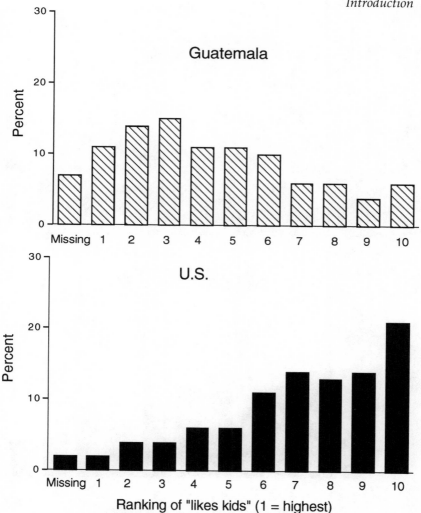

Figure 1. U.S. and Guatemalan adolescent ranking of "likes kids" in selection of opposite-sex ideal person (collapsed across gender).

lescent certainly changes the probability of finding extreme scores on the ranked importance of liking children, but it does not clearly identify a highly likely part of the range of possible ranks.

Similarly, Gibbons et al. (1996) reported a significant difference between adolescents in the United States and in Guatemala in the ranked importance of an opposite-sex ideal person being sexy. Figure 2 shows the data represented as a histogram for each country.

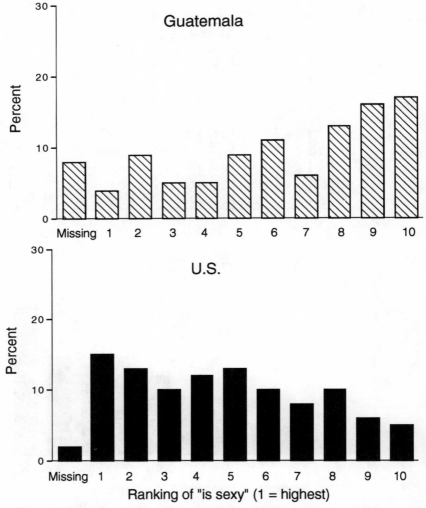

Figure 2. U.S. and Guatemalan adolescent ranking of "is sexy" in selection of oppo-site-sex ideal person (collapsed across gender).

The difference reported is well represented in the figure; the modal importance ranking of being sexy was higher (single most impor-tant) for U.S. adolescents than for Guatemalan adolescents (10th most important). Visual inspection of the figure also reveals that the range of rankings for both countries was the same; all ten rankings were selected. Knowing an adolescent's home country would not al-

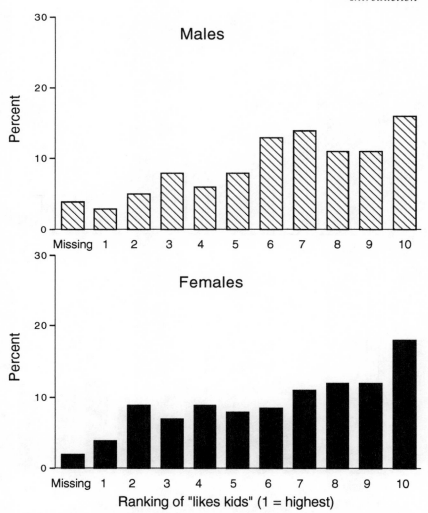

Figure 3. U.S. and Guatemalan adolescent ranking of "likes kids" in selection of oppo-site-sex ideal person (collapsed across country).

low one to rule out any of the possible rankings. Within the U.S. sample there were only small variations in the percent of partici-pants using each rank, varying from about 5% to 15%. Within the Guatemalan sample the variation was slightly greater, ranging from around 4% to slightly under 20%. Again there was substantial over-lap in category use; the middle categories of the ranking scale (ranks

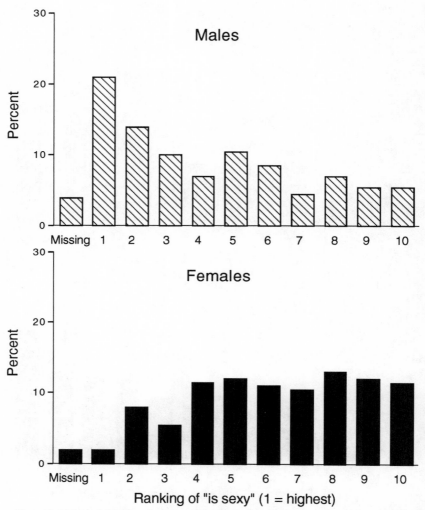

Figure 4. U.S. and Guatemalan adolescent ranking of "is sexy" in selection of opposite-sex ideal person (collapsed across country).

3–8) were used by about 50% of the Guatemalan adolescents and by
about 60% of the U.S. sample. Knowing only the country of origin
for an adolescent certainly changes the probability of finding extreme scores on the ranked importance of being sexy, but it does not
clearly identify a highly likely part of the range of possible ranks.

   The same kind of analysis of group effects was conducted by

gender on the data provided by Judith Gibbons; we combined the U.S. and Guatemalan samples and then divided them into male and female participants, collapsed across country. Figure 3 includes two histograms of the rankings of the importance of an opposite-sex ideal person liking children; one shows the rankings by males, and the other shows the rankings by females. Both the modal rank and the general pattern of the rankings are quite similar for both genders. Gibbons et al. (1996) did not test this difference, but these data would likely not show a mean rank difference between the genders. Figure 4 includes two histograms of the rankings of the importance of an opposite-sex ideal being sexy, and there appears to be a difference in the patterns that is comparable to those found with country. For males the modal ranking is the top category, the single most important category, and about 35% of the male participants ranked being sexy as the 1st or 2nd most important characteristic. Among females there was no clear mode, with about 12% selecting all categories from 4th through 10th most important; a little more than 10% of females rated being sexy as the 1st or 2nd most important characteristic.

Given the similarity of pattern in these rankings and the rankings by country analyzed by Gibbons et al. (1996), it is likely that a test of ranks would yield a gender difference on the importance of being sexy. Like the data divided by country of origin, however, there is substantial overlap in the rankings by men and by women. The full range of rankings was used by participants of both genders, and there was substantial overlap in use of the six middle ranks (3–8); roughly 45% of the males ranked being sexy in the middle range, and roughly 65% of females gave this factor ranks in the middle range. As with the analysis by country of origin, knowledge of gender alone does not substantially narrow the range of likely rank of importance of valuing a sexy opposite-sex ideal; there is a probability shift in the distribution, but there is great diversity in both distributions.

As a final analysis, the two variables (gender and country) were combined to examine the ranking of being sexy. Figure 5 shows separate histograms of those rankings for U.S. males, U.S. females, Guatemalan males, and Guatemalan females. An apparent interaction of the two variables would seem to account for the aggregated data. The lowest rankings of the importance of being sexy came

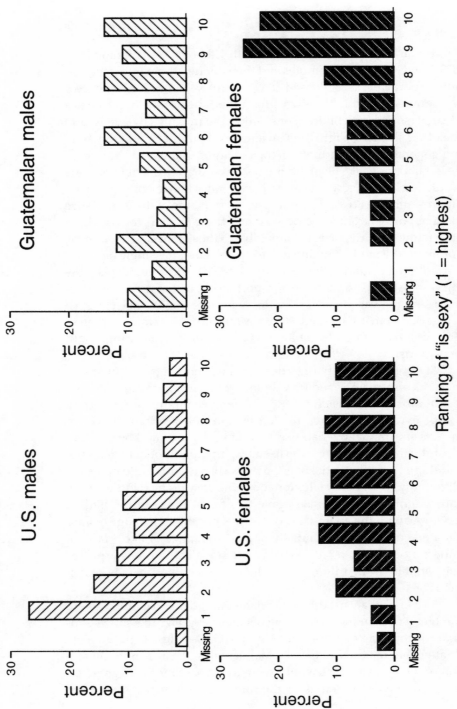

Figure 5. U.S. and Guatemalan adolescent ranking of "is sexy" in selection of opposite-sex ideal person (by gender and by country).

from Guatemalan females, and the highest rankings of importance came from U.S. males. Differences between groups are in fact often quite visible in the comparison of distributions of individual performance. The interaction between gender and country shown in Figure 5 is a good example, and use of this graphical technique may actually strengthen the perception of an important between-group difference.

These separated graphs show the most pronounced variations and yield an important insight into the pattern shown in the aggregate data; yet the figures make clear that there is great diversity in the rankings of the different groups. Three of the four graphs use the full range of ranks (only Guatemalan females do not use the 1st rank), and over the middle range of the ranks there is little systematic variation from an expected flat distribution. Even when a conceptually interesting finding may appear at the group level, there is evidence in the distribution that the group pattern is due to a plurality of individuals whose responses fall in the extremes. The visual representation of the distribution of performance within each group makes it clear that not all individuals show the effect that may be reported as the general finding.

These graphical representations and analyses are neither new nor profound; the suggestion is only that it is useful to present the distribution of data as a complement to any summaries of group differences. This form of data presentation may be useful if it prompts observers to make direct observation of the overlap in the actual performance of the groups being compared. When confronted with the extent of the overlap, including the wide range of scores within each group, readers of the data may be less inclined to create a caricature of a typical group member who is remarkably different from a similarly constructed typical member of the other group(s).

Influencing Readers' Perceptions

One might reasonably ask whether authors who present group data have a responsibility to actively influence how readers construct images of the data. If readers draw inappropriate conclusions from research, whose problem is it? In many cases, responsible authors go to great lengths to warn readers against making the kind of inferences that are described here. For example, the authors of one of the texts

(Smith & Bond, 1993) used in the cross-cultural psychology course described above went to extraordinary lengths to warn readers away from the error of inferring distinct populations. In discussing Hofstede's dimension of individualism and collectivism, they identify the problem specifically: "As applied to the study of cultures, this fallacy would be the mistaken belief that, because two cultures differ, then any two members of those cultures must necessarily also differ in the same manner. For instance, someone might expect that, because America scores higher than Guatemala on individualism, then a particular American is bound to be more independent or individualist than a particular Guatemalan. This is not so" (p. 31). They even provide a diagram of overlapping distributions to highlight the point.

Despite this very clear instruction, however, readers drift into statements that summarize results in ways that ignore the substantial overlap. Perhaps it is in part because the authors report the findings in their field with the shorthand of mean differences found to be statistically significant (presumably for reasons of efficiency and space). When chapter after chapter reports or describes simple differences without showing visually the amount of overlap, the impact of one warning, no matter how clear, is lost. The lesson about a fallacy is overwhelmed by the continuous stream of results presented in language consistent with the notion that differences between groups reflect essential characteristics of the members, rather than slight differences in the modes of very broad distributions.

Another of Woodworth's contributions to psychology was the s-o-r model of learning, in which it is the individual's subjective perception of the world that influences responding. That model presupposes an active person (o for organism) constructing a personal representation of the stimuli (s) perceived, and this model anticipated the contemporary cognitive view of learning a new response (r). Knowing that there are different perceptions of the same stimuli, authors should be interested in any presentation procedures that are more likely to generate subjective representations that are more correct (by the author's standards). I would particularly draw the reader's attention to the visual presentation of data provided by Reed Larson and by Nicki Crick in their chapters on emotion and aggression in this volume; these figures allow the reader to see how the differences reported play out in the context of the diversity of emotionality both between and within genders.

Authors may wish to examine empirically whether a particular visual representation of the performance gives rise to caricatures and stereotypes more or less often than does a numerical representation of central tendency. If there is such an effect, it would also be interesting to ask why it occurs. In principle there could be sufficient information in the numerical data provided to make the same judgment; with means, standard deviations, and measures of skew and kurtosis, an expert judge could draw the same conclusions from either numbers or a graph of the data. Recent work by John Flowers and colleagues (Flowers & Hauer, 1995; Flowers, Buhman, & Turnage, 1997) has demonstrated that observers make very good estimates of correlation from temporally distributed auditory pitch, given sufficient experience with the task. Similar research could examine the tendency of experienced and novice judges to form group caricatures, comparing performance based on visual and numeric representation of the range of individual performance.

Contents of This Volume

The chapters in this book represent analysis by leading scholars whose work is widely appreciated by a variety of audiences. Carol Tavris has done integrative work in many areas of psychology, including gender, health, anger, and critical thinking in higher education. Her textbooks are excellent examples of challenging writing for students, and her writing has earned her both awards and a large readership. Reed Larson does research on adolescence, studying crime, anorexia, mood, leisure, and solitude. His present research on emotionality is especially valuable for its identification of forms of strong emotional experience that are common in men and the ecological approach to observation of emotion in everyday life. Nicki Crick studies aggression that manifests itself in ways other than physical violence, and generates an important account of relational aggression—interpersonal aggression that damages relations rather than body parts. This perspective gives a very different look at the distribution of fundamentally aggressive motivation across genders. Leonore Tiefer is a practicing sexologist whose writing highlights those ways in which gender roles in sexuality are socially constructed. Her perspective is an essential complement to the generally held view that sexual activity is dominated by biological influences. Diane Gill has studied competition and gender in a wide variety of contexts, including identifying the advantages and disadvantages of being competitive. Her work has often highlighted the intensely competitive behavior of elite female athletes.

The authors invited to present papers at the 1997 Nebraska Symposium on Motivation were identified because their scholarship has demonstrated (at least to some readers) that there is overlap in the distributions of male and female performance. It is not the general position of the authors or the editor that gender is an unimportant variable, nor would most of these authors reject the notion that essential differences in the biological nature of men and women may have contributed to whatever distributions of performance emerge. These authors mainly leave that question unanswered or even unaddressed. There is no shortage of writing available that articulates the utility of a biological account of the origin of gender-related patterns of behavior. At issue in the present volume is exactly what can be learned from the magnitude and nature of the differences that are found.

The claim is not being made that biology is totally irrelevant to human life, particularly in the identification of behavior patterns in gender groups. Instead, these authors report those ways in which there is (and should be) remarkable diversity within each gender group. Most psychologists assume that the behavior of an individual is a joint product of nature and nurture, and that point is not at dispute. Regardless of the particular mix of biological and social influences that generated the behavior, the data presented by these authors argue that knowing a person's gender does not allow one to readily or narrowly identify where an individual will fall on a dimension of sexuality, aggression, competition, or emotion. Put another way, knowing how aggressive, competitive, or emotional a person is will not often allow one to state with any certainty the person's gender. Except at very extreme levels, the distributions show remarkable overlap, and that fact is too often lost in conversations dominated by simple reports of measures of central tendency.

In Appreciation

It should be noted that gender studies is not a special professional interest of mine, and I approached the development of this symposium as an opportunity to explore some practical ideas about gender by hearing from people who specialize in that topic. I am deeply grateful to Marcela Raffaelli, Deb Hope, Renee Michael, and Lynn Marcus for their excellent conversations and for suggestions of readings and speakers. I am privileged to have such excellent colleagues who encourage me to continue my education with their assistance. I am also happy to have worked closely with Karen Smith and Kris Veit in the development of the visual analysis of group data. It was a great pleasure to work with interesting and creative people who enjoy solving puzzles and exploring data. Finally, I would like to thank Carol Tavris for her contribution to the development of this symposium. The quality of her conversations about psychology in general, and gender studies in particular, is a model to which we should all aspire. While no single edited volume can be a complete account of any important topic, I believe that the chapters included here provide an interesting and thought-provoking introduction to an important perspective on the relation between gender and motivation.

REFERENCES

Flowers, J. H., & Hauer, T. A. (1995). Musical versus visual graphs: Cross-modal equivalence in perception of time series data. *Human Factors, 37*, 553–569.

Flowers, J. H., Buhman, D. C., & Turnage, K. D. (1997). Cross-modal equivalence of visual and auditory scatterplots for exploring bivariate data samples. *Human Factors, 39*(3), 341–351.

Gibbons, J. L., Richter, R. R., Wiley, D. C., & Stiles, D. A. (1996). Adolescents' opposite-sex ideal in four countries. *Journal of Social Psychology, 136*(4), 531–537.

Smith, P. B., & Bond, M. H. (1993). *Social psychology across cultures: Analysis and perspectives.* New York: Harvester Wheatsheaf.

Woodworth, R. S. (1910). Racial differences in mental traits. *Science, 31*(788), 171–186.

The Science and Politics of Gender Research: The Meanings of Difference

Carol Tavris
Los Angeles, California

Recently something happened to remind me of just how long I have been writing about gender issues and the status of women. Twenty years ago, Carole Wade and I published one of the first texts in women's studies, *The Longest War*. To remind you of what it was like in 1977, many people still believed in penis envy. So, in our book, to make the point that Freud might have been a tad biased in his view that half the human race feels anatomically inferior to the other half, I included a true family story of a 4-year-old English girl who was given a bath with her male cousin for the first time. According to Freud, of course, she should have been deeply shocked by observing the stately penis of a 4-year-old boy, concluding unconsciously that she had been castrated. In this case, however, being a well-mannered English child, she waited before commenting until her mother tucked her into bed that night. "Mummy," she said, "isn't it a blessing he doesn't have it on his face?"

Fade out to a few years ago, when I was teaching psychology at UCLA and told the same anecdote in a discussion of Freud. A graduate student in philosophy who was auditing the class came to see me the next day. She said she had repeated the story to a friend of hers in women's studies, only to be told, "Oh, that! It's an urban legend."

So that's how long I have been writing about gender: long enough for my best stories to have become urban folktales.

Though that story makes me feel pretty old, I have to say it is interesting to be old enough to see how, in my own lifetime, gender research has changed, along with the entrance of women into psychology and with changing social and economic conditions in our society and elsewhere in the world. When I was writing *The Longest War*, most married women could not get credit and mortgages in their own names. No American woman had been a miner, an astronaut, a rabbi, an Episcopalian minister, an attorney general, an armed forces general, a secretary of state, a Supreme Court justice, a "fireman," or a hot-dog vendor at Yankee stadium. Most men and plenty of women believed that women could not and should not run a company or a country, and that men could not and should not diaper a baby or cook for the family. Women were as rare as egrets in law, medicine, business, carpentry, police, politics, and the military. Of course, it was not all bad then: PMS had not been invented.

Much has changed in the past 20 years—and many things have not. One of the things that has not changed is the popularity of the belief that men and women are inherently, unchangeably opposite in their psyches, nature, culture, brains, or biology:

John Gray tells us that *Men Are from Mars, Women Are from Venus*, a book so popular for so long that it has spawned sequels (*Mars and Venus in the Bedroom*), seminars, and therapy franchises.

Jungians tell us that men and women are guided by opposite archetypes, a view popularized by the best-sellers *Iron John* and *Women Who Run with Wolves*.

Neuroscientists tell us that men and women have different brains, and that our brains operate differently.

Sociobiologists tell us that male promiscuity and female chastity are hard-wired reproductive strategies.

Psychiatrists and gynecologists tell us that women have hormones, and therefore moods, but men do not. Hence women have "Premenstrual Syndrome," which, in its extreme form, can become "Premenstrual Dysphoric Disorder" (American Psychiatric Association, 1994). Men, however, do not have "HyperTestosterone Syndrome"; nor have psychiatrists invented a label for "Testosterone Deficiency Dysphoric Disorder."

Cultural feminists, many of whom are academic psychologists and psychotherapists, tell us that women and men speak different languages and have inherently different leadership styles, "ways of knowing," ways of thinking, ways of connecting, ways of feeling, and styles of moral reasoning[1] (Belenky, Clinchy, Goldberger, & Tarule, 1986; Chodorow, 1978; Gilligan, 1982).

If you read enough of these theories, you will surely conclude that women and men are from different planets or at least are different earthly species. The paradox is that even as these notions achieve widespread popularity, men and women are actually becoming more alike—in how they live, what they do, and how they think (Bohan, 1997). In just a few decades, a transformation has been occurring in the social and economic landscape: women's participation in the labor force, and men's in the family, has grown exponentially. The doctrine of "separate spheres"—his for work, hers for family—which guided social science research on gender since the Industrial Revolution, is gone for good. American families consisting of one breadwinning husband and a wife who stays home with children—the postwar ideal that lasted less than a decade—now account for 3% of all families (Barnett & Rivers, 1996; Coontz, 1997).

The entry of women into formerly male-only professions is progressing unmistakably, although erratically and not without efforts—including violent efforts—by the old guard to preserve the traditional ways. Overall, however, there has been a steady change in men's attitudes toward women at work and in politics. Men's endorsement of gender equality has steadily increased; the number of men expressing prejudice toward women executives, for example, declined from 41% in 1965 to only 5% in 1985 (Tougas, Brown, Beaton, & Joly, 1995); and between 1970 and 1995 antiwoman attitudes in general dropped sharply (Twenge, 1997).

As women are moving into the public and political spheres, men are doing more in the private domain of the family (Gerson, 1993). You would never know this by reading all the news stories about men who fear commitment and about deadbeat dads (a real problem, of course), but men's participation in household chores and childcare has been rising steadily, as shown both in community surveys and family studies (Barnett & Rivers, 1996; Coontz, 1997; Stacey, 1996). For example, in her interviews with 300 dual-income couples, Rosalind Barnett found that "the collaborative couple" has become the norm; wives are not the "selfish careerists" of media stereotype, she notes. Nor are today's fathers the remote, work-obsessed dads of the 1950s; most are closely involved in all aspects of their children's care, and when they do not get enough time with their children, their levels of distress rise (Barnett & Rivers, 1996). Judith Stacey (1996), doing qualitative research with working-class families, reported the same thing, somewhat to her own surprise: almost all of the men she observed or heard about routinely performed domestic tasks that her own blue-collar father and his friends would never have even considered.

Differences between males and females are at the greatest at two stages of life: when children are 2 to 6, acquiring the basic cognitive schema of what it means to be male or female, and again in adolescence, when they are learning about dating and mating (Maccoby, 1998). At those two stages, they act like the Gender Police, enforcing rules their own parents have long forgotten. But after that, the story is very different. In studies of cognitive abilities and personality traits, here, too, the overall picture is one of diminishing differences, although of course some studies continue to find differences in some traits, such as self-esteem (Feingold, 1994). Lawrence Cohn (1991) analyzed 65 studies, involving more than 9,000 people, to determine the extent of gender differences in personality, moral reasoning, and other variables. He found that differences were greatest among junior and senior high school students, largely because girls mature earlier than boys. But these differences declined significantly among college students and disappeared entirely among older men and women.

To question the belief that men and women differ in profound and basic ways—their brains, personalities, and abilities—is not to deny that men and women differ at all. Of course they do. They differ in power and resources, life experiences, and reproductive processes. Moreover, to say that men and women are equally capable of sexual pleasure, for instance, does not mean that both sexes have the same sexual experiences, or regard their bodies the same way, or feel equally safe, respected, and attractive. Similarly, to say that the sexes are equally capable of feeling deep emotion does not mean that society encourages them to express those feelings the same way.

Yet why, in spite of incontrovertible evidence about the rapid changes in gender roles and behavior—changes that many people have observed in their own lives—do so many people like to think that the sexes are opposite and unchanging? In *Civilization and Its Discontents*, Freud (1962) observed that European anti-Semitism was at its most virulent during assimilationist periods, when the differences between Jews and the larger society were actually diminishing. The success of theories of difference tells us that they are capturing something that men and women find true or likely about their experiences with one another, and it also tells us that there must be many constituencies that benefit from the belief that men and women are inherently different.

The Study of Gender

The popular theories about sex differences are part of a long tradition of research that takes what is called an *essentialist* approach. Essentialists regard a gender-related attitude, trait, or behavior as being something in the person—internal, persistent, consistent across situations and time (Bohan, 1997). When essentialists say that "Women are more emotional than men" or "Men are more aggressive than women," they are thinking of qualities and behaviors that are located in individuals and bunch up in one sex more often than in the other. Many essentialists, including sociobiologists and evolutionary psychologists, believe that these sex differences are biologically caused and occur regardless of socialization (Lytton & Romney, 1991). But psychodynamic theorists, such as Nancy Chodorow (1978), believe that these differences are caused by unconscious dynamics in the early child-parent relationship; and cultural feminists, such as Carol Gilligan (1982), maintain that they are caused by cultural and environmental experiences.

In contrast, *social constructionist* views hold that there is no "essence" of masculinity and femininity, for these concepts and labels are endlessly changing, constructed from the eye of the observer and the conditions of our lives (Crawford & Marecek, 1989; Gergen, 1985, 1994; Hare-Mustin & Marecek, 1990; Unger, 1990). As Janis Bohan (1997) shows, the difference between essentialist and constructionist views of gender is not an argument between biological and learning explanations; that is, it is not that essentialists think that differences are biologically ordained and constructionists think they are acquired through socialization. The difference between essentialists and constructionists has to do with *where they locate gender*.

Constructionists maintain that although anatomical sex is something that is biologically given, *gender*—all those qualities, actions, and attributes we attach to one sex or the other—is a product of social conventions and agreements. It does not reside in our anatomical sex but in our interactions with one another. As West and Zimmerman (1991) put it, we do not *have* a gender, we *do* gender. Gender is a performance, which is why the behavior of men and women often depends more on with whom they are interacting and their particular situation than on anything intrinsic about the sex they are. In some situations women and men "do" feminine, and in others we "do" masculine, and sometimes we do a combination (Deaux & Major, 1990). A teenage boy on his own at home may "do" feminine by tenderly caring for his baby sister but "do" masculine by behaving in stereotypically male ways when he is out with the guys.

Here is an example of "gender performance." In two recent studies of aggression, men behaved more aggressively than women in a competitive video war game when they were individuated— that is, when their names and background information about them were spoken aloud, heard by all participants, and recorded publicly by the experimenter. Accordingly, the men "did" masculine and the women "did" feminine, as they felt they should. But when the men and women believed that they were anonymous to their fellow students and to the experimenter, they did not differ in how aggressively they played the game (Lightdale & Prentice, 1994). Similarly, a meta-analysis of 64 studies found that gender differences in aggressive behavior drop to almost zero when women are provoked (Bettencourt & Miller, 1996). These studies suggest that when women are provoked enough or when they are anonymous, they forget the "I'm-not-aggressive, I'm-a-girl" gender performance they are supposed to play.

Unlike essentialist theories, which regard gender as the independent variable ("If I know whether you are a man or a woman, can I predict how aggressive you are?"), constructionist approaches regard gender as the dependent variable. Constructionists want to know what factors predict how we come to define ourselves, label ourselves, and behave as a man, a woman, or something else. Why is aggressive behavior "gendered": that is, why do we associate it only with men and overlook it in women? Why are gender categories fluid for some individuals and cultures and rigid for others? Why do the qualities associated with one sex or the other change and vary, historically and cross-culturally? The constructionist view of gender also directs us to pay attention to the social context and uses of research. Why do we pay more attention to some differences than others? Why do we overlook similarities? What are the consequences—for men, women, and society—of the belief that the sexes differ so fundamentally?

Constructionists marshal four main lines of evidence that suggest the limitations of the essentialist approach:

Essentialism Confuses Snapshots with Blueprints As Kay Deaux and Brenda Major (1987) observed a decade ago, "researchers attempting to document and replicate sex differences have often found them elusive, a case of 'now you see them, now you don't'" (p. 369). The reason is that traditional studies of sex differences—in which you round up some men and women, measure their attitudes, behavior, or brains, and hope you find a publishable difference—give us a snapshot of how some men and women are behaving or thinking at any given historical moment (Deaux, 1984).

Snapshots are interesting, of course; it is always fun to look at old photos. They tell us about change, such as the news that men are doing more housework and childcare than ever before. Sometimes they alert us to problems we need to address. For example, although sex differences in verbal and math abilities have declined appreciably over the years, they are not gone. Boys still have more trouble than girls do learning to read, and students who cannot read well are more likely to drop out of high school and get into trouble (Halpern, 1989). Similarly, though girls do as well as boys in meta-analyses that combine studies of all math skills, boys still have a significant advantage in spatial visualization (McGuinness, 1993). These differences—and those between children from different cultures—are important for parents and educators to understand if they want to find better ways of ensuring that all children do well.

The problem occurs when people confuse snapshots with blueprints: when they infer that a difference that turns up in a given study reflects an essential, built-in, unchanging quality attributable to the individual's sex. Many people do not notice the significance of the fact that these snapshots tend to get dated very quickly. The 1996 presidential election, for instance, generated a lot of discussion about the "gender gap," the fact that more women supported Bill Clinton than Robert Dole by a margin of some 15%. The jump from snapshot to blueprint was immediate: Democrats attributed this difference to women's greater compassion and nurturance, and conservative Republicans such as Irving Kristol attributed it to women's greater sentimentality, lack of competitiveness, and aversion to free-market economics. Both sides were assuming that something in women's "nature" makes them vote Democratic. Few recalled that there was no gender gap in the elections won by Dwight Eisenhower and Richard Nixon, and only a small one in the case of George Bush. Few thought that anything other than self-interest was creating the wealth gap, race gap, and sexual orientation gap— all of which were far wider. And few people wondered why marriage and children apparently neutralize women's gene for voting Democratic and make many of them more conservative.

Essentialism Falsely Universalizes The idea that "women are this, and men are that"—although we are all susceptible to using this kind of language—leads to the false impression that the differences are universal and timeless. When I was investigating common beliefs about anger, I would hear all the time that "women" have more problems expressing anger than men do and are more likely to "turn anger inward." Well, which women? The ones screaming at their children in the supermarket? New York women? Mormons? Iraqi women? All Iraqi women? Swedish women today and those of the 14th century?

Biological research is particularly vulnerable to this kind of universalizing. Most psychologists would never dream of generalizing from a study of 14 people to all human beings, but many people have no qualms generalizing from a study of 14 brains to all brains. They forget that brains vary the way fingerprints and noses do. They are also often quick to conclude that any differences they observe are the cause of gender differences, but of course brain differences can also be caused by behavior, drugs and medications, nutrition, degree of environmental stimulation, and life experiences (Diamond, 1993; Fausto-Sterling, 1997; Kolb, 1996).

For example, a famous 1982 study of 14 brains reported a nearly significant sex difference in the size and shape of the corpus callosum, the bundle of fibers that connects the two hemispheres (de Lacoste-Utamsing & Holloway, 1982). This news made the cover of *Science* and all major newspapers, and researchers were quick to speculate that it explained male superiority in art, music, math, and science (Tavris, 1992). Ten years later, William Byne (1993), reviewing all studies, found that only the 1982 study reported the splenium to be larger in women. Two very early studies (in 1906 and 1909) found that it was larger in men, and 21 studies since 1982 have found no sex differences at all. Byne's review did not make the cover of *Science*, or its inside pages either.

Essentialism Fosters Stereotypic Thinking Not only do stereotypes of sex differences inaccurately and inadequately describe actual human beings, but they also influence what researchers see and fail to see. For example, the common stereotypes that "men are aggressive" and "women are nurturant" have caused many to overlook the frequency of male nurturance and female aggression in every culture. When David Gilmore (1990) examined how cultures define manhood, he expected to find masculinity equated with selfishness and hardness. Yet by resisting this stereotype, he was able to see that masculinity frequently entails generosity and sacrifice—two socially important forms of nurturance. Men nurture their families and society, he observed, by bringing home food for their families, by risking or sacrificing their lives to rescue fellow citizens, and by dying if necessary in faraway places to defend their families and nations.

Conversely, the stereotype of women as being nurturant and cooperative overlooks the richly abundant evidence of female aggressiveness and competitiveness, as Nicki Crick and Diane Gill show in other chapters. Women behave as aggressively as men when aggression is defined as saying intentionally hurtful things; as spreading rumors and lies to harm another person's reputation; as slapping, kicking, biting, or throwing objects during disputes; as abusing and humiliating their children; as having bellicose attitudes toward their enemies; and as supporting and participating in war, in whatever ways their societies have permitted (Campbell, 1993; Crick & Grotpeter, 1995; Elshtain, 1987; Gelles & Straus, 1988).

Another good example of the way that essentialism promotes stereotyping may be seen in the example of gender and emotion. There is little evidence from around the world that one sex feels emotions more often than the other; love, grief, anger, fear, shame, and the rest of the human panoply of feeling are evenly distributed (Baumeister, Stillwell, & Wotman, 1990; Fischer, 1993; Hatfield & Rapson, 1996; Oatley & Jenkins, 1996; Shaver & Hazan, 1993; Shields, 1991). But men and women do differ—at present, in some ways, in some cultures—in how they "do" emotion: how they express it, and to whom, and where. In North America, women are more likely than men to express their feelings openly, especially emotions that reveal vulnerability, such as fear, sadness, loneliness, shame, and guilt (Fischer, 1993; Grossman & Wood, 1993; Nolen-Hoeksema, 1990). In general, men learn that expressing emotions of "weakness" will bring them negative consequences.

Starting in childhood, many boys develop a language of depression that differs appreciably from that of girls and women (Cancian, 1987; Stapley & Haviland, 1989). The result is that many mental-health professionals and laypeople alike infer that men suffer less than women when relationships are in trouble, or that men are incapable of love, or that they are cold and unfeeling.

In her study of men and women after divorce, Catherine Riessman (1990) resisted this essentialist impulse to stereotype. The women in her sample were expressing their depression in the culturally approved language of grief for women: crying, talking about their feelings, sleeping too much, overeating, and generally scoring high on the Beck Depression Inventory. The men were suffering just as much, Riessman found, but were expressing it in ways that were stereotypically masculine and thus that they could reveal without conflict or shame—"frantic work," heavy drinking, driving too fast, having difficulties on the job, and having numerous physical ailments and stress symptoms. Other psychologists are now suggesting that the higher rates of drug abuse and violent behavior among men are often masking men's depression and anxiety (Canetto, 1992; Kessler, McGonagle, Zhao, Nelson, et al., 1994).

The essentialist stereotype that men are unemotional or cold and women are emotional and warm also causes us to overlook the situations in which men and women are permitted to be expressive and those in which both must suppress feelings. It causes us to overlook the way culture, social class, occupation, age, and situation affect whether and how people will express their feelings—and to whom. And it ignores the speed of change in rules concerning emotion when conditions change.[2]

Essentialist Theories Conflate Sex with Circumstances Finally, many apparent gender differences vanish when we consider context, power relations, the sex ratio of the group, and other such external factors. Here are a few examples from some of the more famous differences we hear about:

Common belief: Women are more intuitive and better able to read another person's nonverbal signals than men (Hall, 1987). *Evidence*: Actually, women's intuition is more properly called subordinate's intuition; the difference pretty much vanishes when you control for the status and authority of the participants (Fiske, 1993; Henley, 1995; Lakoff, 1990; Snodgrass, 1985, 1992). The powerless person—whether a child, an employee, a captive, or a non-income-earning spouse—needs to know how the powerful partner is feeling in order to know how to behave around him or her. Likewise, women's "ways of knowing"—supposedly more relational and interconnected—are the powerless's ways of knowing (Kanter, 1993).

Common belief: Women speak differently than men do: for instance, women are more likely than men to word their requests as questions ("Would you mind opening the door?"), or they will add delicate little tag questions to their assertions ("Women make less money than men . . . don't you think?"). *Evidence*: Actually, the women who talk this way typically do so only when they are talking to men, not when they are talking to other women. One reason, as Linda Carli (1990) found, may be that men, although more likely to respect a woman who sounds authoritative than one who sounds hesitant, tend to *like* women better when their speech is full of hesitancies, tag questions, and other tentative expressions. Moreover, when men are subordinate—for example, on the witness stand being questioned by an intimidating attorney, or talking to their professors—they tend to speak with the same hesitations, tag questions, and so forth (O'Barr, 1983).

Common belief: Women make moral decisions on the basis of compassion and caring, whereas men make theirs on the basis of abstract rules of justice (Gilligan, 1982). *Evidence*: Men and women base their moral decisions on compassion *and* on abstract principles of justice; they worry about feelings *and* fairness—depending on the situation they are in and what they are reasoning about (Clopton & Sorell, 1993; Cohn, 1991; Friedman, Robinson, & Friedman, 1987; Thoma, 1986; Wark & Krebs, 1996). Women and men use "justice" reasoning when they are thinking about highly abstract ethical dilemmas and "care" reasoning when they are thinking about intimate dilemmas in their own lives (Walker, deVries, & Trevethan, 1987; Clopton & Sorell, 1993). In other words, men and women "do" feminine moral reasoning when they are worrying about their loved ones, and they "do" masculine moral reasoning when they are in law school.

Common belief: Men are more likely than women to express anger directly and abusively. *Evidence*: The difference in expressions of anger pretty much vanishes when you consider the status, culture, and circumstances of the people involved. In the United States, both sexes tend to be indirect and manipulative when they are angry at someone who has more power than they—say, bosses and police officers—and both sexes are equally likely to shout abusively at people with less power than they—say, store clerks and children (Tavris, 1989).

Biology and Constructionism: Bridging the Dualism

Social constructionist approaches to gender are generally thought of as being antithetical to biological explanations, and politically and historically this has certainly been true. At our symposium, it became abundantly clear that more men than women in the audience endorsed sociobiological (or even biobiological) theories of gender differences. Gosh; why would men be favorably disposed toward a theory that male promiscuity and dominance are hard-wired? For their part, many women reflexively reject any research suggesting a biological component in gender differences. Gosh; why would women worry about biological findings suggesting that their hormones make them irrational and that their brains are deficient? Many women in psychology have long held an antipathy toward biological research on sex differences, and for good reason; as Leonore Tiefer (1995) has shown in the case of sexuality, Stephanie Shields (1975) in the case of brain research, and Stephen Jay Gould (1996) in the case of intelligence, it is a history marked by prejudice, reductionism, the misuse of data, and the stigmatizing of groups or individuals thought to be biologically "inferior."

Nevertheless, I think we can understand and accept the important contributions of biological research as long as we resist the temptation to reduce all of the complexities of men's and women's behavior to genes, hormones, and temperament. The evidence today is simply overwhelming for the role of biological factors in temperament, personality traits, some mental disorders, and other domains (Plomin, DeFries, McClearn, & Rutter, 1997). In some cases, as in the study of obesity, ulcers, autism, schizophrenia, or impulsive rage, biological findings are making purely psychological theories passé and have had liberating consequences (Tavris & Wade, 1997). George Gershwin's headaches were caused by a brain tumor, not "repressed rage," as his psychoanalyst thought. Bruno Bettelheim's nonsensical but inflexible notions about the role of "refrigerator mothers" in creating their children's autism, now known to be a neurological disorder, caused thousands of parents unnecessary anguish (Pollak, 1997).

Thus biological research itself is not a problem, any more than psychological research is. Constructionist views invite us always to consider the interpretations, uses, and misuses of research. Michael Bailey (1993), whose studies of possible genetic elements in homosexuality have caused much debate, has pointed out that a society prejudiced against gay men and lesbians will use any research to abet its animosity. Evidence that homosexuality has a biological component can be used to reduce homophobia and make discrimination against gay men and lesbians illegal; or it can be used as evidence of a biological "defect" to be corrected. Conversely, evidence that homosexuality is a fluid category of behaviors that have nothing to do with genetics can be used to reduce homophobia and increase tolerance toward the remarkable diversity of human sexual behavior; or it can be used, as it now is, to implement cruel behavioral techniques to "cure" young boys' "sissy" behavior. Phyllis Burke (1996) describes the behavioral methods currently being used to toughen up boys who are too gentle, who make friends with girls, who don't join with other boys in teasing and hitting the girls, and who play with the "wrong"—i.e., sex-inappropriate—toys. The psychiatrists and psychologists doing this "therapy" diagnose the boys as having Gender Identity Disorder, but the real problem seems to be the adults' fear of homosexuality.

The argument, therefore, is not about biological findings per se; social constructionists do not deny that people have bodies, hormones, emotions, or brains. However, they dispute the assumption of many sociobiologists, evolutionary psychologists, and neuroscientists that biology is somehow fundamental and primary, that biological factors provide a "basic" level of explanation, upon which learning and culture are merely superficial glosses. To constructionists, biology is not the end of the conversation—it is the start. Yes, evolution saw to it that we all eat and that we are programmed to store excess calories as fat, in case another famine comes along. Yes, there is now strong evidence that genetics plays a major role in a person's body shape, disposition to gain weight, and some kinds of obesity (Allison, Heshka, Neale, Lykken, et al., 1994; Bouchard, Tremblay, Despres, Nadeau, et al., 1990). But constructionists are more interested in why so many people do not eat when they are hungry (e.g., to lose weight, to seem appropriately "feminine," or to follow social rules and manners) and why many people do eat when they are not hungry (e.g., to be sociable or to be socially accepted). Constructionists would want to know why we eat only with some classes of people, why some foods become culturally taboo and thus disgusting, and why entire categories of people become defined as inappropriate dining companions (such as, in differing times and places, children, servants, subordinates, and wives) (Harris, 1985).

The chapters in this symposium publication illuminate, in different ways, the limitations of biology in accounting for gender and the gendered behavior of individuals. Their unifying theme can be seen as a critique of what Leonore Tiefer in this volume calls "the shibboleth of naturalism" that is often fostered by sociobiological explanations: the idea that what is natural survives, and that what has survived must be natural.

Reed Larson shows that although emotions certainly have a biological basis, there is no evidence of a sex difference in the frequency with which they are experienced; emotions, he shows, are a *process*, and the differences between men and women are situational and varying.

Nicki Crick shows that aggression is just as "natural" for girls as for boys, depending on what you are looking for and what you are prepared to see. Evolutionary psychologists, defining aggression as the harmful behavior more typical of men than women (hitting, punching, and other physical assaults), overlooked the form that aggression is more likely to take in girls and women—what Crick calls *relational aggression*. Readers of her chapter will be hard-pressed ever to say again that men are "naturally" more aggressive than women.

Leonore Tiefer shows that people like to justify their own culture's sexual practices and beliefs by calling them "natural," but the behavior thus rationalized is historically and culturally enormously variable. Thus some cultures think it is natural that women have the greater sex drive, whereas others think that men naturally have the greater sex drive. In some eras it is natural that children are sexual; in others it is equally natural that children are asexual. Homosexuality is natural in one place and "an act against nature" in another. Diane Gill shows how claims of what is natural about women and competition, and women and physical fitness, have likewise changed over time, with women's changing status in society. In some eras people assumed that it is natural for women to abhor exercise, a fit body, and competition; that only an "unnatural" woman would want to swim the Hudson, race in the Olympics, or achieve perfection in her chosen sport. Today most people assume it is natural for women to exercise and to be fit, though many still believe it is not quite natural for them to compete to win.

Conclusions and New Directions

I began by asking why essentialist theories of opposition are so popular, when many of the important differences between the sexes are diminishing. I suggest several reasons for this paradox:

Offering Certainty in Uncertain Times Precisely because of the dizzying speed of changes in gender roles, occupations, and family constellations, to say nothing of the startling displays of gender variations and performances on the streets and in the media, many people are angry or confused. What to make of an athlete like Dennis Rodman, who sometimes "does" feminine and sometimes "does" masculine? It is no wonder that *The Rules* (Fein & Schneider, 1995) is a best-seller; when the old rules are gone and people are uncertain about how to behave, many want to know the new rules. And what can be more certain than the old rules of dating, dated and dopey though they may be? What can be more certain than claims that men and women are truly, fundamentally different in the old ways we expect them to differ—and that these differences persist even in the face of "superficial" changes?

Reflecting Attributional Habits Our affection for essentialism also stems from two widespread attributional habits in American culture. One is our characteristic individualism, which, unlike collectivist cultures, locates behavior in the individual rather than in the collective, a person's status, or situation (Triandis, 1995). In contrast, in countries such as India, where everyone is embedded in a caste system, and in Japan, China, and Hong Kong, where people are more group oriented than they are in the West, people are more likely to recognize situational constraints on behavior (Lee, Hallahan, & Herzog, 1996; Miller, 1984; Morris & Peng, 1994).

A second attributional habit stems from the normal mental biases and stereotypes we bring to all complex encounters. Because dating, marriage, and family relationships are inherently fraught with emotion and conflict, many people are attracted to theories that attribute the reasons for their unhappiness with a *particular* parent or lover to something inherent in that person's sex: men are pigs, women are gold-diggers, mothers are smothering, fathers are aloof, and so forth. We notice variation within our own group; it is typical to stereotype "the other."[3] But once a stereotype is in place, the confirmation bias kicks in—the normal tendency to notice and remember instances of behavior that confirm our beliefs (another deadbeat dad, another nurturing woman) and to ignore or forget instances that disconfirm them (an aggressive woman, a nurturant father).

Producing Personal Satisfaction It reassures some women and men to think that the reasons for their misunderstandings are that he is from one planet and she is from another; they do not actually have to change anything. Of course, the argument that women are inherently better than men in their ways of knowing and reasoning, and in having kinder and more nurturing natures, is tremendously appealing to many women, who are so eager for pro-woman theories after centuries of misogyny.

Cultural feminists have made important contributions to the study of gender, especially by correcting the biases of excluding women from research and of interpreting their behavior as deficient according to the male norm (Crawford & Marecek, 1989). But what began as a corrective to the way psychology traditionally did business has created new problems (Mednick, 1989; Yoder & Kahn, 1993). Along with revaluing traits traditionally associated with women's work, such as caretaking, this movement has tended to devalue traits or occupations that are associated with men—such as scientific reasoning, ambition, and autonomy. Although the appeal to many women of this inversion of the stereotype is understandable, I believe it exacts too high a price for the temporary good feelings it confers. It commits all the errors of essentialist theories; it alienates men who would be women's allies in the movement toward equality; and it blocks women from recognizing and developing their "masculine" talents, which are only human.

Serving Vested Interests Finally, constructionist approaches always direct us to ask: who benefits from the popularity of certain theories over others? Researchers and the news media alike profit from reporting stories of women's and men's differences; there is no news value (or likelihood of publication) in findings about sex similarities. Drug companies profit (hugely) from the medicalizing of psychological problems and the popularity of medication as treatment; and, with vast resources at their disposal to fund research, they have already succeeded in stifling nonmedical explanations and treatments of mood disorders, "PMS," and sexual dysfunction (Fausto-Sterling, 1997; Tiefer, this volume; Valenstein, 1998). Researchers profit from biological approaches to gender differences because there is more money, fame, and glamor in doing MRI studies than in doing historical, cultural, and sociological studies. Conservatives profit from theories of women's "natural" nurturance and men's "natural" competitiveness, for these ideas support their traditional philosophy that men belong at work and mothers belong at home. Those in power profit from theories that women are naturally more relational and cooperative, naturally adverse to exercising power, because then women who are autonomous, ambitious, and powerful can be excoriated as being "unnatural." And who benefits from that idea?

The constructionist alternative to essentialism helps us think about gender differences in new ways. It directs us to look at gender in context, noting how the qualities and behaviors expected of women and men vary across settings and interactions. It reminds us that women and men develop, learn, have adventures, and have new experiences throughout their lives; gender rules and behavior are not acquired and then frozen, at one moment in life. The way we are as toddlers or adolescents bears no inevitable relation, thank God, to what we are at 30 or 40—or to what we can become.

Constructionism also helps us break the binary habit of polarizing traits into opposites and arguing about which pole is better. Connection and autonomy, dependence and independence, modesty and self-confidence, reason and intuition: all have their place in human life. These are human qualities, not archetypes that typify only one sex; and they are all qualities that contribute to our health and well-being. Numerous studies of men and women across the life span find that the "masculine" trait of agency (focus on the self and independence) and the "feminine" trait of communion (focus on others and connections) are *both* required for optimal well-being (Ryff & Keyes, 1995). Therefore, if we truly value nurturance, competence, and achievement, we should value them in both sexes, expand our definitions of these behaviors to recognize the many forms they take, and make the changes in our work and family lives that will encourage their expression.

Essentialism is appealing, but it cannot account for the nuances, similarities, and variations in women's and men's experiences. It cannot account for the speed of change or for the differences across cultures and historical epochs. It directs attention away from the economic and environmental conditions that perpetuate misunderstanding and conflict between women and men. The war of the sexes, like all other wars, rests on demonizing the enemy—seeing them as hopelessly, fundamentally different and deficient. If and when our popular theories abandon essentialism for a more nuanced reality, we will be taking a big step toward a truce in the longest war.

NOTES

1. American feminism has always been divided between "rights feminists," who regard differences between women and men as being largely

due to history, power inequities, and social and economic factors; and "domestic" (now "cultural") feminists, who regard women and men as being fundamentally different, but with women being morally superior (Lott, 1990). During the movement for women's suffrage, the latter advocated giving women the vote because women would supposedly use it to abolish war and injustice, out of the sweetness of their natures; rights feminists sought the vote because women were entitled to it.

2. With the demise of separate spheres, we would predict that just as women have learned to follow "male" rules of emotion at work, more men will start behaving "like women" in relationships, and I think that is already happening. In the 1970s, as women entered formerly male-only occupations, experts were forever advising them not to cry on the job. Today, experts are telling men it is okay to cry. Both Bill Clinton and Robert Dole cried in public during the 1996 campaign, an act that would once have destroyed their careers, as it did for Edmund Muskie. New Age gurus and conservative Christians alike are encouraging men across America to express their pains and worries. Whatever would John Wayne have said?

3. This aspect of stereotyping—seeing variation in one's own group but not in other groups—starts early. Marilynn Brewer (1993) reported that her daughter returned from kindergarten one day with the observation that "boys are crybabies." The child's evidence was that she had seen two boys crying on their first day away from home. Brewer asked whether any little girls had also cried. Oh yes, said her daughter. "But," she insisted, "only *some* girls cry; *I* didn't cry."

REFERENCES

Allison, D. B., Heshka, S., Neale, M. C., Lykken, D. T., et al. (1994). A genetic analysis of relative weight among 4,020 twin pairs, with an emphasis on sex effects. *Health Psychology, 13*, 362–365.

American Psychiatric Association. (1994). *Diagnostic and statistical manual of mental disorders* (4th ed.). Washington DC: Author.

Bailey, J. M. (1993, March 25). Science and the fear of knowledge. *Chicago Tribune*, opinion page.

Barnett, R. C., & Rivers, C. (1996). *She works, he works: How two-income families are happier, healthier, and better off*. San Francisco: HarperCollins.

Baumeister, R. F., Stillwell, A. M., & Wotman, S. R. (1990). Victim and perpetrator accounts of interpersonal conflict: Autobiographical narratives about anger. *Journal of Personality and Social Psychology, 59*, 994–1005.

Belenky, M. F., Clinchy, B. M., Goldberger, N. R., & Tarule, J. M. (1986). *Women's ways of knowing: Development of self, voice, and mind*. New York: Basic Books.

Bettencourt, B. A., & Miller, N. (1996). Gender differences in aggression as a function of provocation: A meta-analysis. *Psychological Bulletin, 119*, 422–447.

Bohan, J. S. (1997). Regarding gender: Essentialism, constructionism, and feminist psychology. In M. M. Gergen & S. N. Davis (Eds.), *Toward a new psychology of gender: A reader* (pp. 31–47). New York: Routledge.

Bouchard, C., Tremblay, A., Despres, J. P., Nadeau, A., et al. (1990, May 24). The response to long-term overfeeding in identical twins. *New England Journal of Medicine, 322,* 1477–1482.

Brewer, M. (1993). Social identity, distinctiveness, and in-group homogeneity. *Social Cognition, 11,* 150–164.

Burke, P. (1996). *Gender shock.* New York: Basic Books.

Byne, W. (1993). *Sexual orientation and brain structure: Adding up the evidence.* Paper presented at the annual meeting of the International Academy of Sex Research, Pacific Grove CA.

Campbell, A. (1993). *Men, women, and aggression.* New York: Basic Books.

Cancian, F. M. (1987). *Love in America: Gender and self-development.* Cambridge: Cambridge University Press.

Canetto, S. S. (1992). Suicide attempts and substance abuse: Similarities and differences. *Journal of Psychology, 125,* 605–620.

Carli, L. L. (1990). Gender, language, and influence. *Journal of Personality and Social Psychology, 59,* 941–951.

Chodorow, N. (1978). *The reproduction of mothering.* Berkeley: University of California Press.

Clopton, N. A., & Sorell, G. T. (1993). Gender differences in moral reasoning: Stable or situational? *Psychology of Women Quarterly, 17,* 85–101.

Cohn, L. D. (1991). Sex differences in the course of personality development: A meta-analysis. *Psychological Bulletin, 109,* 252–266.

Coontz, S. (1997). *The way we really are.* New York: Basic Books.

Crawford, M., & Marecek, J. (1989). Psychology reconstructs the female: 1968–1988. *Psychology of Women Quarterly, 13,* 147–165.

Crick, N. R., & Grotpeter, J. K. (1995). Relational aggression, gender, and social-psychological adjustment. *Child Development, 66,* 710–722.

de Lacoste-Utamsing, C., & Holloway, R. L. (1982). Sexual dimorphism in the human corpus callosum. *Science, 216,* 1431–1432.

Deaux, K. (1984). From individual differences to social categories: Analysis of a decade's research on gender. *American Psychologist, 39,* 105–116.

Deaux, K., & Major, B. (1987). Putting gender into context: An interactive model of gender-related behavior. *Psychological Review, 94,* 369–389.

Deaux, K., & Major, B. (1990). A social-psychological model of gender. In D. L. Rhode (Ed.), *Theoretical perspectives on sexual difference* (pp. 89–99). New Haven CT: Yale University Press.

Diamond, Marian C. (1993, winter–spring). An optimistic view of the aging brain. *Generations, 17,* 31–33.

Elshtain, J. B. (1987). *Women and war.* New York: Basic Books.

Fausto-Sterling, A. (1997, summer). Beyond difference: A biologist's perspective [Special issue: J. B. James (Ed.), *The significance of gender: Theory and research about difference*]. *Journal of Social Issues, 53,* 213–232.

Fein, E., & Schneider, S. (1995). *The rules: Time-tested secrets for capturing the heart of Mr. Right.* New York: Warner Books.

Feingold, A. (1994). Gender differences in personality: A meta-analysis. *Psychological Bulletin, 116,* 429–456.

Fischer, A. H. (1993). Sex differences in emotionality: Fact or stereotype? *Feminism and Psychology, 3,* 303–318.

Fiske, S. T. (1993). Controlling other people: The impact of power on stereotyping. *American Psychologist, 48,* 621–628.

Freud, S. (1962). *Civilization and its discontents.* New York: Norton.

Friedman, W., Robinson, A., & Friedman, B. (1987). Sex differences in moral judgments? A test of Gilligan's theory. *Psychology of Women Quarterly, 11,* 37–46.

Gelles, R. J., & Straus, M. A. (1988). *Intimate violence: The causes and consequences of abuse in the American family.* New York: Simon & Schuster/ Touchstone.

Gergen, K. J. (1985). The social constructionist movement in modern psychology. *American Psychologist, 40,* 266–274.

Gergen, K. J. (1994). Exploring the postmodern: Perils or potentials? *American Psychologist, 49,* 412–416.

Gerson, K. (1993). *No man's land: Men's changing commitments to family and work.* New York: Basic Books.

Gilligan, C. (1982). *In a different voice.* Cambridge: Harvard University Press.

Gilmore, D. D. (1990). *Manhood in the making: Cultural concepts of masculinity.* New Haven CT: Yale University Press.

Gould, S. J. (1996). *The mismeasure of man* (Rev. ed.). New York: W. W. Norton.

Grossman, M., & Wood, W. (1993). Sex differences in intensity of emotional experience: A social role interpretation. *Journal of Personality and Social Psychology, 65,* 1010–1022.

Hall, J. A. (1987). On explaining gender differences: The case of nonverbal communication. In P. Shaver & C. Hendrick (Eds.), *Sex and gender: Review of Personality and Social Psychology* (Vol. 7, pp. 177–200). Beverly Hills CA: Sage.

Halpern, D. (1989). The disappearance of cognitive gender differences: What you see depends on where you look. *American Psychologist, 44,* 1156–1157.

Hare-Mustin, R. T., & Marecek, J. (Eds.). (1990). *Making a difference: Psychology and the construction of gender.* New Haven CT: Yale University Press.

Harris, M. (1985). *Good to eat: Riddles of food and culture.* New York: Simon & Schuster.

Hatfield, E., & Rapson, R. L. (1996). *Love and sex: Cross-cultural perspectives.* Boston: Allyn & Bacon.

Henley, N. (1995). Body politics revisited: What do we know today? In P. J. Kalbfleisch & M. J. Cody (Eds.), *Gender, power, and communication in human relationships.* Hillsdale NJ: Erlbaum.

Kanter, R. (1993). *Men and women of the corporation* (Rev. ed.). New York: Basic Books.

Kessler, R. C., McGonagle, K. A., Zhao, S., Nelson, C. B., et al., 1994. Lifetime and 12-month prevalence of DSM-III-R psychiatric disorders in the

United States: Results from the National Comorbidity Study. *Archives of General Psychiatry, 51*, 8–19.

Kolb, B. (1996). *Neural plasticity and behavioural development* (State of the art address). Paper presented at the International Congress of Psychology, Montreal, Quebec, Canada.

Lakoff, R. T. (1990). *Talking power.* New York: Basic Books.

Lee, F., Hallahan, M., & Herzog, T. (1996). Explaining real-life events: How culture and domain shape attributions. *Personality and Social Psychology Bulletin, 22*, 732–741.

Lightdale, J. R., & Prentice, D. A. (1994). Rethinking sex differences in aggression: Aggressive behavior in the absence of social roles. *Personality and Social Psychology Bulletin, 20*, 34–44.

Lott, B. (1990). Dual natures or learned behavior: The challenge to feminist psychology. In R. T. Hare-Mustin & J. Marecek (Eds.), *Making a difference: Psychology and the construction of gender.* New Haven CT: Yale University Press.

Lytton, H., & Romney, D. M. (1991). Parents' differential socialization of boys and girls: A meta-analysis. *Psychological Bulletin, 109*, 267–296.

Maccoby, E. E. (1998). *The two sexes: Growing up apart, coming together.* Cambridge MA: Belknap Press of Harvard University Press.

McGuinness, D. (1993). Sex differences in cognitive style: Implications for math performance and achievement. In L. A. Penner, G. M. Batsche, & H. Knoff (Eds.), *The challenge in mathematics and science education: Psychology's response.* Washington DC: American Psychological Association.

Mednick, M. (1989). On the politics of psychological constructs: Stop the bandwagon, I want to get off. *American Psychologist, 44*, 1118–1123.

Miller, J. G. (1984). Culture and the development of everyday social explanations. *Journal of Personality and Social Psychology, 46*, 961–978.

Morris, M. W., & Peng, K. (1994). Culture and cause: American and Chinese attributions for social and physical events. *Journal of Personality and Social Psychology, 67*, 949–971.

Nolen-Hoeksema, S. (1990). *Sex differences in depression.* Stanford CA: Stanford University Press.

Oatley, K., & Jenkins, J. M. (1996). *Understanding emotions.* Cambridge MA: Blackwell.

O'Barr, W. M. (1983). The study of language in institutional contexts [Second International Conference on Social Psychology and Language]. *Journal of Language and Social Psychology, 2*, 241–251.

Plomin, R., DeFries, J. C., McClearn, G. E., & Rutter, M. (1997). *Behavioral genetics* (3rd ed.). New York: W. H. Freeman.

Pollak, R. (1997). *The creation of Dr. B.* New York: Simon & Schuster.

Riessman, C. K. (1990). *Divorce talk: Men and women make sense of personal relationships.* New Brunswick NJ: Rutgers University Press.

Ryff, C. D., & Keyes, C. L. M. (1995). The structure of psychological well-being revisited. *Journal of Personality and Social Psychology, 69*, 719–727.

Shaver, P. R., & Hazan, C. (1993). Adult romantic attachment: Theory and evidence. In D. Perlman & W. H. Jones (Eds.), *Advances in personal relationships* (Vol. 4). London: Kingsley.

Shields, S. A. (1975). Functionalism, Darwinism, and the psychology of women: A study in social myth. *American Psychologist, 30*, 739–754.

Shields, S. A. (1991). Gender in the psychology of emotion: A selective research review. In K. T. Strongman (Ed.), *International review of studies on emotion* (Vol. 1). New York: John Wiley & Sons.

Snodgrass, S. E. (1985). Women's intuition: The effect of subordinate role on interpersonal sensitivity. *Journal of Personality and Social Psychology, 49*, 146–155.

Snodgrass, S. E. (1992). Further effects of role versus gender on interpersonal sensitivity. *Journal of Personality and Social Psychology, 62*, 154–158.

Stacey, J. (1996). *In the name of the family: Rethinking family values in a postmodern age*. Boston: Beacon.

Stapley, J. C., & Haviland, J. M. (1989). Beyond depression: Gender differences in normal adolescents' emotional experiences. *Sex Roles, 20*, 295–308.

Tavris, C. (1989). *Anger: The misunderstood emotion*. New York: Touchstone.

Tavris, C. (1992). *The mismeasure of woman: Why women are not the superior sex, the inferior sex, or the opposite sex*. New York: Simon & Schuster/Touchstone.

Tavris, C., & Wade, C. (1977). *The longest war: Sex differences in perspective*. New York: Harcourt Brace Jovanovich.

Tavris, C., & Wade, C. (1997). *Psychology in perspective* (2nd ed.). New York: Longman.

Thoma, S. J. (1986). Estimating gender differences in the comprehension and preference of moral issues. *Developmental Review, 6*, 165–180.

Tiefer, L. (1995). *Sex is not a natural act, and other essays*. Boulder CO: Westview.

Tougas F., Brown, R., Beaton, A. M., & Joly, S. (1995). Neosexism: Plus ça change, plus c*est pareil. *Personality and Social Psychology Bulletin, 21*, 842–849.

Triandis, H. C. (1995). *Individualism and collectivism*. Boulder CO: Westview.

Twenge, J. M. (1997). Attitudes toward women, 1970–1995: A meta-analysis. *Psychology of Women Quarterly, 21*, 35–51.

Unger, R. (1990). Imperfect reflections of reality: Psychology constructs gender. In R. T. Hare-Mustin & J. Marecek (Eds.), *Making a difference: Psychology and the construction of gender*. New Haven CT: Yale University Press.

Valenstein, E. S. (1998). *Blaming the brain*. New York: Free Press.

Walker, L. J., de Vries, B., & Trevethan, S. D. (1987). Moral stages and moral orientations in real-life and hypothetical dilemmas. *Child Development, 58*, 842–858.

Wark, G. R., & Krebs, D. (1996). Gender and dilemma differences in real-life moral judgment. *Developmental Psychology, 32*, 220–230.

West, C., & Zimmerman, D. H. (1991). Doing gender. In J. Lorber & S. A. Farrell (Eds.), *The social construction of gender*. Newbury Park CA: Sage.

Yoder, J., & Kahn, A. (1993). Working toward an inclusive psychology of women. *American Psychologist, 48*, 846–850.

Hidden Feelings: Emotionality in Boys and Men

Reed Larson
Joseph Pleck
University of Illinois at Urbana-Champaign

When we first began contemplating this chapter, a prominent story in the news regarded a navy admiral who had suddenly taken his own life. The circumstance leading to the suicide appeared to have been public revelation that honors he had received early in his naval career, in Vietnam, were based on false information. People were surprised and shocked that he would commit suicide over what seemed like a trivial issue—the image suggested by the story was of a proud John Wayne figure, torn apart by shame and other strong emotions.

The human interest in this news story was the contradiction it seemed to hold with our general image of adult men as stolid, unreactive, and unemotional. Research has consistently demonstrated that our culture has a stereotype of men as less prone to strong emotions—except anger—than women (Shields, 1991). Indeed, being a "sturdy oak" and being unemotional are seen as part of the definition of masculinity (Brannon, 1976) and are included as components on scales of the male role (Levant et al., 1992; Thompson & Pleck, 1986).

Reed Larson's work on this chapter was partially supported by National Institute of Mental Health grants 1 R01 MH38324 and 1 R01 MH53846. Joseph Pleck's work on this chapter was partially supported by Illinois Agricultural Experiment Station grant 45-0130.

Yet this admiral's suicide cannot be dismissed as an isolated case, since successful suicide is more than three times as frequent for men than for women (Kessler & McRae, 1983; National Center for Health Statistics, 1991). Of course, suicide is not the definitive indicator of emotionality. Nonetheless, this example opens the door to asking whether, beneath the stolid exterior, men and boys may be just as emotional as women and girls.

Studies of emotionality have most often focused on the exterior—on expressed emotion; and, in fact, this research shows that men are typically found to be less emotionally expressive than women, except for expression of anger (Balswick, 1988; LaFrance & Banaji, 1992). This difference is generally attributed to cultural "display rules" that permit women to be more expressive and that inhibit men's expressivity (Shields, 1987). These differences in expressed emotion, however, may say little about gender differences in felt emotion—the type of emotion we are most interested in— since research shows that expressed and felt emotion are only moderately related (Berscheid, 1990). It is possible that men and boys are feeling a wider range of emotion than they are expressing.

Prior discussion of gender and emotionality has largely adopted an "individual differences" perspective, drawn from personality psychology, which asks whether the genders differ in fundamental emotional dispositions or traits. The focus is on a "main effect" for gender, attributable to what emotion theorists call a "top-down" factor, such as biology or childhood socialization—attributable to the x and y chromosomes or to a social order that differentially molds the temperaments of boys and girls. The underlying assumption is that males and females are born with or acquire differences in emotional dispositions that are manifest across all the situations of daily life. We will call this the "gender-as-difference" perspective.

While not fully ruling out these types of top-down main effects, the evidence in this chapter leads us toward a "gender-as-process" perspective that sees gender differences in emotion—where they occur—as emerging "bottom-up" from the transactions of daily life. This perspective acknowledges that top-down factors may influence the nature of daily transactions, but it asserts that the transactions themselves are responsible for gender differences in affective experience. We argue that males and females do not differ in underlying emotional dispositions; however, daily life puts them in situations that can elicit differing emotional responses.

The basis for our conclusion is analysis of data, obtained using a novel time-sampling method, on the daily emotions of adults and adolescents. We first evaluate the overall rates of males' and females' emotions during their daily lives and look at whether the range of males' emotional states is different. Then we turn to examination of emotions within specific categories of daily situations. We give particular attention to adult men's emotional experience in two broad daily contexts: male-male interactions, especially at men's jobs, and male-female interactions in family settings. Our findings indicate that men are as emotional as women, but their emotions occur in somewhat different contexts, as a function of the social processes that they experience in those contexts.

Theories of Emotion

Before presenting our empirical data on emotional experience, we feel it important to provide a framework for thinking about what emotions are, what causes them, and how these causes might create gender differences. We focus on two disparate theoretical accounts: one that sees emotions as biological phenomena, the other as cultural.

EMOTIONS AS BIOLOGICAL PROGRAMS

The first theoretical approach, going back to Darwin, sees emotions as highly functional, built-in systems, evolved to serve survival and social needs. They are biological "programs" designed to motivate, facilitate, and direct an organism's actions. Some emotions, such as fear and anger, clearly prepare an organism for "fight or flight." In response to an urgent situation, the physiological changes that accompany emotions serve to rapidly rearrange behavioral hierarchies, activate physiological support, short-circuit cognitive processes, and coordinate response systems (Levenson, 1994, p. 123). In less urgent circumstances, such as daily social situations, the organismic changes accompanying emotions may have more subtle but equally important functions. Social emotions, such as enjoyment, love, guilt, loneliness, and even mild displeasure, set priorities and direct attention and action (Davidson, 1994, p. 52). Panksepp (1996) argues that emotions provide ingrained values and goals that allow humans to begin operating in the world as spontaneous active organisms (p. 29).

These functional systems or programs are clearly supported by the chemistry and circuitry of the brain. A long tradition of research has focused on the older, subcortical regions as the seat of emotions. During strong emotion these sites alter levels of dozens of chemicals, including neurotransmitters and neuromodulators, which raise arousal levels and facilitate response. Evidence exists for distinct subcortical "circuits" associated with pleasure, rage, fear, and separation distress, among others (Panksepp, 1993, 1996). Recent research indicates that the cortex, particularly the frontal regions, is also important to emotion (Davidson, 1994); indeed, milder emotions may involve cortical activation with little evidence of subcortical changes. The biological paradigm sees these neurological systems as built into the organism in order to prioritize essential survival and social responses.

Scholars studying the biology of emotion focus on the single occurrence of an emotion, but if we are interested in individual differences, such as male-female differences, we need to also be concerned with patterns in repeated rates of emotions: with how often these programs are activated. Research on temperament shows that individuals differ substantially in their dispositions to experience emotions and that these differences tend to be quite stable over time, beginning in infancy (Goldsmith & Rieser-Danner, 1986). Breeding studies with rats and dogs establish a genetic contribution to these dispositions—emotional proclivities can be bred (Davidson, 1994; Goldsmith, 1989). Twin and adoption studies with humans suggest heritability estimates for emotional dispositions ranging from 30% to 80% (Goldsmith, 1989; Lykken & Tellegen, 1996; Plomin, Chipuer, & Neiderhiser, 1994).

Perhaps one of the most thought-provoking evidences of a constitutional contribution to temperament is research showing that, after a period of adjustment, the average emotional well-being of both paraplegic victims of spinal-cord injuries and lottery winners did not differ substantially from that for a normative sample (Brickman, Coates, & Janoff-Bulman, 1978). This suggests that their overall daily rates of positive and negative emotional experience appear to have returned toward an internally set equilibrium level. Findings like this have induced some theorists to propose that each individual has an underlying "set point" for the experience of emotions ranging from happiness to unhappiness that is partly shaped by his or her genes (Diener & Diener, 1996; Hamer, 1996). These theorists argue that an individual's overall emotional patterns are partly determined top-down, as a main effect, from the individual's genetic predispositions.

This leads us to the question of sex differences. Might these physiological systems differ between the sexes, disposing men to be less emotional than women? Clearly genes play a role in putting emotion programs in place and shaping individual differences in emotions and emotionality, but do they create sex differences? Is it possible that the genetic contribution to these set points differs between males and females?

What is curious is that the biological literature is remarkably quiet on this question. We found that books on the physiology of emotion do not even list "gender" or "sex" (as in sex differences) in their indexes (e.g., McNaughton, 1989; Plutchik & Kellerman, 1986). Textbooks on genetics barely mention sex differences of any kind, devoting only a few pages to the role of genes in determining features directly related to physical sexual dimorphism, like genitals or milk production in cattle. Behavioral geneticists are also remarkably mute on sex linkage in emotional traits. Such linkages could easily be assessed with existent twin and adoption data sets, yet the topic is not mentioned—possibly because researchers have tested for these differences and not found them.

Thus, despite the popular belief that men are less emotional than women, such differences do not appear to be jumping out in the wet labs of emotion research. To summarize, there is compelling evidence that biology plays a major role in shaping emotional dispositions, but little existing evidence—at least at this time—that biology shapes these dispositions differently for males and females.

EMOTIONS AS SOCIOCULTURAL SCRIPTS

At a distant pole from the biological view is a theoretical paradigm that sees emotions as social constructions (Lutz, 1988; Harré, 1986;

White, 1994). This perspective begins from the insight that, with the partial exception of the startle response, cognitive appraisals precede and determine emotions, and these appraisals employ cultural rules. Thus, an act that may instigate anger in one culture (a guest failing to remove shoes when entering one's home) may be completely acceptable in another. At a deeper level, societies differ in how emotions are defined. Languages and cultures have differing lexicons of emotions—the meaning of specific emotions cannot be readily translated (Rosaldo, 1989; Shweder, 1993; Van Brakel, 1994). Thus, for example, many non-Western cultures appear to have no state comparable to "depression," and the distinction between angerlike states and sadness is not universal (Heelas, 1986). Beyond this, cultures differ in the values assigned to specific emotions and in their rules for how an emotion should be managed. Lutz (1988) reports that among the Ifaluk of Micronesia, the state of *ker*, roughly equivalent to "happiness" in English, is viewed as amoral if not immoral. The Icelandic sagas lead us to belief that it was normal in that ancient culture for a man learning of the murder of his son to be bedridden with grief for several years and then rise at the end of that period to seek angry revenge (Miller, 1994).

This constructivist position argues, then, that emotions are not biological but, rather, *social* programs—or "social scripts"—that are shaped by cultural rules (Averill & Thomas-Knowles, 1991). These scripts affect felt as well as expressed emotion and reflect the underlying social and moral order of a society: they are embedded in the beliefs, indigenous psychology, and social practices of a group (Harré, 1986). Sociologists have argued that emotions are shaped by relationships of status and power—or subjugation—within a society (Kemper, 1991; Mirowsky & Ross, 1989). A person's experience of fear and distress versus enjoyment and happiness stems, in part, from that person's position in a social order and the experiences that this position creates. Societies construct a system of emotion scripts that embody and reinforce a hierarchical social order (Abu-Lughod & Lutz, 1990).

Like the biological approach to emotions, this constructivist view suggests that individual differences in emotional experience can result from the top down—in this case from the larger social order that socializes individuals to specific emotional scripts. This view also recognizes that society may dictate differing emotional scripts for males and females. Thus, for example, the state of feeling "amok" in New Guinea is confined to males. The state of being "hysterical" in our society was historically associated with women (Brody, 1993). Fear is considered unmanly in Western society but is readily expressed by Ifaluk men (Lutz, 1988). Like the biological approach, these top-down processes could lead to main effects for gender, evident across all the situations of daily life regardless of how we might expect these main effects to vary among societies.

Following this line of argument, we might also expect differences in emotion between males and females to reflect differences in power within a society. Lewin (1938) argued that the characterization of a group as being "emotional" is often made of lower-status groups, such as adolescents and minorities, partly as a means of justifying inequitable distribution of power. A person who is perceived as emotional (whether valid or not) is seen as less able to take responsibility and reason impartially. By extension, our cultural belief that men are less emotional may be interconnected with their comparative position of power in our society.

Gender Similarities in Rates of Emotions

The biological and sociocultural approaches converge in predicting the possibility of cross-situational sex differences in emotional experience. While they diverge greatly in their accounts for the origins of these differences, they are united in acknowledging the possibility that males and females may differ in their overall rates of emotion.

At this point in the chapter, we shift from a theoretical to an empirical mode of analysis to ask whether such differences in overall rates are evident in people's daily lives. Beneath the veneer of being less emotionally expressive, do men and boys really feel less emotion?

PRIOR RESEARCH APPROACHES

Existing knowledge in the field tends to support the thesis that men experience less emotion than women. After reviewing pertinent research, Brody (1996) concludes: "Consistent findings throughout the literature indicate that adult females report more intense emotional experience than do males" (p. 143). Another recent review by LaFrance and Banaji (1992) comes to a similar conclusion, though it notes that the findings are weaker for research using certain methodologies. For example, smaller differences are found when research participants are asked to report on their private rather than public experience, and no differences are found when researchers examine the frequency of emotional terms in spontaneous speech samples. Both reviews note differences by type of emotion. The most consistent finding is that adolescent girls and adult women report higher levels of anxiety; and some studies, though not all, have found that boys and men report more frequent anger. With the possible exception of anger, then, findings from past research tend to confirm the thesis of comparative male unemotionality.

There are methodological reasons, however, to be dissatisfied with these conclusions. The most common methods used involve obtaining people's reports on their emotional experience, either in response to an eliciting situation in a controlled laboratory or as a summary of their usual daily lives. But laboratory studies can be questioned for how adequately the eliciting situations represent people's ordinary experience and whether the types of situations chosen have a bias toward invoking emotional reactions from one gender or the other. The limitation of the second approach, the self-report method, is that it relies on people's ability to reconstruct their past emotional experience from memory. Several studies, for example, have found men to experience less intense emotion than women using the Affect Intensity Measure (AIM), which asks people to generalize about their typical emotional experience (Diener, Sandvik, & Larsen, 1985; Fujita, Diener, & Sandvik, 1991). Yet research by the same investigators demonstrates that people are not very good at recalling past emotional experience (Thomas & Diener, 1990); and it has been shown that when people are asked to recollect or aggregate experience, cultural beliefs and stereotypes, including gender stereotypes, can have a large influence on their judgments (Shields, 1991; Shweder, 1977). In addition, women appear to have more vivid memories of intense positive and negative emotional experiences than men (Fujita et al., 1991), further biasing data obtained from recall.

Research by the first author, Reed Larson, has employed a different methodology that circumvents these concerns by obtaining immediate reports from people on their emotional experience during daily life. To do this we have used a research procedure called the Experience Sampling Method (ESM), in which participants carry electronic pagers for one week and provide reports on their emotions at random times when signaled by the pagers (Larson & Csikszentmihalyi, 1983). The advantage of this technique is that it obtains data on emotions during a representative sample of daily moments. Since individuals report on their immediate experience, distortions related to recall are minimized. This method does not eliminate all possibility of methodological artifact; nonetheless, it may be as close as we can come to an ecologically valid assessment of male and female emotional experience. Indeed, when we examine these samples of immediate daily experience, we obtain different findings than those suggested by prior research.

THE DAILY EMOTIONS OF MEN AND WOMEN

The first data we report come from an ESM study of 110 adults carried out by the first author and his collaborator, Maryse Richards from Loyola University in Chicago. The sample included husbands and wives from 55 working- and middle-class two-parent families in two suburban Chicago communities. All had young adolescent children. We sent them 7–8 signals per day between 7:30 A.M. and 9:30 P.M.; in response, the parents provided 4,734 reports on their experiences.

Each time these people were signaled, they were asked to rate their current state on approximately 40 items dealing with a range of feelings, including those considered "basic emotions" like anger and happiness, as well as other feeling states, like tired, hurried, and free. We have typically focused on a measure of "affect" that well represents the core dimension of positive to negative emotion (Csikszentmihalyi & Larson, 1987; Larson, 1989a). This scale is computed by averaging responses to three 7-point semantic differential items (happy-unhappy, cheerful-irritable, friendly-angry). It demonstrates good psychometric properties, like reliability (alpha = .81–.83), test-retest stability, and construct validity (Larson, 1989a, 1989b).

GENDER AND MOTIVATION

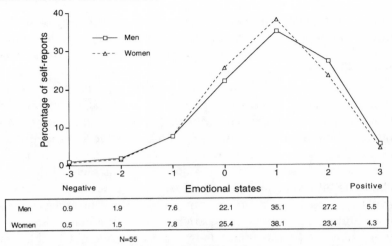

Men	0.9	1.9	7.6	22.1	35.1	27.2	5.5
Women	0.5	1.5	7.8	25.4	38.1	23.4	4.3

N=55

Figure 1. Frequency of emotional states reported by adult men and women. From Larson, R., and Richards, M. H. (1994). Family emotions: Do young adolescents and their parents experience the same states? *Journal of Research on Adolescence, 4,* (4), 567–583.

Do men report less emotion than women? In order to examine gender differences in these data, we first computed the frequency with which each person reported affect at each of seven intervals on this scale, and then we compared these percentages between husbands and wives using match-paired t-tests.[1] Figure 1 shows these comparisons and presents our version of the celebrated overlapping bell curves between genders. One can see that these men and women were remarkably alike in the rates with which they reported different levels of positive and negative emotion. The genders did not differ significantly in their frequency of reporting feelings at any point on the scale, including the extreme ends. When we computed scores for the mean affect and standard deviation for each person, we also found no significant differences between men and women. There was simply no evidence that the husbands were less emotional than their wives.

The absence of notable gender differences was equally striking when we looked at responses for all of the items for individual feeling states. From this list we found no significant difference between husbands and wives for items reflecting basic emotions, including anger and anxiety. Men and women did not differ in rates of feeling worried, nervous, or guilty (Larson & Richards, 1994a, appendix 2.1). Men reported anger slightly *less* often—though the difference was not significant (men, 4.6%, vs. women, 5.4%). We did find significant differences for a few items that are further from the domain of basic emotions. Men reported more often feeling competitive (20% vs. 11%), strong (21% vs. 10%), awkward (6% vs. 2%), and self-conscious (10% vs. 2%). Women more often reported feeling tired (women, 28%, vs. men, 19%), weak (4% vs. 2%), and in love (42% vs. 33%). These differences in feeling states suggest their experience of divergent social roles, an interpretation we develop later in the chapter.

In addition to examining our own data, we reviewed other studies in which adults were asked for immediate reports on their emotions during their daily lives. Using the ESM, McAdams and Constantian (1983) found no sex difference in rates of positive affect and negative affect among 50 college students, and LeFevre, Hedricks, Church, and McClintock (1992) found no differences in variability in mood for a study in which six couples provided ESM data over 30 days. We also note that, in his extensive research on state anger and state anxiety, Spielberger has not found differences between adult men and women, with the one exception that anxiety was found to be somewhat less for women than for men in the 50–69 age period (Spielberger, 1983; Spielberger, Jacobs, Russell, & Crane, 1983).

To summarize, the evidence suggests that once you look at immediate reports of emotion, differences in emotionality between adult men and women largely disappear. Our findings for adolescents are not quite as clear, but we feel they also cast doubt on the thesis of male unemotionality.

DAILY EMOTIONS OF YOUNG ADOLESCENT BOYS AND GIRLS

We carried out an ESM study of 473 randomly selected working- and middle-class young adolescents (Larson & Richards, 1989). These youth came from the same communities as the adult sample just described; in fact, the adult sample was drawn from the parents of a subset of these youth. This sample was composed of European-American fifth- to ninth-graders. These youth provided a total of 17,752 ESM responses and reported their affect on the same scale we used with the sample of parents.

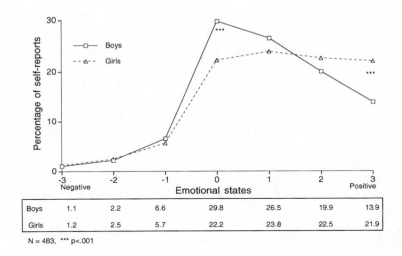

Boys	1.1	2.2	6.6	29.8	26.5	19.9	13.9
Girls	1.2	2.5	5.7	22.2	23.8	22.5	21.9

N = 483, *** p<.001

Figure 2. Frequency of emotional states reported by young adolescent boys and girls.

We found that the bell curves for the boys' and girls' daily emotions were somewhat less overlapping than for the adult men and women (Figure 2). Gender differences for rates of negative affect were not significant, and there were no differences for rates of mild positive affect. The significant difference occurred at two intervals on the scale: boys reported neutral affect 6% more often than girls, and girls reported extreme positive affect 8% more often than boys. When we computed a score for variance in emotions for each individual, girls had slightly higher mean variance, but the difference was quite small, 1.04 versus 0.96 (Greene & Larson, 1991).

Again we looked at differences for a wide variety of specific emotion and feeling state items. From a list of 48 items, 14 differed significantly by gender. Boys reported lower rates for feelings dealing with positive affect, specifically happy, cheerful, and excited. They reported lower rates for several items dealing with anxiety—nervous, worried, and embarrassed. They also reported lower rates for several feelings that are not classic basic emotions: rowdy, in love, kindly, tired, hurt, and weak. As with the adult sample, boys more often indicated feeling competitive and strong. But the genders did not differ significantly for rates of anger (boys, 7.9%, vs. girls, 6.8%; p=.24) nor for many other states.

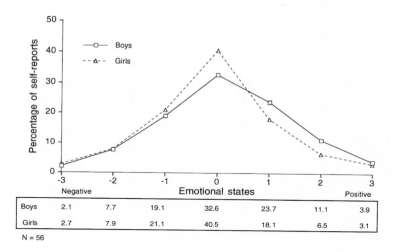

Figure 3. Frequency of emotional states reported by Korean high school boys and girls.

How do we reconcile the finding of differences for the adolescents with the lack of differences for the adult data? Of course, we found more significant differences for the adolescents partly because we had a larger sample size than we had with adults and thus had greater statistical sensitivity. But might these differences reflect an age-specific biological effect, perhaps related to puberty? We were fortunate to have ESM data from a study of Korean high school seniors (from Lee, 1994). If there were biologically based differences between adolescent boys and girls, one would expect them to be evident across cultures. The Korean data, however, show that patterns of emotional experience are not universal (Figure 3). First, the shape of the distribution for both genders is quite different than for U.S. adolescents. There is not the skewness toward happiness that was evident in the American sample. The principal investigator of this study attributes this to the stress Korean adolescents experience preparing for their highly competitive college entrance examination (Lee, 1994).

But what is more important to our topic here is the absence of gender differences for the Korean adolescents. If anything, the patterns for boys and girls are in the opposite direction from the U.S. data, with girls reporting slightly more neutral affect, though none of these differences are significant. Is it possible that younger Korean adolescents might look more like the U.S. young adolescents? We cannot say for certain, but we do know that older U.S. adolescents do not look like these Korean adolescents. We restudied 228 of our young adolescent sample four years later when they were in high school, and the data look quite similar to that in Figure 2.

This leaves us with the conclusion that there may be small differences in the affective experience of U.S. adolescent boys and girls, but these do not appear to apply across cultural settings. Rather than being an indication of a universal sex difference, the patterns for U.S. boys and girls appear to represent an age-specific and culture-specific difference.

TOP-DOWN, CROSS-SITUATIONAL GENDER DIFFERENCES?

On the whole, these findings suggest little or no difference in the daily range of emotions experienced by males and females. For the adults, we found no sex differences for basic emotions, and this was corroborated by other studies of immediate emotions. For U.S. but not Korean adolescents, we found less positive but not less negative affect among boys than girls. Of course, research can never prove the null hypothesis—the absence of differences; nonetheless, this accumulation of findings suggests that overall gender differences are small at best.

A concern that might be raised about these findings is that, although they come from immediate daily situations, they are still based on self-report data, and self-reports, even repeated self-reports, can be influenced by response biases, denial, or individual differences in the ability to detect one's emotions. If such distortions affected these data, however, they are likely to mask, not exaggerate, male emotionality. Western social norms encourage men to control and suppress feelings (LaFrance & Banaji, 1992); thus, if anything, men are likely to underreport strong emotions. What is striking in these findings is that, *by their own admission*, the men in our research are as emotional as women. Several studies indicate that the tendency to suppress or deny strong emotions is particularly evident in children and adolescents, possibly more so in boys (Gilbert, 1969; Brody, 1985; Stapley & Haviland, 1989), which may explain the small gender differences in positive affect that we found for this age group.

It is worth noting that studies using physiological measures of emotion corroborate the conclusion that males are at least as emotional as females. As with expression of emotion, physiological manifestations of emotion may be partly a different elephant—these measures are not highly correlated with reports of experience (Berscheid, 1990). Nonetheless, physiological data from a large number of studies—using a range of measures and testing a wide variety of eliciting situations—are consistent with our findings for immediate self-reports. Nearly all of this research finds either that men and women do not differ in physiological reactivity or that men are more reactive than women (LaFrance & Banaji, 1992). Similar conclusions have been reached for observational studies of temperament in infants: reviewers conclude that either there is no gender difference in infants' emotional dispositions (Buss, 1989; Rothbart, 1989) or that male infants' emotions may be more intense than girl infants' (Brody, 1996).

This accumulation of evidence, we believe, weighs heavily against the thesis that males are constitutionally less emotional than females.[2] Once one goes beyond display of emotion and recall of emotion—both of which are readily influenced by cultural rules and stereotypes—differences between males and females largely disappear. At the level of immediate self-report and physiological reaction, males appear to be as emotional as females. Of course, these findings do not mean that biology does not affect emotionality— much genetic evidence indicates that it does. Rather, these findings suggest that biological factors do not differ for males and females— that the genetic contributions to emotional experience (or set points) are passed from parents to children without regard to a person's sex.

The findings also weigh against the hypothesis of a top-down main effect due to culture and socialization, at least for the groups studied. We did find that U.S. adolescent boys reported strong positive emotion less frequently than girls, but this gender difference was not evident for adults. This lack of consistency across age periods indicates that males and females are not internalizing fundamentally different emotional responses or emotion scripts. American culture appears not to inculcate enduring global dispositions to happiness or unhappiness by gender. The role of culture, however, is suggested when we look in greater detail at *where* emotions are experienced.

Gender Differences in the Contexts of Emotions

The above findings, we feel, rule against the gender-as-difference perspective: they suggest that there are not large, cross-situational differences in emotional dispositions between males and females. Our further findings lead us to a gender-as-process perspective, which sees differences in emotional experience emerging bottom-up within specific contexts—from the gendered nature of transactions in those contexts. This alternate perspective views gender role experience as produced—and reproduced—within daily life. Following the lead of others (Archer, 1996; Ferree, 1990; Hood, 1983), we view gender roles as created and negotiated by people interacting within the social system as manifest in specific contexts. This perspective recognizes that gender is not stable, unitary, nor universal, but rather in flux, multiple, possibly fragmented, and local (Marecek, 1995; Thorne, 1993). It is created on the ground in everyday interactions.

In turning toward this gender-as-process perspective, we reshape the sociocultural account of emotion in a more dynamic mode. Indeed, many contemporary anthropologists have shifted from a focus on culture as static, uniform, and coherent to a focus on "practices" and discourses that stresses the dynamic, fluid, and contested ways in which culture is negotiated in daily life (Abu-Lughod & Lutz, 1990, p. 9). This theoretical paradigm still recognizes the role of history, symbol systems, prior experience, and higher-order social processes in setting the stage for daily interactions. This stage, these factors, may be set differently for males and females, but the scripts are not fixed. Daily interactions—and the resulting emotions—are not predetermined; they are emergent from actors' ongoing negotiations and enactments within the local "culture" of a given daily context (Butler, 1990; Holloway, 1984; Sampson, 1993).

This section provides a preliminary step toward developing the gender-as-process perspective for the domain of emotion. We present data on the frequency of emotions within specific contexts, data that show distinct patterns in males' emotions. In the subsequent sections, we then discuss the processes underlying these patterns.

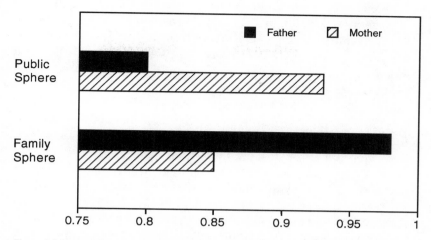

Figure 4. Mean affect scores for mothers and fathers by sphere. From Larson, R., Richards, M. H., & Perry-Jenkins, M. (1994). Divergent worlds: The daily emotional experience of mothers and fathers in the domestic and public spheres. *Journal of Personality and Social Psychology, 67*(6), 1034–1046. Copyright 1994 by the American Psychological Association. Reprinted with permission.

PUBLIC VERSUS PRIVATE SPHERES

For adult men and women, the two broad contexts most often discussed are the home and public spheres (Rosaldo, 1974). In Western society in the past, and some societies in the present, the public sphere outside the home has often been defined as men's domain. Women have been discouraged, and sometimes prohibited, from holding jobs, and their freedom of movement in public has been subject to strictures. By contrast, the home has often been defined as women's domain. In the 19th century, women in the West came to be seen as having greater responsibility over this private sphere. Although there has been a blurring of this division over the last century, we find that it still shapes married adults' emotional experiences.

Our ESM data from married couples show gender differences within emotional experience in the public and private spheres—although it may not be what readers initially expect. We evaluated mean affect scores in these contexts and found that the men reported significantly more positive emotional states in the home sphere than women, and women reported significantly more posi- tive emotional states in the public sphere than men (Figure 4). Women's more positive affect away from home was evident both when we looked at all time away from their role as mother, and when we selected only those couples with employed women and compared the husbands' and wives' emotions when at their jobs (Larson, Richards, & Perry-Jenkins, 1994).

The finding that men experienced more negative emotion at their jobs was also evident when we examined specific emotions. Men reported anger at work more than twice as often as women (men, 5%, vs. women, 2%). They reported feeling bored, awkward, and irritable significantly more often at their jobs than they did in the family sphere. Men were also nervous more often at their jobs (13% vs. 5%) and lonely more often (6% vs. 1%) (Larson & Richards, 1994a). By contrast, men in the study reported significantly more positive affect in the family sphere. They reported feeling happy, cheerful, friendly, and "great" significantly more often when they were at home than at their jobs, differences that were not evident for their wives.

These raw frequencies, then, indicate that men's emotionality— specifically strong negative emotion—is more frequent at their jobs. Home is a context in which negative emotion is rarer and positive emotion is more frequent.

INTERPERSONAL VERSUS IMPERSONAL CONTEXTS FOR EMOTIONS

For the young adolescents, we found no striking gender differences in patterns of emotion at home or in public. This is not surprising, since there is not a recent history, comparable to that for married adults, that differentiates daily life by gender in this way for adoles- cents. However, contextual differences in their experience of emo- tion did show up in two other important ways.

First, boys and girls differed in their affect on occasions when they were with people, in contrast to when they were alone. When we look only at occasions when the young adolescents were with other people (this includes family, friends, and others), the gender differences we noted earlier are somewhat stronger (Figure 5). Boys

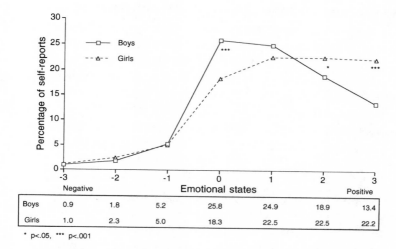

Figure 5. Emotional states of young adolescent boys and girls when with others.

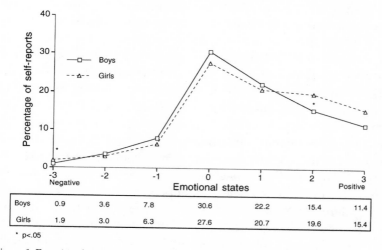

Figure 6. Emotional states of young adolescent boys and girls when alone.

reported significantly more neutral affect than girls; girls reported more extreme positive affect than boys. However, when we look just at times when they were alone, the gender differences in positive affect virtually disappear (Figure 6). A curious difference is that girls report more extreme negative affect in this context, a finding we think might be related to a tendency for girls to engage in rumina-

Table 1. *Percent of strong feelings attributed to different explanations*

	Males %	Females %
Adults		
Self	20.6	25.8*
Social Relationship	19.6	22.9*
Situation	55.9	46.2***
Young Adolescents		
Self	30.0	28.5
Social Relationship	13.6	23.5***
Situation	45.6	38.3***

Note. Percentages add down to 100% within each group, with a small number of "other" responses are not included in the table. *$p < .05$; ***$p < .001$

tion about negative events—a coping pattern that perpetuates rather than relieves negative emotion (Nolen-Hoeksema, 1994). The more germane point, however, is that the difference between boys' and girls' rates of positive emotion that we saw before appears to be largely attributable to occasions when they were with people.[3]

Second, we found gender differences in young adolescents' explanations for their emotions: boys differed from girls as to what they attributed their strong emotions. Participants in our ESM research were asked, when they felt something strongly, to explain why in response to an open-ended item. We coded these responses into three types of causes: self, situation, and social (Larson & Asmussen, 1991). Boys and girls differed significantly in the causes they gave for their strong feelings, including both negative and positive emotions (Table 1). We found that boys more often attributed their emotions to situations. Other people were sometimes elements of these situations, but boys were more likely to attribute their feelings to the circumstances rather than to these other people. For example, they reported more emotions in relation to sporting events (e.g., "happy because I made six tackles in the scrimmage," "disappointed because we lost to a crummy team"), and they reported more emotions in relation to constraints imposed by school ("happy because school is almost over," "mad because I have a lot of homework") or other circumstances ("excited because I'm going to play computer," "angry because I didn't want to recycle papers"). The husbands in our study of adults were also more likely to give these situational explanations for their emotions than were their wives (Table 1). Thus both boys' and men's emotions appear to be more often related to circumstances.

In contrast, girls and women attributed significantly more strong feelings to interpersonal sources—to social interactions (Table 1). They more often attributed their strong feelings to family, same-sex, and cross-sex relationships. This difference is consistent with findings of other studies, which show girls and women to be more emotionally responsive to social interactions (Kessler & McLeod, 1984; LaFrance & Banaji, 1992).

This finding that the emotions of boys and men are less often triggered by interpersonal matters reinforces the methodological caveats we have raised about past research on gender differences in emotionality. Much of this research on emotionality has used data collected in social situations, such as lab experiments, and thus has a built-in bias toward finding greater emotional response in female than male subjects. Even when these studies do not focus on social situations, they often rely on data obtained through social relationships (for example, through peer reports). It is not surprising, then, that males appeared to be less emotional in these studies. However, it is important to give appropriate weight to situations where males are more emotional. We have found that once weight is given to all daily contexts (e.g., Figures 1 and 2), differences in overall rates largely disappear.

The findings of within-context gender differences also give a more complex meaning to our earlier conclusion that the genders differ little in their overall patterns of emotion. These findings suggest that the overall patterns mask differences within specific daily settings.

TOWARD GENDER AS PROCESS

It is these within-context findings that lead us into a gender-as-process orientation. They suggest that gender patterns in emotions emerge, at least partly, bottom-up—from the processes occurring in those contexts. Up to this point we have described this gender-as-process perspective using the language of cultural anthropology. This language suggests that the gender differences we have seen may originate from the daily negotiation of practices, scripts, and discourses that come into play within specific contexts. Cultural scripts may influence females to feel more emotion in response to social situations and males to feel more emotion in response to impersonal situations, such as those involving winning and losing.

We can also use the language of psychology and social interaction to describe the processes shaping within-context gender differences. Roger Barker (1968) coined the term *standing patterns of behavior* to refer to the behavioral regularities he found within contexts. He observed that in given settings—a grocery store, a school classroom, an office— similar patterns of behavior were repeated over and over again. Building on Barker, we would propose that stable factors shaping interaction in specific contexts, including social roles, expectations, and distribution of power, create *standing patterns of emotion*, and that these can vary by gender. For example, differences in the interactions in which husbands and wives participate at home may create differences in the likelihood that each will experience positive emotions. We do not mean that everyone in that setting of a given gender will experience exactly the same emotion, only that their interactions in that setting may have a distinct probability distribution for different emotions—such as the probability distributions that we have just seen (e.g., Figure 5). In the following discussion we mix the language of culture and social interaction, as we see them to be all of one piece.

Our next step is to ask, what are the practices or interactional dynamics that create these within-context differences, these different standing patterns of emotion? We focus on adults and the two broad contexts in which men's emotions differ from those of women. First, we consider what factors shape men's emotions in the public sphere, particularly at their jobs. Historically this has been a sphere of male-male interactions, so we ask, what kind of patterns of interaction have males evolved that shapes their emotional experience in this sphere? Second, we examine men's emotional experience at home in the context of marital relationships. This is a sphere in which males and females directly interact, so we ask how emotion is generated and negotiated within these interactions, and why men's emotions are more positive than women's in this sphere. These sections are inevitably more speculative, combining research findings with exploratory theoretical hypotheses.

Male Culture and the Generation of Emotion in Male-Male Interactions

What happens at men's jobs that creates more frequent negative emotion in this sphere? Some scholars have used the term *emotion culture* to identify the set of practices that dispose a group toward a certain profile of emotions. The emotions men experience at their jobs, we think, can partly be attributed to the emotion culture that organizes men's interactions at their jobs. We discuss this emotion culture, not only as an external milieu, but also as an internalized collection of values, expectations, and goals that animates men's actions and reactions in this setting.

THE WORLD OF MEN'S WORK

The emotion culture surrounding men's experiences at their jobs traces its roots to the 19th century, when females were excluded from most sectors of formal employment. In contrast to the slower-moving commercial life that preceded the Industrial Revolution, the 19th-century male workplace was notable for "its combative energy, its free expression of hostility and self-assertion, and the casual cruelty of its rivalries" (Rotundo, 1993, p. 204). Historian Anthony Rotundo reports that men "engaged in endless small competitions—for business, for advancement, or in the playful competitive testing of wits that formed the cornerstone of male sociability. These constant competitive tests resulted in continuous judgments by peers that, more than anything else, determined a man's status in his profession" (p. 204). This competitiveness at work was paralleled by men's competitiveness in their leisure activities. According to Rotundo, men learned to become psychologically invested in work and leisure, especially sports, as spheres of self-expression and self-validation.

Anger and other negative emotions were a byproduct of this culture of competitive individualism. According to Stearns (1988, 1992), anger was acceptable and even encouraged for men in the work sphere in the 19th century. It was seen as associated with zeal and necessary for surviving in the competitive climate of the workplace. Furthermore, the zero-sum game of daily competitions often bred frustration and anguish among those who lost. The subjugated situation of a large working class led many to levels of distress and despair that were drowned in drink at the end of each day (Thompson, 1963).

Of course, this workplace culture changed in the 20th century.

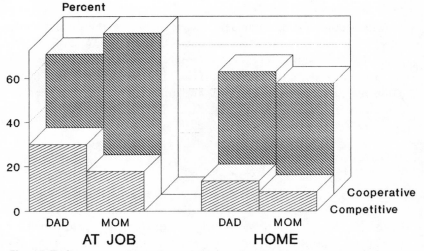

Figure 7. Feeling cooperative and competitive on the job and at home, rated by fathers and mothers.

With the advent of scientific management in the 1920s, there was a deliberate attempt to discourage male expression of anger in the workplace. Frederick Taylor, the guru of scientific management, saw anger as interfering with smooth work operations and incapacitating the individual (Stearns, 1988, 1992). A second change has been a large movement of women into the work setting, although women today often work in different types of jobs than men—thus many men's work lives are still sex-segregated.

Our ESM data indicate that competitive individualism continues to configure men's experience in this sphere. At each self-report, we asked the participants in our study of 55 married couples to rate whether they felt competitive and whether they felt cooperative. Figure 7 shows the rates of reporting these feelings when men and women were at their jobs and at home. Men reported feeling competitive more often at their jobs than women (men, 30%, vs. women, 18%) and cooperative less often. Men also feel more competitive than their wives at home, but this difference is not as great. Similarly, men show lower rates of feeling cooperative at their jobs than women and higher rates of feeling cooperative at home than women feel. The work sphere for men, then, is a context of feeling comparatively more competitive and less cooperative.

Other differences in how men and women experienced their

jobs reinforce the picture of competitive zeal and individualism in men's work life. Men reported deep attention at their jobs significantly more often than women (41% vs. 29%); they reported that they were "the leader" more often (44% vs. 31%); and they felt kindly less often (33% vs. 45%) (Larson & Richards, 1994a). Of course, these differences may be partly due to the fact that, at this point in history, men tend to hold different jobs than women. Nonetheless, they represent the reality in which men participate while at their jobs in the late 20th century.

For some of the men in our study, their investment in their jobs was enthralling and addicting. A boat salesman, for example, reported thinking about how to sell boats on nearly every ESM report, including when he was at home. In an intensive study of successful men, Weiss (1990) found that many men go out of their way to create high challenge at their jobs; one of his interviewees described the "thrill that you can juggle fourteen balls in the air without dropping one of them" (p. 3).

MEN'S EMOTIONS AT THEIR JOBS

This absorbed, hard-driving competitive orientation, we think, is part of what sets the stage for men's frequent negative emotions at their jobs. Again and again, men explained these negative emotions at work as resulting from obstruction or frustration of an activity or goals. Examples include the following statements:

Angry, the computer office was giving me the runaround.
Frustrated, no other business would work at these low margins.
Angry, programmer has not done her job.
Frustrated, I have to do 3 jobs simultaneously.
Irritable, I had a 4:30 appointment and wasn't ready.
Angry, this guy is full of bullshit.
Upset, the equipment I was working on was junk.

These examples come from men working in both white-collar and blue-collar jobs. Men's investment in their tasks—whether it is making steel or selling boats—seemed to set them up for a fall when things did not work out.

This relationship between competitive zeal and negative emotion was confirmed by our quantitative data. The fathers in the study who reported feeling more competitive at their jobs, relative to other parts of their lives, also reported significantly greater frustration, $r(50) = .29$, $p < .05$, disappointment, $r(49) = .27$, $p < .05$, nervousness, $r(50) = .33$, $p < .05$, and anger, $r(48) = .24$, $p < .10$, at their jobs.[4] Similarly, reporting high rates of deep attention at work was related to higher rates of frustration and other negative emotions (Larson & Richards, 1994a). In other words, it was those men who reported feeling most competitive and absorbed in their jobs who most often became upset in this context. These correlations, then, suggest that men's negative emotions at work emerge partly from how they approach their jobs—that their orientation of competitive individualism leads to a higher probability of negative emotions.

BOYS' AND MEN'S INTERACTIONS WITH FRIENDS

We find evidence of these same dynamics in other contexts of male-male interactions. The boys in our young adolescent study reported feeling competitive more often than girls, and these feelings were most frequent in the company of other boys. They reported feeling competitive 44% of the time when they were with other boys, whereas girls reported feeling competitive 29% of the time when they were with girls. Even if we exclude times playing sports and games, boys' rates of feeling competitive were greater (boys, 36%, vs. girls, 25%), and their rates of feeling cooperative were less (34% vs. 47%).

Boys' interactions with other boys may be the context in which the competitive individualism of adult men is bred. Maccoby (1990) has described a distinct culture of interaction that appears to emerge in boys' interactions with other boys. Boys act differently in the presence of other boys than they act when tested individually. This social world of boys is more hierarchical than girls' social world, involving more frequent manipulation of status and more posturing and counter-posturing to assert dominance. In the boys' world, there is more stress on being tough and less emphasis on being nice; social relationships are more competitive, and overt aggression is more common (Crick, this volume; Maccoby, 1988; Thorne, 1993). Reviewing this literature, Hall (1987) concludes that "verbal challenge is a hallmark of boys' interactions." Continuity in this mode of interaction into adulthood is suggested by the finding that men in our study also reported higher rates of feeling competitive when with friends than did women (30% vs. 17%).

This undercurrent of competitiveness in male-male interactions may dampen boys' and men's emotional experience with friends. We have seen that boys reported less positive affect with others than girls (Figure 5)—although this pattern was not exclusive to male-male interactions. Among the adult men, we did find a more discriminate pattern—their emotions with friends were not very positive, on average, and were significantly less positive than were women's emotions with their friends (Larson & Richards, 1994a, p. 74). Using immediate reports, Reis and colleagues also found that adult men experience less satisfaction and pleasantness in their daily social interactions than do women, particularly in interactions with same-gender companions (Reis, Senchak, & Solomon, 1985; Wheeler, Reis, & Nezlek, 1983).

MALE EMOTION CULTURE

The parallels between men's experience with friends and at their jobs suggest to us a general portrait of the conditions under which males negotiate and experience male-male interactions. Sports and warfare are root metaphors of male culture and express a competitive, Social Darwinist moral order. The heros of the male world, from Tiger Woods to Colin Powell, are winners. They are individuals who have fought their way to victory, through extraordinary effort. Sportscasters give their greatest praise to Michael Jordan, not for his incomparable talent, but for his extraordinary work ethic and tenacious competitiveness.

Our data show how this competitive orientation permeates ordinary daily, male-male interactions, suggesting that it sets them up for more frequent negative emotion. At work, men's high rates of absorption and feeling competitive were related to more frequent experience of disappointment, frustration, and anger. Their investment in instrumental goals appears to make them more vulnerable to upset when things stand in their way. The world of competition inevitably produces losers as well as winners: competition is often a zero-sum game, and rewards for one person may often mean disappointments for another.

We also think that this competitive orientation may interfere with men's experiencing some of the positive emotion that women get from social interactions. To the extent that men perceive it as a "dog-eat-dog world," they need to be more guarded among peers and suspicious of intimacy. This orientation gives a more adversarial edge to peer relationships. Reis and associates find that, although men are capable of intimacy, they appear less willing to engage in meaningful, "loneliness-reducing" interactions during daily affiliations (Reis, Lin, Bennett, & Nezlek, 1993; Reis et al., 1985; Wheeler et al., 1983). As we have seen, men are as emotional as women—but male culture inhibits their expression of these feelings. We have also seen that men and boys are focused on, and emotionally responsive to, impersonal aspects of the situation rather than on the relationships (Table 1). It is not surprising, then, that men's relationships with friends have often been found to be shallow, involving little personal disclosure (Brown, 1981; Weiss, 1990).

To summarize, we argue that men's emotions in male-male interactions are not a direct product of emotional scripts—we do not believe that men are programmed, biologically or socially, to have certain emotions in these contexts. Rather, we see them as an indirect result of a male culture that is focused on outcomes, on competition, and on situations rather than people. The standing pattern of frequent negative emotion at men's jobs, we believe, emerges from this culture of competitive interaction.

We would be remiss if we gave the impression that competitiveness does not take place among girls and women. Crick's and Gill's chapters in this volume show us that it does, though often in less overt ways. Thorne (1993) has emphasized that male and female cultures are highly overlapping. What our evidence indicates is that competitiveness is less evident, perhaps less near the surface, for women in the job sphere and for girls in daily interactions with other girls; we think this may allow them to experience more frequent positive emotions in these contexts.

These considerations lead us to the interesting question of what happens when the competitive world view of male culture interacts with the more cooperative and empathetic world view of female culture. We turn, then, to an examination of daily home and marital interactions as another context in which gendered patterns of emotion emerge.

The Politics of Emotion in Male-Female Family Interactions

Why do men experience more positive emotion and less negative emotion than women in the home sphere? Our orientation to gender-as-process suggests that emotions result from daily negotiations within contexts—over the meaning of events, over rights and morality, over obligations, responsibilities, and control of resources. This leads us to consider men's and women's emotions in the home sphere as reflective of their daily bargaining as marital partners. In this section we argue that gendered within-context background factors—specifically marital roles and differences in patterns of emotional communication—set the stage for differences in the daily negotiation of emotion in the home sphere. We propose that emotions result from the interaction of the long-term, historical division of roles between husbands and wives and the short-term, immediate ways in which these are negotiated.

FATHERS' INTERPRETATIONS OF THEIR FAMILY ROLE

The historic evolution of Western marital roles is a key background factor that shapes husbands' and wives' emotional experience in the home sphere. Despite rhetoric to the contrary, evidence indicates that the historic differentiation of male and female family roles is alive and well. Even in households where wives are employed full-time, the husbands are still typically defined as the primary breadwinner for the family (Perry-Jenkins & Crouter, 1990), and primary responsibility for household and family tasks falls to their wives.

This historic interpretation of their role, we believe, leads men to act, think, and thus feel differently than women when they come home from work. Because of their provider responsibility—because they "give at work"—men often claim the right to relax and enjoy themselves at home (Weiss, 1990). After fighting the good fight at work, after engaging in competitive individualism at the office, men feel they have done their part for the family and deserve the right to attend to their own needs. One working-class father in our study would lie down on the couch for a nap in the middle of their small house and insist that no one disturb him. This pattern repeats itself on Saturday afternoon, when men are much more likely than their wives to devote themselves to leisure activities—often watching sports on TV—while their wives are more often doing household work (Larson & Richards, 1994a).

Men's more positive affect in the family sphere follows directly from this interpretation of their role. At home the men in our study spent proportionally more time than their wives in leisure activities, and leisure is associated with more positive emotional experience (Larson et al., 1994). Yet, even when men did family tasks at home, we found that they reported more favorable affect than their wives. This may have been partly because men performed more enjoyable tasks (fixing the deck vs. doing laundry). Closer analyses also suggested that men experience more choice over doing household tasks, which was related to their more favorable affect. Men appeared to perform household tasks when they wanted to; women performed household work when such tasks had to be done (Larson & Richards, 1994a).

The history of fathers' family role also shapes their interactions with their children and the emotions they experience in these interactions. In the 19th and early 20th centuries, the perception that women were more emotionally sensitive than men was seen as making them better suited to providing direct care to children (Pleck, 1987). As a result of this legacy, research now consistently finds that fathers engage in less childcare than mothers, while devoting proportionally more of their time with their children to playful activities (Collins & Russell, 1991; Lamb, 1986; Larson, 1993). Our findings also show that fathers experience more choice about engaging in activities with their children (Larson & Richards, 1994a). Given this choice and given that their activities are more recreational, it is not surprising that fathers also report more favorable emotion during interactions with their children. Perhaps the most intriguing finding was the suggestion in our data that fathers' interactions with their children were partly contingent on the fathers being in a positive mood. Fathering is enjoyable because it is a voluntary activity.

In sum, even before discussing the nature of transactions between husbands and wives, we have seen a basis for men's differing emotional experience in the family. Men's positive emotion in the family sphere derives, at least partly, from their interpretation of their husband-father role and the comparative liberty it gives them in hour-to-hour interactions in this context. In some families, these liberties were contested—wives had not simply granted their husbands freedom and challenged the husbands' claim of entitlement. Role bargaining is ongoing in marriages (Hood, 1983), but these wives often found themselves helpless to do much about it: their husbands contributed to household tasks as they wished and left their wives to fill in the pieces. Men's more positive emotions in the family sphere, then, emerge in part from men's interpretation of their historic role and how it shapes their immediate behavior.

DIFFERENCES IN THE EMOTIONAL COMMUNICATION OF MEN AND WOMEN

Another background factor that shapes the husbands' and wives' differing experiences in the family is differences in patterns of emotional communication and in the underlying dynamics of power. Research suggests a number of gender differences in emotional communication patterns that may affect marital transactions:

Female Sensitivity to Emotional Cues A consistent finding of laboratory research with U.S. samples is that women, on average, are better than men at reading nonverbal cues of emotions in others (Hall, 1987). One might attribute this finding to women's greater investment in interpersonal affairs—to women's socialization in the more empathetic, people-centered values. Girls and women show more empathy than males (Eisenberg & Lennon, 1983). Within a family context, this attunement to others may be accentuated by women's historic role as emotional manager, which gives them responsibility for being sensitive to the emotions of other family members (Rook, Dooley, & Catalano, 1991). It can also be linked to their lesser position of power in the family: in some (though not all) experimental studies, when relative status is manipulated, the person with lower status reads the other's emotions more accurately (Hall,

1987). The common explanation is that people of higher status can afford not to notice what others are feeling, whereas those of lower status need to figure out the others' emotions because these feelings will affect the others' behavior—and thus impact them.

Male Stonewalling The parallel finding is that not only are males less apt to read emotional cues than females, but they are also less inclined to express emotions, with the exception of anger (Balswick, 1988; LaFrance & Banaji, 1992). This pattern, too, can be linked to the power relationship between men and women. Males' emotional inexpressiveness, it has been suggested, increases their control in male-female relationships by withholding information about their vulnerabilities (Sattel, 1976). By giving the appearance that they are unwavering, by not displaying weakness, and by creating the impression that their decisions are made with rationality and efficiency, men maintain and strengthen their power in a relationship. Thus, men more often express anger, the one emotion whose direct expression furnishes power, and less often express other emotions whose expression could reduce power.

Approach-Withdrawal Another difference lies in the value that men and women place on emotional communication. This difference has often been identified with a frequent marital configuration variously labeled the "approach-withdrawal," "pursuer-distancer," or "intrusion-rejection" pattern (Jacobson, 1989). Women are twice as likely to be the pursuer—that is, the person who attempts to initiate intimacy and discussion about matters relevant to the relationship— and men the distancer (Christensen & Heavey, 1993).

This difference in the value attributed to communication may be particularly evident in husbands' and wives' dispositions at the end of the work day. In Blood and Wolfe's (1960) classic study of marriage, wives who reported more frequent communication with their husbands about the husbands' work reported higher satisfaction with marital companionship overall. This suggests that many wives want a husband who expresses his feelings when he comes home from work, as part of a desire for intimacy. However, the husbands' inexpressiveness and their lesser desire for emotional communication may prove an obstacle to this type of interaction, creating a pursuer-distancer type of dynamic.

This dynamic is important, among other things, because of the asymmetry it creates in interactions. The partner wanting less communication can achieve that objective whether the spouse agrees or not, simply by withdrawing. Thus this partner, typically the husband, has more power. But the partner wanting greater closeness can attain it only by requesting and getting the spouse's cooperation. Indeed, all three of the gender differences in communication create asymmetries that affect how emotions are negotiated and transacted in daily marital interactions.

EMOTIONAL TRANSMISSION BETWEEN HUSBAND AND WIFE

Our empirical window for understanding daily marital transactions is the study of "emotional transmission" or "contagion." We are interested in patterns in which one individual's strong emotions have an impact on the subsequent emotional states of another. In order to study emotion transmission, we have selected occasions in our ESM family data when husbands and wives provided pairs of reports close together in time and were in contact during that interval. The question is, does one person's emotion at Time 1 predict the other's subsequent emotion at Time 2? For this analysis, we again used the scale of affect, with values converted to z-scores to remove differences between individuals in means and standard deviations for the scale.

The findings indicate that emotions in husbands significantly influence subsequent emotions in wives, but not the reverse. As Figure 8 shows, there is a significant path from the husbands' emotions at one point in time to their wives' emotions at the subsequent point in time (Larson & Richards, 1994a). However, the path from wife to husband is not significant. Two examples illustrate this emotional transmission from husband to wife. In one case, a father woke up on Saturday morning feeling "crabby" and then blew up because his wife was giving more attention to the children's needs than to his. Although she woke up in a good mood, her husband's outburst at her put her in a negative mood. In the second example, a father became upset during a phone call to make arrangements to run a hot dog stand at a school function ("we're getting a dirty deal," he

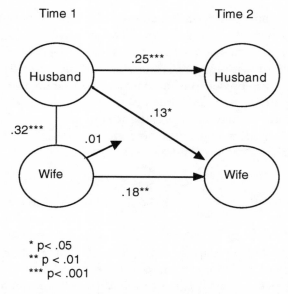

Figure 8. Emotional transmission between husband and wife.

writes). He than shared his anger with his wife, and she became up-set.

This path of transmission from husband to wife has also been found in similar research that uses end-of-the-day diaries, rather than immediate reports. In these diary studies, the husbands' nega-tive events and emotions were more likely to predict wives' subse-quent emotions than the reverse (Bolger, DeLongis, Kessler, & Wethington, 1989; Thompson & Bolger, in press). Laboratory re-search, examining repeated observations of emotion over seconds and minutes, also shows that the husbands' expression of negative emotion more often triggered wives' subsequent expression of neg-ative emotion than vice versa (Notarius & Johnson, 1982; Roberts & Krokoff, 1990), particularly in distressed marriages (Gottman, 1979; Gutherie & Noller, 1988; Katz, Kramer, & Gottman, 1992).

This finding that emotions most often flow from husbands to wives may be attributable to characteristics of the gender differences in emotional communication just discussed. Women's greater skill at detecting others' emotions may make them more susceptible to receiving these emotions; in fact, women are more often susceptible to the emotions of others in nonfamily interactions (Doherty, Orimoto, Singelis, Hatfield, & Hebb, 1995; Hatfield, Cacioppo, & Rapson, 1994). The absence of a path from wife to husband may be attributable to men's lesser skills at reading emotions and the lesser value they place on emotional exchange. They may not read or care about the signals indicating their wives' emotions. As more frequent "distancers" in marital interactions, men may be less interested in their wives' emotions.

This pattern of unidirectional transmission may also stem from differences in women's and men's interpretation of their family roles. Mothers' assumption of the "burden of care" for the family (Rook, Dooley, & Catalano, 1991) may increase their likelihood of being receivers of others' emotions. Wives' "uptake" of their husbands' emotions may be part of their broader "emotion work" in families (DeVault, 1991). In contrast, men may feel that their labor at their jobs excuses them from the role of being sensitive to the feelings of their wives.

What seems likely is that this unidirectional path of emotional transmission not only derives from but also reproduces a power differential between husband and wife. We suspect that the husbands' repeated experience of being a sender and the wives' repeated experience of being a receiver reinforce men's comparative power and thus also reinforce their experience of differing standing patterns of emotion in the family context.

EMOTIONAL TRANSMISSION BETWEEN WORK AND HOME

There is one last piece we would like to add to the puzzle before concluding. This piece shows more fully how immediate transactions—and the emotions they generate—emerge partly from the background factors discussed (gender roles and communication patterns). It also illuminates that the spheres of home and work are not separate but are interrelated.

In our ESM family study, we found that the gender differential in emotional transmission was dramatically heightened at the end of the day when the husbands came home from work. We examined the transmission for intervals in which the husband was at work at Time 1, and both wife and husband were at home at Time 2. These findings show a very strong path of transmission from husband to wife (*beta* = .40). The dominance of the husbands' emotions is suggested by what happens with the wives' emotions. A wife's affect at Time 2 is related to a husband's prior emotion at work, but her prior emotion does not affect his. Furthermore, her affect at Time 2 is unrelated to her *own* affect at the prior report before the husband comes home (Larson & Richards, 1994a).

Two examples illustrate the scenario in which the husbands' emotions affect the wives' emotions during this work-to-home transition. A husband, who had had a bad day at work, refused to stop to get groceries on the way home, which greatly aggravated his wife. A factory worker stopped at the track on the way home and lost a lot of money; he then came home and spread his distress to his wife and daughter.

Research using daily diaries has also found this path of emotional transmission from father's job to home. In several studies, Repetti (1989, 1993, 1997) has found that the stress a father experiences at his job during the day affects his emotional state in the evening and that this stress leads him to be more withdrawn, express more anger, and use more punitive discipline with children in the evening. Bolger and colleagues (1989) found that the husbands' frequency of arguments at work on a particular day was correlated with the frequency of arguments with their spouses on the same evening at $r=.70$, but for wives this correlation was only $r = .20$. Crouter Perry-Jenkins, Huston, and Crawford (1989) found that fathers' stress at work predicted mothers' reports of negative marital interactions in the evening.

We can think about these transactions from the point of view of both the husband and wife. From the man's point of view, the pattern of bringing emotion home from work is part of the historic privilege of his role as family breadwinner. Since the initial negative emotion was caused by his job, the husband may not experience himself as exercising power in this work-to-home transaction. As Turner (1968) wrote in another context, "because the husband must adjust to the demands of his occupation and the family in turn must accommodate to his demands on behalf of his occupational obligations, the husband appears to dominate his wife and children. But as an agent of economic institutions, he perceives himself as controlled rather than as controlling" (p. 282).

There may also be some payoffs for men not to consciously acknowledge the negative emotion they bring home from the workplace. One study found that among male (but not female) caregivers, greater self-awareness of emotions was associated with more health complaints and perception of burden (Gold, Franz, Reis, & Senneville, 1994). Thus, for husbands returning home from work with negative emotions, trying not to experience or express them may serve as a coping function, at least from the perspective that avoiding conscious awareness reduces the potential collateral damage of feeling sick and burdened, feelings that are incompatible with traditional masculinity. Even if the husband's stance is—as expressed in the title of a recent book about men and depression—"I don't want to talk about it" (Real, 1997), it may affect his wife.

Women's response to the return of their husbands is also conditioned by their perception of their family role. They see family care as part of their role: in some cases, wives may be active recipients of their husbands' emotions. When husbands have a "bad day" at work, wives may relieve them of even the limited domestic responsibilities they ordinarily have (Repetti, 1989, 1993). As Bolger et al. (1989, p. 175) note, "the contagion of work stress into the home sets in motion a process of dyadic adjustment, whereby individuals, particularly wives, appear to modify [i.e., increase] their housework efforts to compensate for the work stresses of their spouses." In the case of the factory worker who came home distraught from the track, the subsequent report found his wife massaging her husband's back. At the same time, the husbands' ability to insulate themselves from these negative emotions generated in their wives reduces the potential cost to husbands. Thus, wives respond to their husbands' negative workplace emotions partially by empathically "soaking it up" as well as by not pressing them to do more in the family.

Women may be making a rational and deliberate choice under the circumstances. Thompson (1991) argues that most wives feel the typical division of labor is fair because the "outcome value" they are trying to maximize is not necessarily their own well-being but rather a value of family "care." The emotional dynamics revealed in ESM and other data play a part in this process. The husbands' modal emotional pattern in their role enactment is to use home time for recuperation from the emotional duress of their jobs; if wives pressed

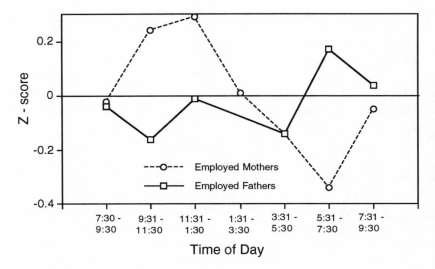

Figure 9. Emotions of employed mothers and fathers across the day.

them to feel greater obligation for family work, it would undermine this compensatory function. Many employed wives correctly perceive that trying to enlist their husbands to do more would only stimulate negative approach-withdrawal interaction. By permitting their husbands to use home time primarily for emotional recuperation, employed wives can be viewed as maximizing "care" consistent with Thompson's conceptualization.

The resulting combination of husbands' and wives' interpretations of their situations is that when dad brings home negative emotion it gets passed to mom. In essence, when husbands return home, they "export" their negative work affect to their wives, reproducing gender differences in the experience at home. The implication of this type of transaction is suggested by the overall pattern of affect by time of day for employed fathers and mothers. One can see in Figure 9 that when fathers come home from work, their emotions rise; when employed mothers come home, their emotions fall. We cannot attribute all of this pattern to emotional transmission—it partly results from differences in husbands' and wives' experience of obligations in the home sphere, as discussed earlier. Nonetheless, the husbands' more positive affect at home might be partly attributable to these transactions. Men bring home negative feelings and transmit these feelings to their wives, which may make them free to derive positive emotional satisfactions from the less interpersonal aspects of their home and family environment.

THE INTERACTION OF MALE AND FEMALE EMOTION CULTURES

What we see in the home sphere, then, is a dynamic in which two differing emotion cultures interact. Men come home from their jobs having participated in an impersonal, competitive, individualistic culture, in which expression of feeling may be viewed with suspicion. This orientation interacts with the more empathetic, intimacy-seeking female emotion culture. In this interaction of cultures, men are more impervious and readily seize the opportunity to relax and recover from the rigors of the day, whereas women are more receptive and thus vulnerable to the emotions that their husbands bring home. The result is differences in the standing patterns of emotion in which husbands experience more positive emotions in this sphere than their wives.

We have argued that emotions in the family emerge from daily transactions, but that this emergence occurs within a context of historic role expectations, gender orientations, family exigencies, and prior interactions between a particular husband and wife. Emotions are negotiated and contested, but a thick history of factors enters into these negotiations—the stage has been set. The emotional patterns that result from these transactions partly derive from differences in spouses' relative power. We think the repeated experience of these transactions also reinforces and re-creates these power differences. Just as the approach-withdrawal dynamic is self-perpetuating and reproduces gender differences, the transmission and reception of emotion may also be a mechanism that reproduces gender differences within this context.

This view of emotion as fluid and negotiated suggests that men's and women's emotions in this sphere may change as the daily ecology of transactions changes. Our data suggest that the daily emotional patterns of wives' lives change when they become employed. One-parent families and gay and lesbian families represent other family variants that are important to study. While not well represented in our sample, another increasingly frequent pattern in conjugal households is the situation in which parents work different shifts, so wives are not present to receive their husbands' emotions when they come home (Pleck & Staines, 1985; Presser, 1989). Scholars have also noted that fathers in two-shift families are more involved in their children's care, a potentially positive correlate, but we know little about this asynchrony of parents' schedules, which may alter the emotional exchange between marital partners. Further research might examine how this and other variations in family ecology change the emotional politics between husbands and wives and the resulting emotional profiles at home.

Conclusion

Before summarizing our conclusions, we want to do a reality check to ascertain that we have not exaggerated the extent of gender differences suggested by our findings. Our data definitely take the form of highly overlapping bell curves. The gender differences we found represent slivers of difference in these overlapping curves. There is enormous variation *within* each gender: women and girls who participate in a culture of competitive individualism, and men who participate in a culture of interpersonal relationships and nurturing. We need to recognize that there are "multiple masculinities," conflicting voices, counterpoint, and "double-voiced style," even within a single individual (Thorne, 1993). Likewise, there is enormous variation within marriages and between marriages. We have described a modal type of husband-wife transaction, but many dyads may not follow this script; and within any one dyad, the negotiation of emotion may vary greatly from day to day.

In qualifying our conclusions, we also note the limitations of our methodology. Our time-sampling procedure provides a window on experienced emotions but little direct information on expressed emotion. If we are discussing the daily negotiation of feelings, surely the two need to be discussed hand-in-hand. It would be valuable to combine our "inside-the-head" data with observational data that provide a narrative account of what is said and expressed in these daily transactions between people.

Having emphasized these limitations, we pull together the main points we have been trying to make. First, we have found little evidence of consistent cross-situational gender differences in felt emotion during daily life. Although prior research indicates gender differences in expressed emotion, with males being less expressive, our data indicate that, by their own admission, men and boys differ little from women and girls in the range of emotions they feel. The only marked difference we found was that American adolescent boys experienced less frequent positive emotion than girls, but this was not the case in Korea.

This absence of substantial cross-situational gender difference, we argue, suggests that there are not fundamental—inside the person—temperamental or trait differences in emotional experience between males and females. Although we know that genetics makes a substantial contribution to emotionality, these findings suggest that these innate dispositions are passed from parent to child without regard to a person's sex. Likewise, these findings weigh against an interpretation that little boys and little girls are socialized into differing core emotional scripts or emotional dispositions. Although there is consistent evidence of gender differences in *expression* of emotion in our culture—attributable to gender-based display rules—our data indicate that beneath the veneer, males are just as emotional in what they experience. To summarize, our evidence fails to support the presence of top-down, cross-situational main effects.

Instead, what our findings show are more subtle gender differences in emotional experience *within contexts*. We give particular attention to findings that adult men experience more negative affect than women at their jobs, and men experience more positive emotion at home. These findings, we argue, suggest gender differences in emotional experience that are generated, not top-down, from inherited temperaments or learned traits, but bottom-up, from the hour-to-hour transactions of daily life. We suggest that the greater negative emotions that men feel at their jobs and the lesser positive emotions that boys and men feel in interactions with same-gender peers emerge from a male subculture of competitive individualism, a subculture in which the focus on instrumental achievement sets men up for frustration, in which one person's triumph is gained at the cost of another's defeat, and in which a more adversarial relationship to peers may impair intimacy and limit the experience of positive emotion. We also suggest that married men's greater positive affect at home, relative to their wives, is attributable partly to negotiation of roles between husbands and wives and to a resultant mode of transaction in which the husbands' negative emotions from their work are transmitted to their wives.

For the domain of emotional experience, then, we reject a gender-as-difference model in favor of a gender-as-process model. We argue that the gender differences in emotional experience that we have seen within contexts do not inhere in maleness or femaleness; rather, they are emergent from the types of transactions that males and females experience. We cannot rule out the possibility that the nature of these transactions results from *other* top-down genetic or socialized differences that we have not discussed. And we definitely recognize that these transactions do not occur in a vacuum: they are affected by background factors—by the historical evolution of male and female subcultures, communication patterns, and the social negotiation of roles and power between men and women. Our basic point, however, is that causality goes both ways between immediate interactions and larger-order structures, and just as these background factors affect the daily differences in experience of males and females, daily experience affects and reproduces power relationships and the larger societal construction of gender.

NOTES

1. This use of aggregated scores for each individual as the unit of analysis could be seen as a conservative test, since the degrees of freedom for the repeated measurements within each person are not being used. An alternative approach is to use multilevel modeling (ML), a new statistical procedure that allows us to use each report as the unit of analysis, while modeling the fact that these reports are nested within people (Goldstein, 1987). To evaluate this, we employed ML for all the analyses in Figures 1–6 and came up with identical findings to those based on aggregate scores.

2. There is another concern about our findings that might be raised by an experimentalist. We argued that it is a virtue of the ESM that it obtains emotions during the natural contexts of people's lives, yet an experimentalist might see this as a vice: possibly the similarities between males and females in these data result from differential choice of daily situations. Our comparison of genders may be confounded by niche picking, in which people with differing temperaments and dispositions choose daily settings that moderate or facilitate their tendencies. Indeed, there is evidence that emo-

tionally reactive people prefer situations of lower stimulative value, whereas less emotionally reactive people prefer more stimulating situations; extroversion is associated with spending more time in social recreation, sensation seeking with sensation-provoking situations (Van Heck, 1991, p. 168). Might lower innate or acquired emotional reactivity in males be offset by a tendency to put themselves in more emotionally arousing situations?

It is difficult to fully address this concern. True, men may be somewhat more likely to walk down dark alleys at night, but then men are on average larger and heavier than women, making the situation different for them. Is it really possible to talk about the equivalence of situations between men and women? It goes against our ecological perception to try to conceptualize the individual as separate from the daily situations in which he or she lives. While acknowledging that males and females do choose and find themselves in different daily life situations, we are not sure how one could really control for this, or even whether that would be meaningful.

3. This pattern of gender difference related to being alone versus being with others did not occur for our sample of adults.

4. These analyses were conducted using variables that were z-scored within each person. We report the correlation between a person's average z-score for competitive feelings when at work with that person's average z-score for frustration and other negative emotions when at work.

REFERENCES

Abu-Lughod, L., & Lutz, C. (1990). Introduction: Emotion, discourse, and the politics of everyday life. In L. Abu-Lughod & C. Lutz (Eds.), *Language and the politics of emotion* (pp. 1–23). New York: Cambridge University Press.

Archer, J. (1996). Comparing men and women: What is being compared and why? *American Psychologist, 51,* 153–154.

Averill, J. R., & Thomas-Knowles, C. (1991). Emotional creativity. In K. T. Strongman (Ed.), *International review of studies on emotion* (Vol. 1, pp. 269–299). New York: John Wiley & Sons.

Balswick, J. (1988). *The inexpressive male.* Lexington MA: Lexington Books.

Barker, R. G. (1968). *Ecological psychology.* Stanford CA: Stanford University Press.

Berscheid, E. (1990). Contemporary vocabularies of emotion. In A. M. Isen & B. S. Moore (Eds.), *Affect and social behavior* (pp. 22–38). New York: Cambridge University Press.

Blood, R. O., & Wolfe, D. M. (1960). *Husbands and wives: The dynamics of married living.* New York: Free Press.

Bolger, N., DeLongis, A., Kessler, R. C., & Wethington, E. (1989). The contagion of stress across multiple roles. *Journal of Marriage and the Family, 51,* 175–183.

Brannon, R. (1976). The male sex role: Our culture's blueprint for manhood and what it's done for us lately. In D. David & R. Brannon (Eds.), *The forty-nine percent majority: The male sex role* (pp. 1–48). Reading MA: Addison-Wesley.

Brickman, P., Coates, D., & Janoff-Bulman, R. (1978). Lottery winners and accident victims: Is happiness relative? *Journal of Personality and Social Psychology, 36*(8), 917–927.

Brody, L. R. (1985). Gender differences in emotional development: A review of theories and research. *Journal of Personality, 53*, 102–149.

Brody, L. R. (1993). On understanding gender differences in the expression of emotion. In S. L. Ablon, D. Brown, E. J. Khantzian, & J. E. Mack (Eds.), *Human feelings: Explorations in affect development and meaning* (pp. 87–121). Hillsdale NJ: Analytic Press.

Brody, L. R. (1996). Gender, emotional expression, and parent-child boundaries. In S. Fein, R. D. Kavanaugh, & B. Zimmerberg (Eds.), *Emotion: Interdisciplinary perspectives* (pp. 139–170). Hillsdale NJ: Lawrence Erlbaum.

Brown, B. B. (1981). A life-span approach to friendship: Age-related dimensions of an ageless relationship. In H. Lopata & D. Maines (Eds.), *Research on the interweave of social roles: Vol. 2. Friendship* (pp. 23–50). Greenwich CT: JAI Press.

Buss, A. (1989). Temperaments as personality traits. In J. E. Bates, G. A. Kohnstamm, & M. K. Rothbart (Eds.), *Temperament in childhood* (pp. 49–58). New York: John Wiley & Sons.

Butler, J. P. (1990). *Gender trouble: Gender and the subversion of identity.* New York: Routledge.

Christensen, A., & Heavey, C. L. (1993). Gender differences in marital conflict: The demand/withdraw interaction pattern. In S. Oskamp & M. Constanzo (Eds.), *Gender issues in contemporary society* (pp. 113–142). Newbury Park CA: Sage.

Collins, W. A., & Russell, G. (1991). Mother-child and father-child relationships in middle childhood and adolescence: A developmental analysis. *Developmental Review, 11*, 99–136.

Crouter, A. C., Perry-Jenkins, M., Huston, T. L., & Crawford, D. W. (1989). The influence of work-induced psychological states on behavior at home. *Basic and Applied Social Psychology, 10*(3), 273–292.

Csikszentmihalyi, M., & Larson, R. (1987). The Experience Sampling Method. *Journal of Nervous and Mental Disease, 175*, 526–536.

Davidson, R. J. (1994). On emotion, mood, and related affective constructs. In R. J. Davidson & P. Ekman (Eds.), *The nature of emotion* (pp. 51–55). New York: Oxford University Press.

DeVault, M. L. (1991). *Feeding the family: The social organization of caring as gendered work.* Chicago: University of Chicago Press.

Diener, E., & Diener, C. (1996). Most people are happy. *Psychological Science, 7*(3), 181–185.

Diener, E., Sandvik, E., & Larsen, R. J. (1985). Age and sex effects for emotional intensity. *Developmental Psychology, 21*(3), 542–546.

Doherty, R. W., Orimoto, L., Singelis, T. M., Hatfield, E., & Hebb, J. (1995). Emotional contagion. *Psychology of Women Quarterly, 19*, 355–371.

Eisenberg, N., & Lennon, R. (1983). Sex differences in empathy and related capacities. *Psychological Bulletin, 94*(1), 100–131.

Ferree, M. (1990). Beyond separate spheres: Feminism and family research. *Journal of Marriage and the Family, 52*, 866–884.

Fujita, F., Diener, E., & Sandvik, E. (1991). Gender differences in negative affect and well-being: The case for emotional intensity. *Journal of Personality and Social Psychology, 61*(3), 427–434.

Gilbert, D. C. (1969). The young child's awareness of affect. *Child Development, 40*, 629–640.

Gold, D. P., Franz, E., Reis, M., & Senneville, C. (1994). The influence of emotional awareness and expressiveness on care-giving burden and health complaints in women and men. *Sex Roles, 31*, 205–224.

Goldsmith, H. H. (1989). Behavior-genetic approaches to temperament. In G. A. Kohnstamm, J. E. Bates, & M. K. Rothbart (Eds.), *Temperament in childhood* (pp. 111–132). New York: John Wiley & Sons.

Goldsmith, H., & Rieser-Danner, L. A. (1986). Variation among temperament theories and validation studies of temperament assessment. In G. A. Kohnstamm (Ed.), *Temperament discussed: Temperament and development in infancy and childhood* (pp. 1–9). Lisse: Swets & Zeitlinger.

Goldstein, H. (1987). *Multilevel models in educational and social research.* New York: Oxford University Press.

Gottman, J. M. (1979). *Marital interactions: Experimental investigations.* New York: Academic Press.

Greene, A. L., & Larson, R. (1991). Variations in stress activity during adolescence. In E. M. Cummings, A. L. Greene, & K. H. Karraker (Eds.), *Life span perspectives on stress and coping* (pp. 195–209). Hillsdale NJ: Lawrence Erlbaum.

Gutherie, D. M., & Noller, P. (1988). Spouses' perceptions of one another in emotional situations. In P. Noller & M. A. Fitzpatrick (Eds.), *Perspectives on marital interaction* (pp. 153–181). Philadelphia: Multilingual Matters.

Hall, J. A. (1987). On explaining gender differences. In C. Hendrick & P. Shaver (Eds.), *Sex and gender* (pp. 177–200). Newbury Park CA: Sage.

Hamer, D. H. (1996). The heritability of happiness. *Nature Genetics, 14*, 125–126.

Harré, R. (1986). An outline of the social constructionist viewpoint. In R. Harré (Ed.), *The social construction of emotions* (pp. 2–14). New York: Basil Blackwell.

Hatfield, E., Cacioppo, J. T., & Rapson, R. L. (1994). *Emotional contagion.* New York: Cambridge University Press.

Heelas, P. (1986). Emotion talk across cultures. In R. Harré (Ed.), *The social construction of emotions* (pp. 234–266). New York: Basil Blackwell.

Holloway, W. (1984). Gender differences and the production of subjectivities. In J. Henriques, W. Holloway, C. Urwin, C. Venn, & V. Walkerdine (Eds.), *Changing the subject* (pp. 26–59). London: Methuen.

Hood, J. (1983). *On becoming a two-job family.* New York: Praeger.

Jacobson, N. (1989). The politics of intimacy. *Behavior Therapist, 12*(2), 29–32.

Katz, L., Kramer, L., & Gottman, J. M. (1992). Conflict and emotions in marital, sibling, and peer relationships. In C. U. Shantz & W. W. Hartup (Eds.), *Conflict in child and adolescent development* (pp. 155–185). New York: John Wiley & Sons.

Kemper, T. D. (1991). An introduction to the sociology of emotions. In K. T. Strongman (Ed.), *International review of studies on emotion* (pp. 301–349). New York: John Wiley & Sons.

Kessler, R., & McRae, J. (1983). Trends in the relationship between sex and attempted suicide. *Journal of Health and Social Behavior, 24*, 98–110.

Kessler, R. C., & McLeod, J. D. (1984). Sex differences in vulnerability to undesirable life events. *American Sociological Review, 49*, 620–631.

LaFrance, M., & Banaji, M. (1992). Toward a reconsideration of the gender-emotion relationship. In M. S. Clark (Ed.), *Emotion and social behavior* (pp. 178–201). Newbury Park CA: Sage.

Lamb, M. E. (1986). The changing roles of fathers. In M. E. Lamb (Ed.), *The father's role: Applied perspectives* (pp. 3–27). New York: John Wiley & Sons.

Larson, R. (1989a). Beeping children and adolescents: A method for studying time use and daily experience. *Journal of Youth and Adolescence, 18*(5), 511–530.

Larson, R. (1989b). The factor structure of moods and emotions in a sample of young adolescents. Unpublished manuscript, University of Illinois at Urbana-Champaign.

Larson, R. (1993). Finding time for fatherhood: The emotional ecology of adolescent-father interactions. In S. Shulman and W. A. Collins (Eds.), *Father-adolescent relationships* (New Directions for Child Development, no. 62, pp. 7–18). San Francisco: Jossey-Bass.

Larson, R., & Asmussen, L. (1991). Anger, worry, and hurt in early adolescence: An enlarging world of negative emotions. In M. E. Colton and S. Gore (Eds.), *Adolescent stress: Causes and consequences* (pp. 21–41). New York: Aldine de Gruyter.

Larson, R., & Csikszentmihalyi, M. (1983). The Experience Sampling Method. In Harry Reis (Ed.), *New Directions for Naturalistic Methods in the Behavioral Sciences* (pp. 41–56). San Francisco: Jossey-Bass.

Larson, R., and Richards, M. (Eds.). (1989). The changing life space of early adolescence [Special issue]. *Journal of Youth and Adolescence, 18*(6), 501–626.

Larson, R., and Richards, M. H. (1994a). *Divergent realities: The emotional lives of mothers, fathers, and adolescents.* New York: Basic Books.

Larson, R., & Richards, M. H. (1994b). Family emotions: Do young adolescents and their parents experience the same states? *Journal of Research on Adolescence, 4*(4), 567–583.

Larson, R., Richards, M. H., & Perry-Jenkins, M. (1994). Divergent worlds: The daily emotional experience of mothers and fathers in the domestic and public spheres. *Journal of Personality and Social Psychology, 67*(6), 1034–1046.

Lee, M. (1994). *Cultural differences in the daily manifestation of adolescent depression: A comparative study of American and Korean high school seniors.* Unpublished doctoral dissertation, University of Illinois at Urbana-Champaign.

LeFevre, J., Hedricks, C., Church, R. B., & McClintock, M. (1992). Psychological and social behavior of couples over a menstrual cycle: "On-the-spot" sampling from everyday life. In A. J. Dan & L. L. Lewis (Eds.), *Menstrual health in women's lives* (pp. 75–82). Champaign: University of Illinois Press.

Levant, R. F., Hirsch, L. S., Celentano, E., Cozza, T. M., Hill, S., Mac-Eachern, M., Marty, N., & Schnedeker, J. (1992). The male role: An investigation of contemporary norms. *Journal of Mental Health Counseling, 14*(3), 325–337.

Levenson, R. W. (1994). Human emotion: A functional view. In R. J. Davidson & P. Ekman (Eds.), *The nature of emotion* (pp. 123–126). New York: Oxford University Press.

Lewin, K. (1938). Field theory and experiment in social psychology: Concepts and methods. *American Journal of Sociology, 44,* 868–896.

Lutz, C. A. (1988). *Unnatural emotions: Everyday sentiments on a Micronesian atoll and their challenge to western theory.* Chicago: University of Chicago Press.

Lykken, D. T., & Tellegen, A. (1996). Happiness is a stochastic phenomenon. *Psychological Science, 7*(3), 186–189.

Maccoby, E. E. (1988). Gender as a social category. *Developmental Psychology, 24,* 755–765.

Maccoby, E. E. (1990). Gender and relationships: A developmental account. *American Psychologist, 45,* 513–520.

Marecek, J. (1995). Gender, politics, and psychology's way of knowing. *American Psychologist, 50,* 162–163.

McAdams, D. P., & Constantian, C. A. (1983). Intimacy and affiliation motives in daily living: An experience sampling analysis. *Journal of Personality and Social Psychology, 45,* 951–961.

McNaughton, N. (1989). *Biology and emotion.* Cambridge: Cambridge University Press.

Miller, W. I. (1994, 14–17 July). The politics of emotion display in heroic society. In N. H. Frijda (Ed.), *Proceedings of the 8th Conference of the International Society for Research on Emotions.* Cambridge: ISRE, Fitzwilliam College, Cambridge University.

Mirowsky, J., & Ross, C. E. (1989). *Social causes of psychological distress.* New York: Aldine de Gruyter.

National Center for Health Statistics. (1991). *Vital statistics of the United States, 1988: Vol. 2. Mortality.* Hyattsville MD: Author.

Nolen-Hoeksema, S. (1994). An interactive model for the emergence of gender differences in depression in adolescence. *Journal of Research on Adolescence, 4*(4), 519–534.

Notarius, C. I., & Johnson, J. S. (1982). Emotional expression in husbands and wives. *Journal of Marriage and the Family, 44,* 483–489.

Panksepp, J. (1993). Neurochemical control of moods and emotions: Amino acids to neuropeptides. In J. M. Haviland & M. Lewis (Eds.), *Handbook of emotions* (pp. 87–107). New York: Guilford Press.

Panksepp, J. (1996). Affective neuroscience: A paradigm to study the animate circuits for human emotions. In S. Fein, R. D. Kavanaugh, & B. Zimmerberg (Eds.), *Emotion: Interdisciplinary perspectives* (pp. 29–60). Hillside NJ: Lawrence Erlbaum.

Perry-Jenkins, M., & Crouter, A. C. (1990). Men's provider-role attitudes: Implications for household work and marital satisfaction. *Journal of Family Issues, 11*, 136–156.

Pleck, J. H. (1987). Men in domestic settings: American fathering in historical perspective. In M. S. Kimmel (Ed.), *Changing men: New directions in research on men and masculinity* (pp. 83–97). Newbury Park CA: Sage.

Pleck, J. H., & Staines, G. (1985). Work schedules and family life in two-earner couples. *Journal of Family Issues, 6*(1), 61–81.

Plomin, R., Chipuer, H., & Neiderhiser, J. (1994). Behavioral genetic evidence for the importance of nonshared environment. In E. M. Hetherington, D. Reiss, & R. Plomin (Eds.), *Separate social worlds of siblings: The impact of nonshared environment on development* (pp. 1–31). Hillsdale NJ: Lawrence Erlbaum.

Plutchik, R., & Kellerman, H. (Eds.). (1986). *Emotion: Theory, research, and experience* (Vol. 3). Orlando FL: Academic Press.

Presser, H. B. (1989). Can we make time for the children? The economy, work schedules, and child care. *Demography, 26*, 523–543.

Real, T. (1987). *I don't want to talk about it: Overcoming the secret legacy of male depression.* New York: Simon & Schuster.

Reis, H. T., Lin, Y., Bennett, M. E., & Nezlek, J. B. (1993). Change and consistency in social participation during early adulthood. *Developmental Psychology, 29*(4), 633–645.

Reis, H. T., Senchak, M., & Solomon, B. (1985). Sex differences in the intimacy of social interactions: Further examination of potential explanations. *Journal of Personality and Social Psychology, 48*(5), 1204–1217.

Repetti, R. L. (1989). Effects of daily workload on subsequent behavior during marital interaction: The roles of social withdrawal and spouse support. *Journal of Personality and Social Psychology, 57*(4), 651–659.

Repetti, R. L. (1993). Short-term effects of occupational stressors on daily mood and health complaints. *Health Psychology, 12*(2), 125–131.

Repetti, R. (1997). *The effects of daily job stress on parent behavior with preadolescents.* Paper presented at the biennial meeting of the Society for Research in Child Development, Washington DC.

Roberts, L. J., & Krokoff, L. J. (1990). A time-series analysis of withdrawal, hostility, and displeasure in satisfied and dissatisfied marriages. *Journal of Marriage and the Family, 52*, 95–105.

Rook, K., Dooley, D., & Catalano, R. (1991). Stress transmission: The effects of husbands' job stressors on the emotional health of their wives. *Journal of Marriage and the Family, 53*, 165–177.

Rosaldo, M. Z. (1974). Woman, culture, and society: A theoretical overview. In M. Z. Rosaldo & L. Lamphere (Eds.), *Woman, culture, and society* (pp. 17–42). Stanford CA: Stanford University Press.

Rosaldo, R. (1989). *Culture and truth: The remaking of social analysis* (Rev. ed.). Boston: Beacon Press.

Rothbart, M. K. (1989). Temperament and development. In J. E. Bates, G. A. Kohnstamm, & M. K. Rothbart (Eds.), *Temperament in childhood* (pp. 187–247). New York: John Wiley & Sons.

Rotundo, A. E., (1993). *American manhood: Transformations in masculinity from the revolution to the modern era.* New York: Basic Books

Sampson, E. E. (1993). Identity politics: Challenges to psychology's understanding. *American Psychologist, 48,* 1219–1230.

Sattel, J. W. (1976). The inexpressive male: Tragedy or sexual politics? *Social Problems, 23*(4), 374–382.

Shields, S. A. (1987). Women, men, and the dilemma of emotion. In C. Hendrick & P. Shaver (Eds.), *Sex and gender* (pp. 229–250). Newbury Park CA: Sage.

Shields, S. A. (1991). Gender in the psychology of emotion: A selective research review. In K. T. Strongman (Ed.), *International review of studies in emotion* (pp. 227–245). New York: John Wiley & Sons.

Shweder, R. A. (1977). Likeness and likelihood in everyday thought: Magical thinking in judgments about personality. *Current Anthropology, 18*(4), 637–658.

Shweder, R. (1993). The cultural psychology of the emotions. In M. Lewis & J. M. Haviland (Eds.), *Handbook of emotions* (pp. 417–431). New York: Guilford Press.

Spielberger, C. D. (with Gorsuch, R. L., Jacobs, G. A., Lushene, R., & Vagg, P. R.). (1983). *State-Trait Anxiety Inventory.* Palo Alto CA: Consulting Psychologist Press.

Spielberger, C. D., Jacobs, G., Russell, S., & Crane, R. S. (1983). Assessment of anger: The State-Trait Anger Scale. In J. N. Butcher & C. D. Spielberger (Eds.), *Advances in personality assessment* (pp. 161–189). Hillsdale NJ: Lawrence Erlbaum.

Stapley, J. C., & Haviland, J. M. (1989). Beyond depression: Gender differences in normal adolescents' emotional experiences. *Sex Roles, 20*(5/6), 295–308.

Stearns, P. N. (1988). Anger and American work: A twentieth-century point. In C. Z. Stearns & P. N. Stearns (Eds.), *Emotion and social change: Toward a new psychohistory* (pp. 123–149). New York: Holmes & Meier.

Stearns, P. N. (1992). Gender and emotion: A twentieth-century transition. In D. D. Franks and J. V. Gecas (Eds.), *Social perspectives on emotion* (Vol. 1, pp. 127–160). Stamford CT: JAI Press.

Thomas, D. L., & Diener, E. (1990). Memory accuracy in the recall of emotions. *Journal of Personality and Social Psychology, 59,* 291–297.

Thompson, A. T., & Bolger, N. (in press). Transmission of emotion in couples facing a major stressful event. *Journal of Marriage and the Family.*

Thompson, E. H., Jr., & Pleck, J. H. (1986). The male role: The structure of male role norms. *American Behavioral Scientist, 29*(5), 531–543.

Thompson, E. P. (1963). *The making of the English working class.* New York: Vintage.

Thompson, L. (1991). Family work: Women's sense of fairness. *Journal of Family Issues, 12,* 181–186.

Thorne, B. (1993). *Gender play: Girls and boys in school.* New Brunswick NJ: Rutgers University Press.

Turner, R. (1968). *Family interaction.* New York: Macmillan.

Van Brakel, J. (1994). Emotions: A cross-cultural perspective on forms of life. In D. D. Franks (Series Ed.) & W. M. Wentworth & J. Ryan (Vol. Eds.), *Social perspectives on emotion* (Vol. 2, pp. 179–237). Stamford CT: JAI Press.

Van Heck, G. L. (1991). Temperament and the person-situation debate. In A. Angleitner & J. Strelau (Eds.), *Explorations in temperament* (pp. 163–175). New York: Plenum Press.

Weiss, R. S. (1990). *Staying the course: The emotional and social lives of men who do well at work.* New York: Fawcett Columbine.

Wheeler, L., Reis, H., & Nezlek, J. (1983). Loneliness, social interaction, and sex roles. *Journal of Personality and Social Psychology, 45*(4), 943–953.

White, G. M. (1994). Affecting culture: Emotion and morality in everyday life. In S. Kitayama & H. S. Markus (Eds.), *Emotion and culture* (pp. 219–239). Washington DC: American Psychological Association.

Childhood Aggression and Gender: A New Look at an Old Problem

**Nicki R. Crick,
Nicole E. Werner,
Juan F. Casas,
Kathryn M. O'Brien,
David A. Nelson**
University of Minnesota–Twin Cities

Jennifer K. Grotpeter
University of Colorado at Boulder

Kristian Markon
University of Minnesota–Twin Cities

What are little boys made of?
Snips and snails and puppy dog tails,
That's what little boys are made of.

What are little girls made of?
Sugar and spice and everything nice,
That's what little girls are made of.

Mother Goose

Because of its deleterious effects on individuals and society, and the important role that it has been given in several theories of human behavior (e.g., psychoanalytic theory, social learning theory; Freud, 1930; Bandura & Walters, 1959, 1963; Bandura, 1986), aggression has

Preparation of this chapter was supported by a FIRST award from the National Institute of Mental Health (#MH53524) and a Faculty Scholars Award from the William T. Grant Foundation to the first author. Special thanks to Daniel Bernstein, Maureen A. Bigbee, W. Andrew Collins, and Craig H. Hart for their comments on earlier drafts. Send correspondence to the first author at the Institute of Child Development, 51 East River Road, University of Minnesota, Minneapolis MN 55455.

been one of the most widely researched topics in the past several decades. Although many important advances have been made in our understanding of aggressive behavior, most of this knowledge has been gained through the study of aggressive males only (Crick & Dodge, 1994; Parke, 1992; Robins, 1986) and through the study of forms of aggression that are more characteristic of males than of females (i.e., physical forms of aggression). Not surprisingly, this approach to the study of aggressive behavior has fostered the stereotype of females as nonaggressive (Bjorkvist & Niemela, 1992). Or, in the words of Mother Goose, women and girls have been viewed as "sugar and spice and everything nice."

Recently, however, a new perspective on this issue has emerged, one that posits males and females to be equally aggressive. Investigators basing their work on this hypothesis have noted the significant gender bias apparent in past studies of aggression and have called for the systematic assessment of forms of aggression that are relevant for both sexes. Toward this goal, a relational form of aggression has been identified that has been shown to be more characteristic of females than the physical forms of aggression that have captured most of the previous empirical attention (Cairns, Cairns, Neckerman, Ferguson, & Gariepy, 1989; Galen & Underwood, 1997; Crick & Grotpeter, 1995; Feshbach, 1969; Lagerspetz, Bjorkvist, & Peltonen, 1988; Owens, 1996).

Our goal for the present chapter is to provide an overview of the current state of knowledge of relational aggression (both empirical and conceptual), with an emphasis on the roles of gender versus aggression form (physical vs. relational) in children's development. The first topics addressed include the definition of relational aggression, the distinction between relational aggression and other types (and subtypes) of aggression, evidence regarding the damaging nature of relationally aggressive acts, and the ways in which relational aggression has been assessed. Second, we provide an overview of the developmental manifestations of relational aggression across the life span. Third, we describe empirical evidence regarding gender differences in relational aggression at different developmental periods. The fourth section includes a discussion of cross-cultural research on relational aggression, and the fifth focuses on factors that may contribute to the development or maintenance of relationally aggressive behavior patterns. Finally, social-psychological adjustment problems that have been shown to be associated with relational aggression are reviewed.

What Is Relational Aggression?

Although specific definitions have varied somewhat over the past few decades, aggression has generally been defined as behaviors that are intended to hurt or harm others (e.g., Brehm & Kassin, 1990; Gormly & Brodzinsky, 1993; Myers, 1990). Using this general definition as a starting point, Crick and her colleagues defined *relational aggression* as behaviors that harm others through damage (or the threat of damage) to relationships or feelings of acceptance, friendship, or group inclusion (Crick, 1996; Crick & Grotpeter, 1995; Crick, Bigbee, & Howes, 1996). These behaviors include acts such as giving someone the "silent treatment" to punish them or to get one's own way, using social exclusion as a form of retaliation, or threatening to end a friendship unless the friend complies with a request. In contrast, *physical aggression* harms through damage (or the threat of damage) to another's physical well-being (Crick & Grotpeter, 1995). These behaviors include acts such as hitting, shoving, kicking, or threatening to beat up another unless she or he does what is requested. Another type of aggression that is distinct from relational aggression is *verbal aggression*. Typically, behaviors classified as verbally aggressive in past research have included threats to another's physical well-being (behaviors that we consider part of physical aggression) and verbal insults (e.g., calling a peer mean names). These behaviors are distinct from relational aggression in that they do not focus specifically on damage to relationships.

In addition to its distinctiveness from physical and verbal aggression, relational aggression can also be distinguished conceptually from other, more similar forms of hostile behavior, including *indirect aggression* and *social aggression*. As the term conveys, indirect aggression involves covert behaviors in which the target is not directly confronted (Buss, 1961; Feshbach, 1969; Lagerspetz et al., 1988). As such, it includes some behaviors that overlap with relational aggression, such as ignoring or rumor spreading. However, it does not include more direct relationally aggressive behaviors, such as overtly manipulating friendships to get one's own way (e.g.,

"You can't be my friend if you don't give me a bite of your ice cream cone"). Further, indirect aggression can include behaviors that are not relationally aggressive, such as practical jokes (indirect physical aggression; Buss & Perry, 1992). In sum, whereas indirect aggression focuses on the nonconfrontational nature of hostile behavior, relational aggression includes all hostile acts in which relationships are the vehicle of harm, regardless of the direct or indirect nature of the behaviors.

Relational aggression can also be contrasted with social aggression, a term coined by Cairns et al. (1989). Social aggression has been defined by Galen and Underwood (1997) as behaviors that damage another's self-esteem or social status. Thus, social aggression includes some relationally aggressive behaviors, such as rumor spreading or social exclusion. However, according to Galen and Underwood, it also includes nonverbal behaviors, such as negative facial expressions or body movements (e.g., rolling one's eyes). Although probably not intended by these authors, it also appears that many additional types of aggressive behaviors would be encompassed by their definition of social aggression (e.g., verbal insults, behaviors that are likely to damage self-esteem; physical aggression, acts that can be used to impact social status). Thus, social aggression appears to be a much broader construct than relational aggression. Of particular importance for the present chapter is that, in contrast to relational aggression, social aggression does not specifically focus on damage to relationships.

In this chapter, research on indirect aggression and social aggression is reviewed, in addition to studies of relational aggression, due to the partial overlap in the behaviors encompassed by each of these constructs and due to the relatively few studies yet available in this area. However, it is important to keep in mind that these three forms of aggression are relatively distinct; thus, studies of one form may not completely generalize to the other forms.

SUBTYPES OF RELATIONAL AGGRESSION

Theories of aggressive behavior and empirical studies of physical aggression indicate the existence of reactive (hostile) and proactive (instrumental) subtypes of aggression (Dodge, 1990; Dodge & Coie,

1987; Hartup, 1974; Price & Dodge, 1989). The reactive subtype of aggression, posited as part of the frustration-aggression model (Berkowitz, 1993; Dollard, Doob, Miller, Mowrer, & Sears, 1939), is an angry or defensive response to a perceived frustration or provocation. Thus, the intent of the reactively aggressive act is to retaliate (or defend) against the provocateur (e.g., slapping someone after they push you). The proactive subtype of aggression, suggested via social learning models of aggression (Bandura, 1973), is a deliberate behavior that is controlled by external contingencies. Thus, proactively aggressive behaviors are a means for achieving a desired (not necessarily aggressive) goal (e.g., shoving someone out of the way in order to reach the water fountain).

Although previous investigations have focused primarily on subtypes of physical aggression, it seems likely that reactive and proactive subtypes of relational aggression also exist (and preliminary evidence to support this hypothesis has been generated; McNeilly-Choque, Hart, Robinson, Nelson, & Olsen, 1996). Reactive relationally aggressive behaviors may include acts such as spreading hostile rumors about a peer in order to get even with him or her or using social exclusion as a form of retaliation. In contrast, proactive relationally aggressive behaviors may include strategies such as using friendship as a bargaining chip (e.g., "You can't be my friend unless you help me with my homework") or threatening to divulge personal secrets to gain control over a peer.

ARE RELATIONALLY MANIPULATIVE BEHAVIORS AGGRESSIVE?

Several studies have been conducted to evaluate empirically whether relationally aggressive acts, similar to physical forms of aggression (and in keeping with the definition of aggression described above), cause significant damage to others. The most direct evidence to support this hypothesis comes from a series of studies in which children have been asked to describe aggressive behaviors that occur frequently among their peers. In the first set of these studies, 9- to 12-year-old children were asked to describe "things that other girls/boys do when they are mad" (study one) and "things other girls/boys do when they want to be mean" (study two) (Crick et al., 1996). These studies were conducted to identify the normative behaviors that children view as enacted in anger (study one) and as intended to harm others (study two), two components commonly associated with aggressive acts (e.g., Aronson, 1988; Berkowitz, 1993; Dodge & Coie, 1987; Maccoby, 1980; Myers, 1990). Results showed that children cited relational aggression as the most common angry, hurtful (i.e., aggressive) behavior enacted in girls' peer groups. (In contrast, physical aggression was the most normative angry, hurtful behavior cited for boys' peer interactions.)

Additional evidence for the aggressive nature of relationally manipulative behaviors was generated in a study of 9- to 13-year-old sibling pairs who were asked to describe what they (or their brother or sister) do when they want to be mean to their sibling (O'Brien & Crick, 1997). Results revealed that, regardless of birth order (younger or older sibling) or gender, relational aggression was cited more frequently than physical aggression and verbal insults as the kind of mean behaviors that occur within the sibling dyad. A similar methodology was used in a recent study of older adolescents (college-aged students) who were asked to describe what most males (females) do to be mean to other males (females) (Crick, Werner, & Schellin, 1998). Similar to children, adolescents cited relational aggression as a form of mean behavior that occurs frequently within their peer groups.

These findings provide evidence that, similar to researchers, children and adolescents view relationally manipulative acts as mean and hurtful—and, thus, "aggressive"—and as behaviors that occur relatively frequently in some peer and sibling contexts. Similarly, studies in which children have been asked to indicate how upset or hurt they would be if they were the target of a peer's relationally aggressive behavior (Crick, 1995) or socially aggressive behavior (Galen & Underwood, 1997) provide evidence that girls view this treatment as a relatively distressful event. Additionally, girls are more likely than boys to report that they dislike peers who exclude others (i.e., a type of relational aggression; Foster, DeLawyer, & Guevremont, 1986).

Other, more indirect, evidence also points to the harmful nature of relationally aggressive acts. Studies of the children who are the frequent targets of relationally aggressive behaviors have shown that relational victimization is associated with serious adjustment problems such as depression, rejection by peers, problematic friendships, loneliness, low self-esteem, and emotional distress for preschoolers and grade-schoolers (relational victimization: Crick & Bigbee, 1998; Crick, Casas, & Ku, in press; Crick & Grotpeter, 1996; Grotpeter, Geiger, Nukulkij, & Crick, 1998; social victimization: Paquette & Underwood, in press). These results are consistent with the hypothesis that relational aggression is harmful for the recipients. However, because these studies are limited by their correlational design, firm conclusions await future longitudinal research. Taken together, these studies provide evidence that relationally aggressive behaviors are indeed harmful and "aggressive."

ASSESSMENT OF RELATIONAL AGGRESSION

Numerous different approaches to the assessment of relational aggression have been followed in recent years, including self-report, peer report, teacher report, parent report, and observation. The personal, relatively covert nature of relational aggression poses unique problems for measurement not encountered in the assessment of physical aggression. For example, because relationally aggressive behavior is often experienced only within the dyad of target and aggressor (and as a result, may be invisible or hard to interpret for others), relational aggression may sometimes be difficult for a non-victim to observe and, thus, assess. In fact, victims themselves may not always be aware of relational aggression. In this section we briefly review and evaluate the various approaches to the assessment of relational aggression, discuss the agreement among different informants, and highlight important issues.

Peer Reports The assessment tool used most frequently in past research to assess relational aggression is a peer nomination instrument. Three versions of this instrument have been developed, corresponding with three developmental periods: preschool, middle childhood, and late adolescence (Crick, Casas, & Mosher, 1997; Crick & Grotpeter, 1995; Werner & Crick, in press). All of these instruments involve asking children or adolescents within a stable peer group (e.g., classroom, sorority) to nominate peers who fit a number of behavioral descriptors. These descriptors (i.e., items) generally fall into at least three categories: relational aggression (e.g., "Name three kids who tell friends they will stop liking them unless the friends do what they say"), physical aggression (e.g., "Name three kids who hit and push others"), and prosocial behavior (e.g., "Name three kids who do nice things for others").

The psychometric properties of this instrument have been shown to be favorable. For example, the internal consistency of both aggression subscales has been shown to exceed .80 in numerous samples of various ages (e.g., Crick, 1996; McNeilly-Choque et al., 1996). Further, high test-retest reliability has been demonstrated over a four-week interval for a middle-childhood sample (i.e., for boys, $r = .86$ for relational aggression and $r = .93$ for physical aggression; for girls, $r = .80$ for relational aggression and $r = .81$ for physical aggression; Crick, 1996; Rys & Bear, 1997). Additionally, factor analyses have consistently yielded separate factors for relational versus physical aggression, supporting the relatively distinct nature of these two forms of aggression. One advantage of peer reports, relative to other informant types, is that they yield scores based on multiple individuals, a circumstance that may increase reliability and validity. A second advantage of peer reports is that peers may be privy to instances of relational aggression that are unobservable to other informants (e.g., episodes that occur in the school bathroom).

Teacher and Parent Reports Two versions of a teacher report instrument have been used in past research, one appropriate for preschoolers and the other for grade-schoolers (Crick, 1996; Crick, Casas, & Mosher, 1997). Three of the subscales on this rating instrument were designed to parallel those included in the peer report instrument described above: physical aggression (e.g., "This child hits, shoves, or pushes peers"), relational aggression (e.g., "This child spreads rumors or gossips about some peers"), and prosocial behavior (e.g., "This child tries to cheer up peers when they are sad or upset about something"). Similar to the peer nomination instrument, teachers' reports of relational and physical aggression have been shown to be internally consistent, and factor analyses have yielded separate factors for the two forms of aggression for both preschool and grade school samples (e.g., Crick, 1996; Crick, Casas, & Mosher, 1997; Rys & Bear, 1997; Tomada & Schneider, 1997).

The teacher rating instrument was recently adapted for use with parents of grade-schoolers (i.e., the item stem "This child . . ." was changed to "My child . . ." for each item of the middle-childhood version of the teacher measure; Crick, 1997). Thus far, parents' reports of relational and physical aggression appear to be internally consistent. However, because this conclusion is based on only one sample, additional studies are needed to evaluate the generalizability of these findings.

Self-Reports A self-report measure, the Children's Peer Relations Scale, has also been used to measure relational aggression in middle childhood. This instrument consists of three subscales that parallel the relational aggression (e.g., "Some kids tell their friends that they will stop liking them unless the friends do what they say. How often do you tell friends this?"), physical aggression (e.g., "Some kids push and shove other kids at school. How often do you do this?"), and prosocial behavior (e.g., "Some kids say or do nice things for other kids. How often do you do this?") subscales of the peer nomination instrument. Evidence for the internal consistency of each subscale has been demonstrated; however, the instrument has been included in only one study thus far (Crick & Grotpeter, 1995). The relative unpopularity of this measure is primarily attributable to the lack of correspondence between self-reports and other reports of relational aggression. However, given the difficulty of obtaining information from other informants in certain contexts (e.g., clinical settings), it will be important to investigate further the utility of self-reports of relational aggression in future research (see MacDonald & O'Laughlin, 1997, for an example).

Observation Naturalistic observation was used to assess relational aggression in a recent study of preschoolers (McNeilly-Choque et al., 1996). Although interobserver reliability was satisfactory in this research, the authors concluded that adequate observations of relational aggression will likely require sophisticated observational techniques that make it possible to hear clearly all verbal exchanges. Additionally, as we have argued elsewhere (Crick & Grotpeter, 1995), efforts to obtain valid observational assessments of relational aggression may be hampered unless the observers have current insider knowledge about the existing relationships within the observed peer group (e.g., a lack of interaction between two children

Table 1. *Association between Relational and Physical Aggression for Various Informants*

Informant	Pearson Correlation Coefficient
Peers	.62
Teachers	.63
Parents	.38
Observation	.16

may be due to one child actively ignoring a friend, an instance that would reflect relational aggression, or it could be due to the lack of a relationship between the two children).

ASSOCIATION BETWEEN RELATIONAL AND PHYSICAL AGGRESSION

To evaluate the association between relational and physical aggression, a meta-analysis was conducted based on available published and unpublished data. Results of this analysis are listed in Table 1. The values in this table represent Pearson correlations (averaged over studies wherever information from more than one sample was available), weighted by sample size according to procedures reported in Snedecor and Cochran (1989). As Crick and Grotpeter (1995) have noted, a modest correlation between relational and physical aggression is to be expected: relationally and physically aggressive behaviors, after all, are both forms of aggression and should be correlated somewhat. That the correlation between relational and physical aggression does not approach scale reliabilities, even with different informants, supports the distinction between the two forms—an observation supported by factor analysis and sundry examples of criterion validity (e.g., Crick, 1996; Crick & Grotpeter, 1995; Grotpeter & Crick, 1996; McNeilly-Choque et al., 1996; Rys & Bear, 1997).

The connection between relational and physical aggression was somewhat higher for males, relative to females (not shown in the table; with the teacher report, $r = .73$ for males, .61 for females, significantly different at $p < .05$; with the peer report, $r = .75$ for males, .60 for females, significantly different at $p < .05$). This may result from greater actual co-occurrence of the two forms of aggression in males or from a co-occurrence of extreme physical aggression and rela-

Table 2. *Interinformant Agreement for Assessments of Relational and Physical Aggression*

Informants	Relational Aggression	Overt Aggression
Peer - Teacher	.47	.60
Peer - Parent	.28	.64
Peer - Observation	.10	.30
Teacher - Parent	.19	.47
Teacher - Observation	.20	.30

tional aggression in general, with the sex difference arising from the sex difference in physically aggressive behavior. Correlations between the two forms of behavior may also differ in males and females because of an error caused by the effect of physical aggression on measurement. That is, it is possible that extreme physical aggression may tend to bias observers toward reporting increased relational aggression, regardless of actual levels of the latter.

Interinformant Agreement To examine the agreement among the previously described informants, Pearson correlation coefficients were computed as outlined above, averaged across studies where appropriate (Table 2). Results of this analysis indicate that different informants tend to agree more on individual differences in physically aggressive behavior than on individual differences with regard to relational aggression. This is not surprising given that physical aggression is less covert than relational aggression and, thus, more easily observed. Situational variability in either the extent or appearance of relational aggression could also account for the lower consensus, with different informants being particularly privy to certain types of relational aggression, or relationally aggressive behavior occurring to different extents in the presence of different observers, or both. Adults, for instance, may be more aware of indirect forms of aggression than children, who may tend to be more aware of direct forms. For example, a teacher may be more likely to hear gossip about a victim of relational aggression, and to better identify it as gossip, than the victim or a friend of the victim. A child, often personally involved in interactions involving threats of ostracism, may find direct forms of relational aggression more salient than an adult.

Although the comparatively small correlation between parent and teacher assessments of relational aggression suggests that lower interinformant agreement is probably not entirely due to differences in age, such an interpretation cannot entirely be ruled out. Low convergence may partially result from differences in the ability of children and adults to discriminate between relational and physical aggression, or from differences in the ability of each to accurately appraise social cues (e.g., Younger, Schwartzman, & Ledingham, 1985, 1986). To examine empirically the possible moderating role of age in teacher-peer agreement, a contrast analysis (Hall & Rosenthal, 1991) of correlation size by sample grade was carried out on the studies included in the meta-analysis reflected in Table 1. Contrasts were significant in each case ($p < .001$ for each): sample grade was negatively correlated with the size of the correlation between peer reports of physical and relational aggression ($r = -.30$ for the whole sample, $-.14$ for males, and $-.35$ for females), suggesting increasing ability to distinguish between relational and physical aggression with age. Moreover, grade was positively correlated with the size of the peer-teacher correlation for both relational aggression ($r = .63$) and physical aggression ($r = .50$), suggesting increasing convergence of peer and teacher assessments with age. As one would predict, the correlation between sample grade and the size of the correlation in the teacher assessment of physical and relational aggression, although statistically significant, was relatively small in magnitude ($r = .11$). Teachers' ability to distinguish between relational and physical aggression apparently does not change dramatically with classroom age.

The size of the correlation between the peer report of physical aggression and teacher report of relational aggression also increased with sample grade, as did the correlation between the peer report of relational aggression and the teacher report of physical aggression, although the effect was much stronger for the former than for the latter ($r = .65$ for the former; $r = .28$ for the latter). This pattern suggests that, with older students, teachers tend to rate those individuals identified by peers as physically aggressive as also being relationally aggressive. A sex difference in this trend ($r = .79$ for males, $r = .56$ for females), as well as in the moderating effect of grade on the size of the correlations between teacher identification of relational and physical aggressions ($r = .32$ for males, $r = -.05$ for females), hints that teachers increasingly tend to see physically aggressive boys as relationally aggressive also, as the boys grow older. Although boys may manifest increasing comorbidity with age, it is also possible that teachers or other observers suffer a bias toward perceiving physically aggressive boys or extremely physically aggressive individuals in general as also being relationally aggressive. In other words, ratings of relational aggression may be "washed out" by severe physically aggressive behavior. Important, in this regard, is the absence of increasing correlations between physical and relational aggression with age in boys when assessed by peers rather than teachers.

We have proposed elsewhere that, at least in middle childhood, peers may provide better, or at least more generalizable, measures of relational aggression than teachers or parents (Crick & Grotpeter, 1995). Evidence to support this premise was obtained in a recent study of third-grade children (Crick, 1997; $n = 57$) in which hierarchical regression analyses showed that neither parent nor teacher ratings of relational aggression significantly added to the prediction of the other beyond that accounted for by peer reports ($p > .90$ for each). In contrast, peer reports either significantly added to the prediction of each or did so at the level of a trend ($p < .01$ and $p < .10$). These results suggest that peer nominations may represent the most cross-situationally applicable measure of relational aggression, at least at those ages where peers are able to distinguish adequately between physical and relational aggression. For young children, who have the most difficulty discriminating between physical and relational aggression, teacher or other adult ratings may be the most valid assessment modality. As children age, however, with interactions that are out of view of adults becoming more common and, perhaps, more situationally differentiated, peers themselves may become the best informants.

Ultimately, the best measure of relational aggression may be a composite averaged over multiple informants and contexts, an approach recommended by other investigators for physical aggression (e.g., Achenbach, McConaughy, & Howell, 1987). Of course, this option is relatively costly and may not be possible in many circumstances (e.g., some researchers may not have access to children's peer groups and thus may be unable to obtain peer reports of relational aggression). Clarifying the ways that relational aggression is manifested in various contexts, such as in the home, in school, or at work, should help to better identify those individuals who engage in relationally aggressive behavior only in specific situations, those who do so cross-situationally, and those who do so rarely, regardless of the context.

Developmental Manifestations of Relational Aggression

INFANCY, TODDLERHOOD, AND THE PRESCHOOL YEARS

As many investigators have noted (e.g., Ladd & Mars, 1986; Levy-Schiff & Hoffman, 1989; Olson & Lifgren, 1988; Wasik, 1987), early identification of children's aggressive behavior problems is crucial for the prevention and treatment of childhood adjustment problems and for furthering our understanding of the etiology of these maladaptive behaviors. As of yet, no studies have been conducted to assess whether children exhibit relationally aggressive behaviors during the first three years of life. It will be important to generate this information in future research to determine when and how relationally aggressive strategies first appear in children's behavioral repertoires. Studies in this area are likely to be difficult, however, due to the cognitive and social limitations of infants and toddlers. For example, it is during this period that children first develop the capacity for language. As currently defined, most relationally aggressive acts are verbal (and those that are not, such as actively ignoring another, may require even more sophistication than the verbal behaviors). Thus, relatively advanced language, cognitive, and social abilities may be prerequisites for engagement in relationally aggressive behaviors, skills that are likely to be lacking during most of this age period. Another developmental issue that may impact the assessment of relational aggression during the first three years of life can be seen in the area of play behavior. During this period, children begin to make the transition from parallel play to more interactive, social play (Mueller & Lucas, 1975). It may be that the acquisition of these interaction skills (i.e., when children begin interacting with each other and start forming meaningful relationships) is required before relational aggression can become an effective strategy.

We are not proposing that relational aggression does not exist during the first three years of life, but rather that there may be important developmental milestones that must be achieved before relationally aggressive behaviors can develop, and also before valid assessments of them can be obtained. However, because young children may be exposed to relational aggression during this period, by either their parents or their siblings (and thus they may learn some aspects of it), this age period is an important one for future research. Specifically, it will be important to identify which developmental milestones are necessary precursors to the acquisition of relationally aggressive behavior patterns.

In contrast to infancy and toddlerhood, several investigations have been conducted with preschoolers from 3 to 5 years of age and have demonstrated that children at these young ages *do* exhibit relationally aggressive behaviors (Crick, Casas, & Mosher, 1997; McNeilly-Choque et al, 1996). Of course, because preschoolers are still relatively immature, the manifestations of relational aggression at these ages are also relatively unsophisticated. Additionally, preschoolers are only beginning to learn social skills during these years; thus, when they engage in relationally aggressive behaviors, they tend to do so in relatively simple, obvious ways (e.g., directly telling a peer that they will not play with them unless certain conditions are met), whereas, as discussed in more detail later in the chapter, older children are more adept at using complex and subtle forms of relational aggression (e.g., getting other children to agree not to play with a particular child). Furthermore, relational aggression by preschoolers is most often enacted in response to immediate problems. That is, the behaviors tend to reflect children's current situation rather than being a response to some transgression in the past. For example, consider the following illustration of relational aggression (and physical aggression) yielded via naturalistic observations conducted in preschool classrooms:

> Child A (a girl), who wants to climb on some plastic blocks, pushes child B (a boy) who is currently climbing on the plastic blocks. Child B yells "don't push me!" and pushes her back. Child A yells back "don't scream!" Child C (a girl), who was standing near them, moves away. Child A then moves beside child C and says "I have to tell you something!" She then whispers something to child C, excluding child B. Child B watches, looking very uncomfortable.

Another important feature of preschoolers' social behavior is that it often centers around preferred activities rather than pair bonds. For example, a child wants to play blocks, but a second child is already playing with them. The first child has been told by a third child not to play with the second child but will likely go ahead and play with the blocks anyway (i.e., the immediate activity may take precedence over loyalty to an absent peer). Thus, these types of coalitional, relationally aggressive behaviors may be less effective during the preschool years than during older age periods.

It seems plausible that at these very young ages, verbal abilities might be related to the use of relational aggression, particularly given the wide range of individual differences in language development during the preschool years. Research has shown that girls' verbal development tends to precede boys' verbal development (Keenan & Shaw, 1997). These findings would seem to fit with the gender differences in relational aggression mentioned earlier. However, in our first study of preschoolers (unpublished data) we failed to find a significant correlation between relational aggression and children's scores on the Peabody Picture Vocabulary Test—Revised (Dunn & Dunn, 1981). Further research is needed to clarify whether verbal abilities are an important factor in the development of relationally aggressive behaviors.

Bjorkvist, Osterman, and Kaukiainen (1992) have argued that young children (those less than 8 years of age) are incapable of engaging in indirect aggression. The studies described above provide strong evidence that, in contrast, relational aggression is exhibited by children as young as 3 years of age. As discussed above, the relationally aggressive behaviors used during this period of development are relatively direct in nature. These discrepancies highlight another important difference between indirect aggression and relational aggression and indicate that relational aggression is likely to impact a broader range of developmental periods than indirect aggression (i.e., because relational aggression includes direct, as well as indirect, behaviors).

MIDDLE CHILDHOOD

To date, the majority of studies of relational aggression have focused on the middle-childhood period, particularly children from 9 to 12 years of age. These studies indicate that, in contrast to the relatively simple, direct types of relationally aggressive behaviors characteristic of preschoolers (e.g., "I won't be your friend if you don't share that crayon"), the relationally aggressive acts exhibited by grade-schoolers are much more sophisticated and complex. For example, consider the following descriptions of relationally aggressive events cited by grade-school participants in response to the question "What do most boys/girls do when they want to be mean to another boy/girl? (Crick, Bigbee, & Howes, 1996):

> Tell a lie about them that they didn't do.
> They say "We're going to be a group and you're not going to be in it."
> They pretend they don't see the kid.
> They don't talk to them and write nasty notes and talk behind their back.

The relationally aggressive acts employed by grade-schoolers likely reflect the social and cognitive developmental advances of the middle-childhood period. Although important at any age, needs for acceptance by peers and for mutually satisfying friendships become increasingly salient during the grade-school years and are typically met through relationships with same-gender peers (Bukowski & Hoza, 1989; Hartup, 1983; Maccoby, 1990; Thorne, 1986). It seems likely that the increase in the salience of these social issues, in addition to the language and cognitive skills acquired during middle childhood (e.g., increases in memory and vocabulary, the ability to view one's own thoughts, feelings, and behavior from another person's perspective; Ford & Keating, 1981; Kail, 1990; Selman, 1976), contributes to the children's ability to use the peer group as an effective means for hurting others. Accordingly, the relationally aggressive behaviors employed during this period often involve manipulation or mobilization of a relevant (typically same-gender) peer group against another child (i.e., to withdraw actual peer acceptance or to make the child feel excluded; e.g., "Tease a girl in front of her friends and it will embarrass her and no one will play with her").

Another feature of relational aggressive acts employed during the middle-childhood period involves their relatively covert nature. In contrast to the relationally aggressive behaviors typical of the preschool-age child, those employed during middle childhood often involve less confrontation of the target and may focus instead on interactions with other peer group members regarding the target child (e.g., "They tell their friends not to be that kid's friend"). Covert forms of relational aggression such as these require a certain degree of cognitive complexity not only by the aggressor (i.e., to recognize that this will be an effective strategy) but also on the part of the victim (i.e., to recognize that others are being mean to them on "behalf" of the aggressor). However, despite the appearance of these less confrontational behaviors, direct strategies are also still apparent during this developmental period (e.g., as cited by a 9-year-old: "I'm not going to play with you because you're mean and I'm going to play with someone else except for you"). Another characteristic of relationally aggressive acts during this developmental period is that these behaviors, when used as retaliatory strategies, are more likely than those used by younger children to represent retribution for an act that occurred in the past, as opposed to the immediate present (e.g., "I'm not going to be your friend anymore because you did something to me last time"). The development of this "ability" likely serves to prolong anger and emotional upset among those children involved in the event because the distressing episode is not immediately resolved.

It is important to note that, to our knowledge, no studies have been conducted in which relational aggression has been studied among children from kindergarten to second grade. This is a significant empirical gap given that this period marks the beginning of formal schooling and, for many children, the initial experience with a stable, same-age peer group. Future research directed toward understanding the manifestation of relational aggression for these age groups seems warranted.

ADOLESCENCE AND ADULTHOOD

Relative to the preschool and middle-childhood periods, few studies have investigated relational aggression during later stages of development. However, recent efforts have been made to extend prior work on relational aggression (and indirect aggression) into the periods of adolescence and adulthood (e.g., Bjorkqvist, Osterman, & Lagerspetz, 1994a, 1994b; Owens, 1996; MacDonald & O'Laughlin, 1997; Werner & Crick, in press). These studies are significant because they have demonstrated that adolescents and adults, similar to children, use relational aggression to harm others. This work is also important because it illustrates the ways in which relational aggression among older individuals differs from the relationally aggressive behaviors identified in the early- and middle-childhood periods.

To investigate older adolescents' normative beliefs about aggression, Crick and colleagues asked undergraduate students to generate responses to four questions regarding what people do when they want to be "hurtful" or "mean" to others (Crick, Werner, & Schellin, 1998). One pattern that emerged in students' responses involved the utilization of opposite-gender relations as vehicles for relational aggression. For example, a large number of participants cited damaging a peer's romantic relationship as a strategy for harming the person (i.e., "stealing" a person's boyfriend or girlfriend, sleeping with a person's best friend, sharing potentially harmful information with a friend's dating partner). In addition, whereas relationally aggressive children have been found to manipulate others' feelings of acceptance in the *same*-sex peer group, older adolescents described ways in which peers threaten others' feelings of acceptance by *opposite*-sex peers: "Women hurt other women by the amount of affection from men they receive. For example, saying, 'Mark called and he likes me better than you'" (Crick, Werner, & Schellin, 1998). Although this type of strategy differs from those typically used by younger children in terms of its focus on opposite-gender relations, it is similar to children's strategies in its direct, confrontational nature. This indicates that direct forms of relational aggression are used even during late adolescence, in addition to more indirect forms.

The emergence of the use of opposite-gender relations in relational aggression is consistent with changes in the structure of the peer group that take place during adolescence. Whereas peer relationships in early and middle childhood involve almost exclusively same-gender friendships and acquaintanceships, interest in opposite-gender friendships and romantic relationships increases significantly during early and middle adolescence (Maccoby, 1990). Developmental research has also shown that intimacy, affection and love, having romantic involvements, providing nurturance, and receiving support are "personal needs" and social goals that emerge or intensify during adolescence and adulthood (e.g., Buhrmester, 1996; Ford, 1982; Jarvinen & Nicholls, 1996). In light of these developmental changes, it is not surprising that the thwarting of these goals through relational aggression was apparent in the responses of college students in the Crick, Werner, and Schellin (1998) study.

Another pattern observed in adolescents' responses in this study involved the contexts in which relational aggression was utilized. Whereas same-gender friendships have been found to be an important context for relational aggression in middle childhood (Grotpeter & Crick, 1996), cross-gender relationships (friendships and romantic relations) appeared as unique dyadic contexts befitting the expression of relational aggression in late adolescence. In addition, Bjorkqvist et al. (1994b) found that some relationally aggressive behaviors were used among adults in another context—the workplace. Aside from the uniqueness of these contexts, however, the majority of relationally aggressive behaviors mentioned by adolescents in the Crick, Werner, and Schellin (1998) study were remarkably similar to those typical of younger children. For example, two commonly cited hostile behaviors involved developmentally appropriate variations of the "silent treatment" and rumor spreading:

> Sometimes women will ignore the man, the "silent treatment" which can be very hurtful depending on the surrounding circumstances. Women will also use love or friendship withdrawal and be distant, but not quite to the extent of a silent treatment.
>
> Women build up a "coalition" of other people against the woman. They spread rumors about her reputation.
>
> Men are hurtful to women through withdrawing their attention or ignoring their needs.

CONCLUSION

Examination of studies in which relational aggression has been assessed within different developmental periods illustrates both continuity and discontinuity in the structure and form of the relationally aggressive behaviors used by individuals of varying ages. Although relational aggression can be seen in the behavioral repertoires of preschoolers, it appears that with age children become progressively more adept at using subtle, complex, and nonverbal relationally aggressive behaviors, in addition to verbal behaviors. These advances likely occur as a function, in part, of the cognitive and social changes that take place with development during childhood. Changes in the social contexts in which relational aggression is expressed also appear to reflect normative developmental patterns. For example, the increasing salience of peer relations during middle childhood, the shifting gender composition of peer groups in early adolescence, and the central role of romantic and workplace relations in late adolescence and adulthood all influence the topography of relational aggression during each of these developmental periods. Despite these age-related changes in relational aggression, however, there also appear to be some prototypical acts of relational aggression that can be seen at all ages, such as ignoring and social exclusion. The descriptive information obtained from the studies described here demonstrates the importance of using age-appropriate assessments of relational aggression, as well as the need for viewing relational aggression within a developmental framework.

Gender Differences in the Expression of Aggression

THE PRESCHOOL YEARS

Based on our work with elementary-school-age children and our naturalistic, pilot observations of preschool children, we conducted the first study of gender differences in relational aggression among young children ($n = 65$; Crick, Casas, & Mosher, 1997). Results based on teachers' assessments of aggression indicated that preschool girls were significantly more relationally aggressive and less physically aggressive than preschool boys. These findings provided the first evidence of gender differences in the relationally aggressive behaviors of young children. It should be noted, however, that peer assessments of aggression did not yield any significant effects due to gender. This study was then replicated (Casas & Crick, 1997) with a larger and more diverse sample ($n = 120$). Results from this second investigation showed that, for both peer and teacher assessments of relational aggression, preschool girls were significantly more relationally aggressive and less physically aggressive than preschool boys.

A third study, conducted by Hart and colleagues (McNeilly-Choque et al., 1996), also found gender differences in relational aggression among a large sample of preschoolers ($n = 241$). Moreover, this investigation also included naturalistic observations of relational aggression. Observations and teacher assessments showed that preschool girls were significantly more relationally aggressive and significantly less physically aggressive than preschool boys. Results from peer assessments showed that preschool boys were significantly more physically aggressive than girls. No gender differences were obtained for peer reports of relational aggression. Hart and colleagues also attempted to make a distinction between verbal and nonverbal forms of relational aggression. Results from teacher assessments indicated that preschool girls displayed significantly more verbal forms of relational aggression than preschool boys; however, no gender differences were obtained for nonverbal forms of relational aggression.

These studies illustrate that relationally aggressive behaviors can be seen in the behavioral repertoires of young children. Moreover, they demonstrate that relational aggression is more characteristic of young girls' aggressive behavior, whereas physical aggression is more typical of young boys' aggressive behavior. That these gender differences can be detected at such a young age is significant, as they point to the potential role of early socialization by parents, siblings, and peers in the development of children's relationally aggressive behavior and may also possibly suggest biological influences. Of course, both of these premises are highly speculative and await future research.

MIDDLE CHILDHOOD

Similar to research on preschool-age children, gender differences in relational aggression have also been investigated for children during middle childhood. Three approaches have generally been taken to evaluate this issue. The first approach has focused on evaluation of gender differences in children's continuous relational aggression scores. Thus far, the findings resulting from these evaluations have been mixed. For example, although girls have been found to be significantly more relationally aggressive than boys in two studies (Crick, 1997, peer and teacher reports; Crick & Grotpeter, 1995, peer reports), no gender difference was obtained in a third study (Rys & Bear, 1997, peer and teacher reports).

The second way that gender differences in relational aggression have been evaluated has involved identification of peer-identified extreme groups of relationally and physically aggressive children and computation of the percentage of boys versus girls classified into aggressive versus nonaggressive groups (i.e., physically aggressive, relationally aggressive, physically plus relationally aggressive, and nonaggressive). Generally, research based on this approach has demonstrated that, in contrast to previous research focusing primarily on physical aggression, aggressive boys and girls are identified with almost equal frequency when both forms of aggression are assessed (Crick & Grotpeter, 1995; Rys & Bear, 1997). Furthermore, it has been shown that the physically aggressive group is composed primarily of boys (e.g., 15.6% of the total number of boys; 0.4% of the girls), the relationally aggressive group is composed primarily of girls (e.g., 2.0% of the boys; 17.4% of the girls), and the physically plus relationally aggressive group is composed of both boys and girls but tends to include more boys than girls (e.g., 9.4% of the boys; 3.8% of the girls) (Crick & Grotpeter, 1995).

The third approach to the evaluation of boys' versus girls' engagement in relational aggression has involved directly asking children about the types of aggressive behaviors they view as most typical of their male and female peers (Crick, Bigbee, & Howes, 1996). Consistent with several of the studies described above, findings from this research show that the majority of children viewed girls as more relationally aggressive than boys, regardless of whether the target was a girl (48.4% of girls vs. 10.7% of boys) or a boy (25.8% of girls vs. 7.1% of boys).

Considered together, the available evidence indicates that girls are more relationally aggressive than boys during middle childhood, although this was not demonstrated in every study. Perhaps the most important message to glean from the studies in this area, however, is that the "gender gap" in aggressive behavior narrows considerably during middle childhood when relational aggression is considered, in addition to physical aggression (e.g., 27% of boys vs.

22% of girls; Crick & Grotpeter, 1995). This finding provides important evidence to counter the stereotype of the "sugary, nonaggressive female."

ADOLESCENCE AND ADULTHOOD

Several recent studies have addressed the question of whether the gender differences in relational aggression and other forms of non-overt aggression found in early and middle childhood extend to later stages of development (Bjorkqvist, Osterman, & Lagerspetz, 1994b; Bjorkqvist, Osterman, & Kaukiainen, 1992; Crick, Werner, & Schellin, 1998; Owens, 1996). The majority of this research has been conducted outside of the United States (e.g., in Finland and Australia) and has focused on assessing gender differences in indirect aggression and physical aggression (e.g., Bjorkqvist et al., 1994b; Owens, 1996). In the United States, two recent studies of relational aggression have focused on the period of adolescence (Crick, Werner, & Schellin, 1998; MacDonald & O'Laughlin, 1997).

When peer reporting procedures have been used with adolescents, studies have found that females are more indirectly aggressive than males, whereas rates of physical aggression tend to be higher for males than females (Bjorkqvist, Osterman, & Kaukiainen, 1992; Lagerspetz & Bjorkqvist, 1994; Owens, 1996). Using a different approach in which adults were asked to report how often they were the targets of aggressive behaviors at work, Bjorkqvist, Osterman, and Lagerspetz (1994b) found that females were more likely than males to use "social manipulation" (e.g., not speaking to a coworker or making insulting comments about a coworker's personal life). Using self-reports of aggression, MacDonald and O'Laughlin (1997) found that mid-adolescent females reported higher levels of relational aggression than did males; however, Crick, Werner, and Schellin (1998) failed to find gender differences in self-reports of relational aggression in a sample of late adolescents.

In general, these studies provide evidence that older females do tend to engage in higher levels of relational aggression than do males. However, it is important to note that these studies differed widely in their conceptualizations of aggression (i.e., indirect vs. re-

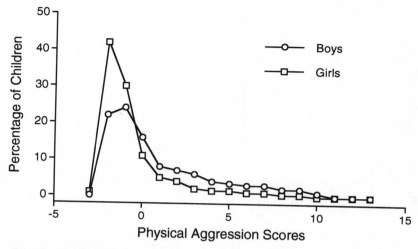

Figure 1. Distribution of standardized physical aggression scores by gender. From Werner, N. W., Bigbee, M. A., and Crick, N. R. (1998). In M. Schäfer and D. Frey (Eds.), *Aggression und gewalt unter kindern und jugendlichen* [Aggression and violence among children and adolescents] (pp. 153–177). Göttingen: Hogrefe.

lational aggression) and in the methods used to measure aggression (e.g., peer reports of aggression, self-reports of victimization). Moreover, unlike studies in preschool and middle childhood, the age of participants in these studies was quite wide, ranging from 15 to 45 years. Additional information in the form of longitudinal studies of relational aggression is greatly needed before firm conclusions can be drawn regarding changes in relational aggression or the relative stability of gender differences in relational aggression from childhood through adolescence and adulthood.

CONCLUSION

Taken together, the previously described studies provide strong evidence that gender differences in aggression are minimal (or nonexistent) when both physical and relational forms of aggression are considered. Another way to illustrate this point is to consider the

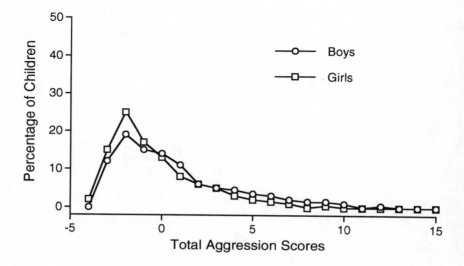

Figure 2. Distribution of standardized total aggression scores by gender (relational and physical aggression). From Werner, N. W., Bigbee, M. A., and Crick, N. R. (1998). In M. Schäfer and D. Frey (Eds.), *Aggression und gewalt unter kindern und jugendlichen* [Aggression and violence among children and adolescents] (pp. 153–177). Göttingen: Hogrefe.

distribution of children's aggression scores when physical aggression is assessed, but not relational aggression (i.e., the approach used in most past research), and when both physical and relational aggression are assessed. Figure 1 depicts boys' and girls' standardized physical aggression scores obtained through peer nominations, whereas Figure 2 depicts boys' and girls' combined (and standardized) physical and relational aggression scores (n = 2,342; 8–10 years of age). Figure 1 shows a relatively high degree of nonoverlap in girls' versus boys' aggression scores, indicating that boys are more physically aggressive than girls. In sharp contrast, Figure 2 shows that the distribution of aggression scores is almost identical for boys and girls when both forms of aggression are considered. These two graphs clearly demonstrate that both boys and girls are aggressive, results that shatter the myth of the nonaggressive female (Bjorkvist & Niemela, 1992).

Cross-Cultural Studies of Relational Aggression

The studies conducted with Finnish and Australian adolescents described previously are not the only examples of cross-cultural work on relational and indirect aggression. Based on the assumption that these behaviors may be universal, several other recent studies have originated in cultures outside the United States. The research described below has been conducted with children in preschool and middle childhood. Studies conducted in Finland, Russia, Italy, Australia, and China are outlined.

THE PRESCHOOL YEARS

In addition to work with preschoolers in the United States, research on relational aggression has also been conducted with Russian and Chinese nursery school children. The definition of relational aggression, using relationships as the vehicle of harm, is consonant with some of the methods consistently employed under former and current communist states to foster loyalty to a collectivist ideology. For example, Bronfenbrenner (1970) reported that peer pressure and the threat of exclusion from group membership were widely used in Russian (Soviet) classrooms in order to promote conformance to societal norms while diminishing individualistic desires. Similarly, Ho (1986) reported that shaming and the threat of ostracism or abandonment by the group are preeminant socialization strategies used with Chinese children. Therefore, early research in Russia and China has been based on the expectation that relational aggression would be a particularly salient feature in children's interactions.

Russia and China Consistent with these expectations, Hart and colleagues have recently completed research efforts in Russia and China. In the Russia study (Hart, Nelson, Robinson, Olsen, & McNeilly-Choque, 1998; Hart et al., in press), a sample of ethnic Russian nursery school children (corresponding in age with preschoolers and kindergartners in the United States) participated. Teacher ratings and peer nominations were used to assess relational and physical aggression (Nelson, Hart, Robinson, & Olsen, 1998), based on instruments and procedures developed in the U.S. samples cited above (Crick, Casas, & Mosher, 1997; McNeilly-Choque et al., 1996). All items were translated both forward and backward by Russian linguists in order to ensure accuracy. Factor analyses of the teacher and peer measures yielded separate factors for relational and physical forms of aggression. Therefore, both Russian nursery school children and their teachers were able to reliably distinguish relational from physical forms of aggression.

In regard to gender differences in relational aggression, consistent with U.S. studies, peer assessments indicated that boys were significantly more physically aggressive, whereas girls were significantly more relationally aggressive (Nelson et al., 1998). Teacher assessments, however, did not yield significant gender differences for instigators of either relational or physical aggression (Hart, Nelson, et al., 1998a; Nelson et al., 1998).

In a cross-cultural comparative study involving Chinese children, confirmatory factor analysis of teacher reports of young children's aggression also yielded separate factors for relational and physical aggression. Findings indicated that Chinese preschool teachers can reliably distinguish these subtypes of aggression (Hart, Yang, et al., 1998). Evaluation of gender differences in the Chinese sample indicated that boys were more physically aggressive and girls tended to be more relationally aggressive.

MIDDLE CHILDHOOD

The study of relational aggression (or related constructs) in middle childhood is ongoing in numerous cultures outside the United States, including Finland, Italy, and Australia.

Finland The most prominent study of behaviors that overlap with relational aggression in middle childhood is the work of Bjorkqvist and colleagues described previously. In addition to the adolescent studies, these investigators have also focused on two samples of children in middle childhood. In their first study (Lagerspetz, Bjorkqvist, & Peltonen, 1988), 11- and 12-year-old children were asked to describe what they and their classmates do when angry with another peer (boys rated boys; girls rated girls). Specific peer nomination items were then generated from these responses, and each child was asked to rate the behavior of classmates on each item. A factor analysis produced three factors: indirect aggression, physical aggression, and prosocial behavior. Furthermore, Finnish girls tended to use indirect aggression, whereas Finnish boys tended to employ physical aggression.

In a follow-up study, Bjorkqvist, Lagerspetz, and Kaukiainen (1992) replicated the initial factor structure for a group of 8- and 15-year-olds. Further, boys scored significantly higher on items related to more physical aggression. However, no significant differences for indirect aggression were obtained.

In contrast with the research in other countries outside of the United States (cited above and hereafter), the Finnish studies are unique. The Finnish data were not based on translated items from U.S. measures (or vice-versa). On the contrary, the Finnish and U.S. researchers began and proceeded quite independently of each other in developing a framework for understanding gender differences in aggression. Yet surprisingly similar results have emerged from separate research efforts, distinct cultural backgrounds, and different definitions of aggression.

Italy One of the most recent efforts to test the cross-cultural validity of the construct of relational aggression is the work of Tomada and Schneider (1997) with a group of Italian children 8 to 10 years of age. Peer and teacher nominations were utilized to assess relational and physical aggression, based on items and procedures derived from Crick and Grotpeter (1995). All items were translated into Italian by the first author and translated back into English by the second author to ensure accuracy.

Peer nominations were obtained for physical aggression, relational aggression, and prosocial behavior. A confirmatory factor analysis was performed, testing both the three-factor model reported by Crick and Grotpeter (1995) and a two-factor model (single aggression factor). The three-factor model was found to be the most viable. A similar approach was taken for the teacher nominations, and once again, the data best fit the three-factor model. Therefore, relational and physical aggression were clearly delineated by both peers and teachers as specific subtypes of aggression.

Results based on the peer nomination instrument indicated that boys scored significantly higher than girls for physical aggression.

Counter to expectations, however, boys also scored significantly higher on items related to relational aggression. Girls scored significantly higher for prosocial behaviors. Analyses with the teacher nominations revealed the same pattern. However, the gap between genders was much smaller for relational than for physical aggression—there was a substantial percentage (9.1%) of girls who were nominated as relationally aggressive.

Australia Indirect aggression has been observed with an Australian sample. Owens (1996) enlisted 2nd-grade (8-year-olds), 6th-grade (12-year-olds), 9th-grade (15-year-olds), and 11th-grade (17-year-olds) subjects in his recent study (results for the 9th- and 11th-grade samples were reported earlier). Owens adapted the measure used by Bjorkqvist, Osterman, and Lagerspetz (1994a) to assess direct physical aggression, direct verbal aggression, and indirect aggression. A factor analysis satisfactorily yielded the expected three factors. Therefore, as in other cultures, indirect and physical aggression were reliably distinguished by peers as separate forms of aggression in Australia. Results also demonstrated that, at both the 2nd- and 6th-grade levels, boys' direct forms of aggression (both physical and verbal) toward other boys were higher than girls' physical aggression toward other girls. However, at these grade levels there were no significant differences between boys and girls in their use of indirect aggression.

FUTURE WORK IN CROSS-CULTURAL STUDIES

The above studies basically affirm the cross-cultural validity of the concept of relational aggression. The results also suggest that measures of relational aggression, developed with samples in the United States, are general enough in nature to be translated and constructively used across varied cultural settings. However, although it is encouraging that these items are readily understood in what seem to be drastically different cultures, cultural nuances for these behaviors are certainly expected. Qualitative research methods (e.g., open-ended questions and observation) will be necessary in order to define the possibly unique character of relationally aggressive behaviors in each of these cultures.

Factors That May Contribute to Relational Aggression

Theories of human development and motivation, in addition to empirical studies, have identified numerous factors that may contribute to the use of physically aggressive strategies in social contexts (e.g., Bandura, 1973; Berkowitz, 1993; Dodge, 1980; Grych & Fincham, 1990; Patterson, 1982). Although an exhaustive review of the research in this area is beyond the scope of the present chapter, a brief discussion of several factors is provided below. Our goal for this overview is to describe the current state of research on possible antecedents of relational aggression and also to illustrate how past studies of the antecedents of physical aggression may inform research on the development of relational aggression (and vice-versa). First we discuss individual child characteristics that may impact relational aggression (social information-processing mechanisms, emotion), and then we turn to contextual factors (parent-child and interparental relationships, sibling relationships, friendships).

SOCIAL INFORMATION-PROCESSING MECHANISMS

One important component that has been shown to influence the use of aggressive behavior in childhood is children's social information-processing (SIP) (Dodge & Crick, 1990; Parke & Slaby, 1983). Research in the past decade has consistently demonstrated the utility of SIP models of children's social behavior for increasing our understanding of the development and maintenance of aggressive behavior problems (for a review, see Crick & Dodge, 1994). As with most of the past literature in this area, the majority of previous SIP studies have focused on physical aggression and on aggressive boys. These studies have shown that physically aggressive children (primarily boys have been studied) perceive, interpret, and make decisions about social stimuli in ways that increase the likelihood of their engaging in physically aggressive acts (Crick & Dodge, 1994). Further, through the use of experimental and intervention designs, it has been demonstrated that these social information-processing mechanisms play an important causal role in the generation of children's physically aggressive behavior (e.g., Bierman, 1986; Dodge, Bates, & Pettit, 1990; Guerra & Slaby, 1989; Hudley & Graham, 1993; Rabiner & Coie, 1989).

In one SIP model, it has been posited that children's social behavior, including aggression, is a function of several cognitive steps: (1) encoding of social cues; (2) interpretation of those cues; (3) selection of a goal; (4) response access; and (5) response decision (Crick & Dodge, 1994). Application of this social information-processing model to relationally aggressive behavior problems has only recently been initiated and has focused on two SIP components thus far. One of these components (step 2: interpretation of social cues) involves inferring the motives of others (e.g., determining whether peers are acting with hostile or benign intent; Crick & Dodge, 1994). Numerous studies have documented that physically aggressive children hold hostile attributional biases; that is, they are significantly more likely than other children to infer hostile intent in peers even when such intent is not intended (for a review, see Crick & Dodge, 1994). According to social information-processing models, hostile attributions increase the likelihood that a child will behave aggressively (i.e., because the aggressive act serves as a defense against a peer who is perceived as a threat).

In past studies of children's intent attributions, social cognitions have been assessed for one specific type of social context, situations that involve peer conflicts of an instrumental nature (e.g., a situation in which a peer takes a child's preferred spot in line; Crick & Dodge, 1996; Sancilio, Plumert, & Hartup, 1989; Waas, 1988). However, in recent studies of the intent attributions of relationally aggressive children, we posited that instrumental conflicts, although problematic for physically aggressive children, would not be particularly salient or provoking for relationally aggressive children. Rather, we hypothesized that peer conflicts of a relational nature would be particularly troublesome for relationally aggressive children (i.e., conflicts that involve potential relationship slights such as failing to receive an invitation to a peer's birthday party; Crick, 1995). Thus far, findings from three studies of 9- to 12-year-old children provide evidence to support this view (Crick, 1995; Crick, Grotpeter, & Bigbee, 1998, study one and study two). Specifically, these investigations showed that relationally aggressive children exhibited hostile attributional biases for relational conflicts but *not* for instrumental conflicts. In sharp contrast, physically aggressive children exhibited hostile attributional biases for instrumental conflicts but *not* for relational conflicts.

The second SIP component that has been assessed in studies of relational aggression is the response decision step (step 5). According to social information-processing theory, at this step children are faced with a decision that involves evaluation of possible responses to a social situation (e.g., the desirability of the likely outcomes to accrue) and selection of the most favorable response for enactment. Past research on the response decision step has shown that physically aggressive children evaluate physically aggressive responses more positively than do their peers (evaluations that are likely to result in the enactment of physical aggression; Crick & Dodge, 1994).

Similar to past research on the intent attributions of physically aggressive children, previous studies of response decision processes have been assessed for instrumental, but not relational, conflicts. We addressed this issue in a recent study of 9- to 12-year-olds in which we were interested in whether relationally aggressive children evaluate relationally aggressive responses in relatively positive ways (i.e., a response decision pattern that might contribute to their use of relational aggression). Results indicated that relationally aggressive boys, but *not* relationally aggressive girls, evaluated relationally aggressive responses in relatively positive ways (Crick & Werner, in press). Further, the response decision bias exhibited by relationally aggressive boys was apparent for instrumental, but not for relational, conflicts (i.e., a context that has been shown to be particularly salient for boys; Block, 1983). These findings provide initial evidence that gender, aggression form, and social context may all moderate the association between social information processing and aggressive behavior in childhood. Findings from this study also revealed a lack of response decision deficits for relationally aggressive girls (i.e., they did not differ from nonaggressive peers in their evaluations of aggression for either instrumental or relational conflicts). These results suggest that this particular processing step may be less salient for some aggressive children than for others. Of course, additional research will be necessary before firm conclusions about this issue can be offered.

Taken together, findings from these studies provide preliminary evidence for the utility of social information-processing models for enhancing our understanding of relational aggression. However, they also highlight the necessity of generating new approaches to the study of SIP patterns, beyond those employed in past research, to obtain an adequate understanding of the sip–relational aggression link and to better understand the processing patterns of aggressive girls (e.g., inclusion of relational conflicts, in addition to instrumental conflicts, when assessing children's processing). Clearly, a great deal of research remains to be done in this important area, including longitudinal studies, research with different age groups, and investigation of other social information-processing steps, to name only a few.

EMOTION

Although negative emotions such as anger have been afforded a major role in several theories of aggression (e.g., Berkowitz, 1993; Dollard et al., 1939), almost no research has focused on the impact of emotion in the development or enactment of relationally aggressive behaviors. To our knowledge, only two studies to date have generated evidence to support this relation. In these studies, children were presented with hypothetical vignettes that depicted relational or instrumental peer conflicts. Participants were asked to rate how angry or upset they would be if the situation depicted in each vignette happened to them. Findings from both studies showed that relationally aggressive children were significantly more angry and upset by relational conflicts (but not by instrumental conflicts) than were their nonaggressive peers (Crick, 1995; Crick, Grotpeter, & Bigbee, 1998). The emotional distress that relationally aggressive children experience when confronted with relational conflicts may play a role in their enactment of aggressive responses (i.e., being angry may lead to retaliatory aggression), particularly for children who exhibit reactive types of relational aggression problems. However, additional research is needed, including richer, more extensive assessments of emotion and longitudinal or experimental designs.

PARENT-CHILD AND INTERPARENTAL RELATIONSHIPS

Numerous previous studies have demonstrated the important role that parents may play in children's physically aggressive behavior problems (Patterson, 1982; Cummings & Cummings, 1988; Grych & Fincham, 1993; Davies & Cummings, 1994; Patterson & Dishion, 1988). Although little information is currently available regarding the family relationships of relationally aggressive children, it seems likely that past theoretical and conceptual models of physical aggression may be useful in guiding future research in this area. Below, a few of these models are described briefly, along with relevant knowledge, albeit limited, about the families of relationally aggressive children, information we obtained recently from a U.S. sample (also see research by Hart, Nelson, et al., 1998; Hart et al., in press; Hart, Yang, Nelson, Jin, Bazarskaya, & Nelson, 1998, for findings obtained with Chinese and Russian samples). Before we describe our research in this area, it is important to point out that it was necessary in many instances to adapt and expand existing measures of the parent-child and interparental relationships to adequately apply existing theories to the study of relational aggression (e.g., it was necessary to generate ways to assess parental modeling of relational aggression).

Social Learning Theory: Interparental Relationships For several decades, social learning theory has guided a great deal of research on physical aggression (Bandura, 1973). This model posits that children learn to be aggressive by observing and imitating others who serve as models for aggressive behavior, a premise that has been well supported in research on physical forms of aggression. Parents can be powerful models because of their salience, affective relationship, and importance to their children (Grych & Fincham, 1990; Easterbrooks & Emde, 1988). One way that parents may model aggressive behavior is through their interactions with each other (i.e., a modeling "opportunity" that is applicable only to children whose families include two or more parents or caretakers). In a recent investigation of third-graders, we sought to assess whether, as has been demonstrated repeatedly for physical aggression, children's peer-directed relational aggression would be related to their parents' modeling of relational aggression within interparental relationships (Grotpeter & Crick, 1997). Results of this investigation indicated that, relative to nonaggressive children, those who were relationally aggressive in their peer groups had parents who were more relationally aggressive toward each other (as reported by the children) and who were also more physically aggressive toward each other (as reported by both the children and their mothers). Though these findings show that aggression in interparental relationships is related to children's use of relational aggression in the peer group, they also indicate that the processes by which children learn relational aggression may be more complex than modeling alone (i.e., because relationally aggressive children observe physical aggression in their homes but do not tend to use these strategies within their peer interactions).

Social Learning Theory: Parent-Child Relationships Another way that parents can serve as models of aggressive behavior is through their direct interactions with their children (i.e., by directing aggressive behaviors toward their children). Thus far, the limited evidence available indicates that both relationally aggressive and physically aggressive children are more likely than nonaggressive children to have a parent or parents who direct relationally aggressive behaviors toward them (Grotpeter & Crick, 1997). These findings indicate that, as would be predicted by social learning theory, relational aggression in the parent-child relationship is related to children's use of relational aggression in the peer group. However, it also appears that parental modeling of relational aggression within the parent-child relationship is not specific to children's use of relational forms of aggression. Thus, it seems likely that, similar to the interparental relationship, modeling processes within the parent-child relationship do not fully account for children's learning (and use) of relational *or* physical aggression within the peer group. Additional research on this topic is needed to clarify the role of parent modeling of aggression in children's use of aggression in the peer group (e.g., it is possible that children model only their same-sex parent, or the parent that they most admire, etc.).

Cognitive-Contextual Framework: Interparental Relationships Over the past decade, a great deal of research has been conducted on the impact of marital conflict on children. Studies have shown marital conflict to be a significant predictor of physical aggression in boys (for reviews, see Emery, 1982; Grych & Fincham, 1990; and Cummings & Cummings, 1988). The cognitive-contextual framework posits that marital conflict that is frequent, hostile, and poorly resolved and that concerns the child is particularly disruptive and distressing for children, resulting in adjustment difficulties such as aggression (Grych & Fincham, 1990). Of particular importance in this model are children's own perceptions and attributions of their parents' conflict (Grych, Seid, & Fincham, 1992).

Thus far, research on children's perceptions of their parents' interactions has shown that, relative to nonaggressive peers, relationally aggressive children view their parents as more physically aggressive toward each other and as more relationally aggressive toward each other (Grotpeter & Crick, 1997). Further, relationally aggressive children tend to blame themselves more for their parents' conflicts than do other children. In contrast, and consistent with past research, physically aggressive children view their parents' conflicts as relatively frequent and intense and unlikely to be resolved (Grotpeter & Crick, 1997). Physically aggressive children also view their parents' interactions as less warm than do nonaggressive children.

The findings from this study are highly consistent with those found in past research for physically aggressive children and with the predictions of the cognitive-contextual model. In contrast, the specific findings for relational aggression are inconsistent with the model. In general, these results suggest that children's general perceptions of interparental conflict may be related to children's use of both relational and physical aggression in the peer group, but that different, specific perceptions may be uniquely related to each of the two forms of aggression. Further research is needed to evaluate whether revision of the cognitive-contextual model is warranted, in order to account for relational, as well as physical, forms of aggression.

Coercion Theory: Parent-Child Relationships For 17 years, Patterson's (1982) coercion theory has been used to describe the family processes of physically aggressive boys. In this theory it is posited that family members reinforce aggressive behavior in each other via harsh and inconsistent discipline, little positive parental involvement with the child, and poor monitoring and supervision of the child's activities—premises that have gained a great deal of empirical support in recent years (Patterson, 1982; Loeber & Dishion, 1983). The social-interactional perspective on these findings is that family members directly train the child to perform antisocial behaviors through their inconsistent discipline of negative behaviors and their inconsistent reinforcement of positive behaviors (Patterson, 1982; Patterson, DeBaryshe, & Ramsey, 1989). The impact of these processes over time is that levels of aggression within the family typically increase, and family members' views of the family become more negative (Patterson, 1982).

Thus far, relational aggression research related to coercion theory indicates that relationally aggressive children's relationships with their mothers are characterized by relatively low levels of warmth and relatively high levels of physical aggression directed at the mother by the child (Grotpeter & Crick, 1997). Physically aggressive children's relationships with their mothers are characterized by conflict resolution difficulties, relatively low levels of warmth, and relatively high levels of relationally aggressive behaviors directed at the child by the mother (Grotpeter & Crick, 1997).[1] Taken together, these findings provide indirect evidence that coercive family processes may be present in the families of relationally aggressive as well as physically aggressive children (e.g., high levels of aggression exist in both family types, which may indicate inconsistent parental discipline); however, observational methods that can take into account the sequential nature of family interactions are needed before firm conclusions can be offered.

Importance of Relationships Model: Parent-Child Relationships
The previously discussed theoretical frameworks have traditionally been used to assess family correlates or antecedents of physical aggression in children, particularly aggressive boys. However, research on the nature of relationally aggressive children's dyadic peer and family interactions provides initial evidence that children may become relationally aggressive via a different process than their physically aggressive peers, one that is characterized by a relatively intense focus on the importance of relationships to themselves and to others.

Research on relationally aggressive children's dyadic friendships has shown these relationships to be characterized by relatively high levels of intimacy, jealousy, and desires to keep their friendships exclusive (e.g., not wanting their friends to have other important peer relationships; Grotpeter & Crick, 1996). Additionally, a recent study of mother-child relationships revealed that, in contrast with developmental norms in which children typically start to disengage from parents as they approach adolescence (Sullivan, 1953), preadolescent relationally aggressive children reported being significantly closer to their mothers than did younger children (Grotpeter, Crick, & O'Brien, 1996). Finally, a study of mother-child and father-child relationships showed that relationally aggressive children reported significantly higher levels of exclusivity with both their mothers and their fathers than did other children (Grotpeter & Crick, 1997), indicating that the parents of relationally aggressive children desired high levels of closeness in the parent-child relationship. Additionally, the fathers of relationally aggressive children reported using relatively high levels of control strategies involving love withdrawal with their children (e.g., "I won't love you unless you do what I want"), behaviors that may teach children about the use and effectiveness of relational aggression (Crick & Grotpeter, 1997). In contrast, for this same sample, physically aggressive children reported significantly lower levels of closeness and intimacy with their mothers than did other children.

Taken together, evidence from the above studies suggests that relationally aggressive children continue to maintain close relationships with their mothers into their preadolescent years while also maintaining close, intense relationships with their peers. Based on these findings, we offer the hypothesis that relationally aggressive children learn that close, intimate relationships are highly valued (e.g., by their parents), and that the manipulation of these relationships is an effective means for achieving desired goals (e.g., as modeled by their fathers). If this is the case, then relationally aggressive children may become aggressive through a different process than physically aggressive children. Thus, a different framework may be needed to fully address the development of relational aggression (i.e., a framework that focuses on the importance of relationships).

SIBLING RELATIONSHIPS

Another family subsystem that has been shown to play a critical role in the development of physically aggressive behaviors is the sibling relationship (Dunn & McGuire, 1992). Given that children are most likely to imitate models who are similar to them (Bandura, 1973, 1977), and that children spend more time with siblings than with parents (Crouter & McHale, 1989), interactions with siblings may be even more influential than those with parents in the acquisition of aggressive behaviors. Two theories that have guided many of the investigations of sibling influence in the development of physical aggression are social learning theory and coercion theory. According to social learning theory, children's early interactions and observations with siblings (particularly older siblings) provide a fruitful context for the learning of social behaviors, including aggression (Bandura, 1973; MacDonald & Parke, 1984; Parke, MacDonald, Beitel, & Bhavnagri, 1988; Putallaz, 1987). Patterson's (1982, 1986) coercion theory builds on social learning theory through its specific emphasis on dyadic contexts. According to Patterson (1986), the sibling relationship may serve as a type of "training ground" for the learning of aggressive behaviors. For example, an older sibling may act in a physically aggressive way toward the younger child, and as a result, the younger child may model this behavior and respond in kind. Moreover, Patterson suggests that the maintenance of physically aggressive behaviors is exacerbated through interactions with siblings as children attempt to control and influence the behaviors of their siblings (i.e., pushing a sibling in order to obtain the sibling's game or toy).

A great deal of evidence has been generated to support the premises of both of these theories. For example, observational studies of sibling interactions have demonstrated that physically aggressive behavior exhibited by one sibling is highly correlated with physical aggression by the other sibling (Beardsall, 1987; Brody, Stoneman, & Burke, 1987; Dunn & Munn, 1986). Similarly, studies of antisocial children have revealed that the siblings of these children exhibit similar behavioral problems (Patterson, 1982; Neilsen & Gerber, 1979). Further, evidence indicates that older siblings are more frequently the initiators of aggressive behaviors (and thus may serve as models of aggression), with younger siblings more often being the imitators of these particular behaviors (Abramovitch, Corter, & Lando, 1979; Dunn & Kendrick, 1982). Additionally, Patterson's (1982) studies have shown that frequent and intense coercive exchanges occur at significantly high levels within the sibling dyads of aggressive children.

Both social learning theory and coercion theory posit that, similar to parents, older siblings may provide their younger siblings with modeling and "training" in the use of physical aggression. It seems plausible that a similar pattern of transmission may occur for the development of relational aggression. To our knowledge, only one study to date has been conducted in this area. This study is described below, along with several conceptual issues that we hope will serve as a framework for future research.

Does Relational Aggression Occur within the Sibling Context? Because past sibling research has focused on physical forms of aggression, no information has been generated regarding the use of relational aggression within the sibling context. Thus, we recently conducted a preliminary investigation designed to determine whether children view relationally aggressive acts as behaviors that occur frequently within their sibling relationships. Toward this goal, we interviewed 50 third-grade children and their older siblings (9 to 12 years of age; O'Brien & Crick, 1997) using procedures developed in prior research (Crick, Bigbee, & Howes, 1996). Both older and younger siblings were independently asked open-ended questions about the kinds of mean behaviors that occur most frequently in their sibling interactions (e.g., "What kinds of things do you do when you want to be mean to your sister/brother?" "What kinds of things does your sister/brother do when she/he wants to be mean to you?"). Content analyses of children's responses revealed that relationally aggressive behaviors were cited more often than physically and verbally aggressive acts (i.e., the forms of aggression traditionally studied in past sibling research) as a type of aggressive (i.e., mean) behavior likely to be used by one sibling toward the other. These findings provide the first evidence that relational aggression is employed within the sibling context and, more importantly, that children view it as a relatively frequent aggressive event.

Unique Features of the Sibling Relationship and Relational Aggression The unique features that characterize the sibling relationship clearly distinguish it from children's relations with parents and peers. Because of these distinct characteristics, children's relations with siblings may provide unique opportunities for the learning, maintenance, and expression of relationally aggressive behaviors.

According to Buhrmester (1990), one important factor that is likely to influence siblings' interactions (including aggressive behavior) is the biosocial structure of the relationship (i.e., birth order, age spacing between siblings, gender composition of dyad). Throughout early and middle childhood, older siblings tend to be physically stronger than their younger siblings. Given that physical strength has been shown to be associated with children's engagement in physical aggression against a weaker peer (Olweus, 1993), older siblings may be in a position to successfully direct physically aggressive behaviors toward their younger siblings, whereas the reverse may not be true. If so, other forms of aggression (e.g., relational aggression) may be relatively more effective and less costly for younger siblings.

The gender of each child within the sibling dyad may also impact the use of physical versus relational forms of aggression. For example, although societal norms concerning gender-appropriate behavior may encourage the use of physical aggression for boys, engagement in these types of behaviors is likely to be highly discouraged for girls. However, in mixed-sex sibling dyads, the use of physical aggression by boys may not be encouraged (or tolerated) when the intended target is a female sibling. If not, other forms of aggression (including relational aggression) may be used as alternative strategies in these circumstances.

In addition to the biosocial structure of the sibling dyad, another feature that may impact children's use of relational aggression against their brothers or sisters concerns the closed nature of the relationship (i.e., whereas a child may select her friends, she does not have a choice regarding her siblings). This feature may contribute to siblings being less likely to inhibit aggressive acts toward one another, because such behaviors will not result in the termination of the relationship as it may with friends. Consistent with this premise, studies have shown that there are indeed higher levels of aggressive behaviors within sibling interactions than within dyadic peer interactions (Berndt & Bulleit, 1985). These findings suggest that research on the sibling context may be crucial for understanding the acquisition and maintenance of relationally aggressive behavior patterns.

The sibling relationship is embedded within the larger hierarchical family structure, a context that may provide unique opportunities for the expression of relational aggression. For example, past research has demonstrated that younger children are likely to solicit assistance from parents when their older siblings are physically attacking them (Felson & Russo, 1988; Sutton-Smith & Rosenberg, 1968). It seems likely that younger siblings may sometimes use parental intervention as an opportunity to relationally aggress against their older siblings (i.e., by negatively manipulating the relationship between the parent and the older sibling). Additionally, unlike peers or friends, siblings typically live in close proximity to one another and, as a result, are privy to an abundance of private information about each other. Threatening to share this information with individuals from another context (e.g., the sibling's friends at school) may be a particularly powerful relationally aggressive strategy within the sibling relationship. The following quotes from children illustrate some of the expressions of relational aggression within the sibling relationship that surface when children are asked, "What does your sister/brother do when she/he wants to be mean to you?" (from O'Brien & Crick, 1997):

> Shane does something in the house that I'll get in trouble for but he really did it.
> Emily takes my friend and doesn't let me play with them.
> Steffan will listen to the radio instead of me.
> Cathey tells mom about things I shouldn't be doing to get mom mad at me.
> Jill goes in her room and ignores me.
> Kodi talks about me behind my back to my friends.

In future research, it will be important to consider the relatively unique expressions of relational aggression within the sibling dyad (relative to the peer group) in studies of the development of aggressive behavior, with particular attention given to identification of the function and meaning of these behaviors when exhibited within this specific context.

FRIENDSHIPS

Although it has been well documented that children's overall level of acceptance in the peer group is a significant predictor of social-psychological adjustment (e.g., Parker & Asher, 1987), researchers have only recently begun to pay attention to the important role of dyadic peer relationships, namely friendships, in children's social development (e.g., aggression). The few existing studies on the developmental significance of friendships have emphasized the positive functions afforded to children by having friends versus not having friends. Recent theoretical and empirical extensions of this work, however, suggest that the quality of a child's friendships (e.g., degree of closeness, symmetry) and the identity of the child's friends (e.g., variations in behavioral characteristics or reputation) have an even greater impact on developmental outcomes (see Hartup, 1996). Some research driven by this new, multidimensional perspective has generated findings that question previous notions of friendships as developmental assets (e.g., Dishion, Patterson, & Griesler, 1994; Dishion, Andrews, & Crosby, 1995).

One line of such research involves the study of physically aggressive children's peer relationships. Drawing on prior evidence that aggressive behavior is the single strongest predictor of problematic relations in the larger peer group (Parker & Asher, 1987), some investigators have hypothesized that the peer relationship difficulties of aggressive children would extend into their friendships. This research has demonstrated that aggressive children are just as likely to have friends as are nonaggressive children. However, physically aggressive children tend to establish friendships with other, similarly aggressive peers, and it appears that children who associate with antisocial peers tend to engage in higher levels of antisocial behavior over time (Cairns et al., 1989; Dishion et al., 1994; Dishion et al., 1995). These findings are significant in that they suggest that children's close friendships may serve as a context in which aggression is facilitated or maintained.

Not surprisingly, prior studies on aggression and friendship have focused almost exclusively on physical forms of aggression and on aggressive boys (Grotpeter & Crick, 1996). The lack of theoretical and empirical attention to the friendships of relationally aggressive children is problematic for several reasons. First, there is ample evidence that relationally aggressive children, like physically aggressive children, experience serious peer relationship difficulties. Specifically, several studies have found that relationally aggressive children and adolescents are highly rejected by the larger peer group (e.g., Crick & Grotpeter, 1995; McNeilly-Choque et al.,

1996; Werner & Crick, in press). Based on this evidence, we hypothesized that, similar to the difficulties of physically aggressive children, the difficulties of relationally aggressive children in the peer group might "carry over" into their friendships.

Our second reason for embarking on the investigation of relationally aggressive children's friendships derived from studies of gender differences in the structure and nature of children's peer relationships during middle childhood and adolescence (e.g., for a review, see Buhrmester & Prager, 1995; Maccoby, 1990). This research has demonstrated that girls tend to emphasize communal over agenetic concerns in their interactions with peers and to report higher levels of intimacy, emotional closeness, and support in their friendships compared with boys. Given these qualitative differences in the nature of girls' friendships and in their social goals, it is not surprising that their peer networks are more likely to consist of dyads or triads than are boys' networks. In contrast, boys' interactions with same-gender peers tend to be directed toward the enhancement of individual status, and their social networks are typically larger, and less tightly knit, than those of girls. Given that relational aggression is more prevalent among girls' interactions, we hypothesized that the structure and function of girls' friendships would provide a unique context for the expression, and perhaps maintenance of, relational aggression. For example, a child who discloses high levels of personal information to her friend is in a potentially vulnerable position, to the extent that her friend could use this information as "ammunition" against her in anger or as a means of control. Boys, who have been found to disclose relatively little to even their best friends, are less likely to find themselves in a similar position.

In a first attempt to extend the literature on aggression and friendships, we conducted two studies investigating relationally aggressive children's participation in friendships and the qualities of these friendships (Grotpeter & Crick, 1996). We used the criteria specified by Parker and Asher (1993) to identify the mutual friendships of relationally aggressive and physically aggressive children in the third through sixth grades. Further, the qualitative features of children's friendships (e.g., levels of exclusivity, conflict, validation, and caring) were assessed using a revised version of the Friendship Qualities Questionnaire (FQQ; Parker & Asher, 1993). The specific hypotheses and associated findings from these two studies are described below, using Hartup's (1996) model for understanding the developmental significance of friendships as a conceptual framework (i.e., having friendships, the quality of one's friendships, and the individual characteristics of one's friends).

Having Friends To test the hypothesis that relationally aggressive children would be as likely as other children to have mutual friendships, in our first study we compared the percentage of children with mutual best friendships by aggression status (Grotpeter & Crick, 1996). Overall, our hypothesis was supported; however, an unexpected gender difference was found. Whereas relationally aggressive girls did not differ from nonrelationally aggressive girls with respect to their participation in friendships, relationally aggressive boys were less likely than nonrelationally aggressive boys to have a mutual friend. It appears that the social difficulties of relationally aggressive boys may be more extensive than those of relationally aggressive girls. Moreover, these findings suggest that, for boys, engaging in relational aggression is more problematic, in terms of social adjustment, than is physical aggression (i.e., relationally aggressive boys, but not physically aggressive boys, have fewer friendships). These findings are consistent with a recent study in which Crick (1997) reported that children who engage in nonnormative forms of aggression for their own gender (e.g., physically aggressive girls, relationally aggressive boys) were more socially and emotionally maladjusted than were children who engage in normative forms of aggression.

Friendship Quality Our findings regarding friendship quality showed that, relative to nonaggressive peers, relationally aggressive children's friendships were characterized by high levels of intimacy (i.e., closeness and self-disclosure; Grotpeter & Crick, 1996). Further, friends of relationally aggressive children perceived their friendships to be characterized by relatively high levels of conflict, betrayal, relational aggression, and demands for exclusivity. In sharp contrast, our findings showed that physically aggressive children's friendships were typified by relatively low levels of intimacy and by coalitional acts in which the two friends joined forces to gang up aggressively on other children. These findings suggest that relationally aggressive children's friendships may be relatively intense or enmeshed, whereas physically aggressive children's friendships may be characterized by a lack of closeness. However, it is also important to note that aggressive children's friendships did *not* differ from those of their nonaggressive peers on several positive dimensions of friendship, such as companionship or validation and caring, suggesting that, even for aggressive children, friendships may provide some supportive functions.

The Friends' Identity A final consideration of researchers interested in friendships concerns the identity of the peers whom children befriend (Hartup, 1996). In comparison to studies of individual differences in friendship participation and friendship quality, this dimension has received relatively little theoretical and empirical attention (Hartup, 1996), and consequently, the developmental significance of this dimension is not yet understood. Nonetheless, there is increasing evidence that suggests that behavioral and attitudinal concordances between some friends may contribute to the development or maintenance of behavior problems. For example, friends tend to be more similar than are nonfriends in terms of antisocial behavior (e.g., Cairns & Cairns, 1994; Haselager, Hartup, Van Lieshout, & Riksen-Walraven, 1995). Moreover, although children tend to report that negative peer influence is minimal (Brown, Clasen, & Eicher, 1986), several studies have found instead that association with deviant peers can lead to significant increases in the frequency with which some children engage in antisocial behaviors (e.g., Dishion, 1990; Dishion et al., 1994). These findings illustrate the importance of assessing the behavioral characteristics of a child's friends in order to understand some forms of aggressive behavior (i.e., physical aggression).

Unfortunately, very little empirical information is currently available regarding the characteristics of the friends of relationally aggressive children; however, several hypotheses can be generated on the basis of past research. For example, we might expect relationally aggressive children, similar to physically aggressive children, to be more likely to associate with other relationally aggressive children than would nonrelationally aggressive children. Preliminary descriptive information in one sample, however, showed that relationally aggressive children were just as likely to have a nonrelationally aggressive friend (52%) as they were a relationally aggressive friend (O'Brien & Werner, 1997). Physically aggressive children, on the other hand, were somewhat more likely to be friends with nonphysically aggressive children (60%) than with physically aggressive children. One avenue for future research will be to investigate developmental differences in concordances between friends' engagement in relational and physical aggression. Perhaps, through the processes of selection or mutual socialization, older relationally aggressive children (i.e., adolescents) will be more likely to associate with other relationally aggressive children.

We also examined the possibility that differences in social status might differentiate relationally aggressive children's friends from those of nonrelationally aggressive children. For example, given that the friends of relationally aggressive children have been found to report relatively high levels of conflict and betrayal, relational aggression, and demands for exclusivity, one might ask why these children would maintain friendships with relationally aggressive children. One hypothesis might be that these friends are in a vulnerable position in the peer group (i.e., low social status) and, as a result, have fewer friendship choices than do higher-status children. The finding that relationally aggressive children reported receiving high levels of self-disclosure from their friends, whereas they did not report that they reciprocated this self-disclosure (Grotpeter & Crick, 1996), suggests that the friends of relationally aggressive children are in a somewhat vulnerable position within their friendship. In contrast to our expectations, however, no consistent patterns were found with respect to the sociometric status of the children befriended by relationally aggressive children. Clearly, additional research is needed to further our understanding of the significance of the identity of relationally aggressive children's friends for their social and emotional development.

Social-Psychological Adjustment and Relational Aggression

In addition to the lack of gender-balanced assessments of aggressive behavior in past research, previous investigations have been limited by the tendency to evaluate adjustment outcomes that are more likely to be linked with aggression for boys than for girls (Zahn-Waxler, 1993). This gap in our knowledge is not surprising, given that males have been the focus of most past research. However, to build an understanding of the risk associated with aggressive behavior patterns for females, we must consider adjustment outcomes that are likely to be particularly salient for this gender group, in addition to those that have been traditionally studied. Although work in this area has only recently been initiated, a variety of social-psychological adjustment indices have been evaluated. Thus far, three approaches to the identification of appropriate adjustment correlates are apparent in these investigations. The first approach involves inclusion of adjustment indices that have been shown to be related to physical forms of aggression in past investigations (e.g., peer rejection, externalizing problems). Other indices have been included because research indicates that they may share features in common specifically with relational aggression (e.g., borderline personality features). Finally, exploratory studies have been conducted in which adjustment indices have been assessed because they are more prevalent among females and thus may be related to aggressive behavior for females (e.g., eating problems and disorders). It is important to note that, to date, most of the research in this area has been correlational in design, and thus inferences about causal links await future longitudinal investigations.

THE PRESCHOOL YEARS

Thus far, our understanding of the associations between relational aggression and adjustment difficulties in early childhood is limited. Nevertheless, the few studies that have been completed have been consistent in finding significant associations between relational aggression and social-psychological adjustment problems. Moreover, these associations have been found for both peer nominations and teacher ratings of relational aggression. These initial studies suggest the importance of looking at relational aggression, in addition to physical aggression, for a more complete understanding of young children's adjustment problems.

One important adjustment index included in many studies of aggression has been children's peer status (i.e., acceptance and rejection). Past investigations have demonstrated that physical aggression is one of the best known predictors of concurrent and future rejection by peers (for reviews, see Asher & Coie, 1990; Parker & Asher, 1987). Based on this evidence, several studies have been conducted to determine whether relational forms of aggression show similar associations.

Investigations of relational aggression during the preschool years have shown it to be highly related to children's peer status (e.g., acceptance and rejection). Peer assessments of relational aggression have been found to be significantly correlated with peer rejection, for both boys and girls, in Russian as well as American samples (Crick, Casas, & Mosher, 1997; Casas & Crick, 1997; Nelson et al., 1998). Teacher assessments of relational aggression have also been found to be associated with peer rejection for girls, but not for boys (Casas & Crick, 1997; Nelson et al., 1998; McNeilly-Choque et al., 1996).

Associations have also been found for relational aggression and prosocial behavior among preschoolers. Teacher ratings of relational aggression have been found to be negatively correlated with teacher assessments of prosocial behavior for both boys and girls (Crick, Casas, & Mosher, 1997; Casas & Crick, 1997). Peer assessments of relational aggression have also been shown to be negatively correlated with teacher assessments of prosocial behavior for boys and girls in one study (Casas & Crick, 1997), but only for girls in an earlier investigation (Crick, Casas, & Mosher, 1997). Although longitudinal studies are needed, these results have important implications for young children's adjustment, given that research with older children has shown that a lack of prosocial behavior is a significant predictor of future social adjustment difficulties beyond what would be predicted from engaging in physical and relational aggression (Crick, 1996).

Although it has been assessed in two studies (Crick, Casas, & Mosher, 1997; Casas & Crick, 1997), we have not found a significant association between relational aggression and loneliness. It is possible that the structure of the preschool classroom, with its emphasis on group activities, makes social isolation a relatively rare experience. It is also possible that feelings of loneliness may be attenuated by the fact that many preschoolers are in school for relatively short periods of time.

Finally, our investigations have also shown an association between young children's use of relational aggression and teachers' reports of depressed affect. Significant correlations have been obtained for teacher ratings of depressed affect and teacher ratings of relational aggression among girls, but not boys (Crick, Casas, & Mosher, 1997; Casas & Crick, 1997). Although caution is needed when interpreting these correlational findings, it is possible that children's depressed affect is a result of being rejected by peers for their use of relational aggression. Why these results are found for girls but not boys is not entirely clear. It is possible that preschool boys may not be as perceptive as their female counterparts in detecting when they are being rejected by their classmates, especially in relatively subtle ways. As boys' perceptual abilities develop, the association between depression and relational aggression may strengthen. The results of studies with elementary-school-age children are consistent with this hypothesis, demonstrating that relational aggression is associated with higher levels of internalizing problems, such as depression, for both girls and boys (Crick, 1997; Crick & Grotpeter, 1995).

Taken together, the results of these studies underscore the importance of assessing relational aggression in the early detection of young children's adjustment difficulties. There is one important caveat, however, that must be considered when interpreting these results—namely, that all the information gathered to date has been collected within the preschool context. It will be important for future research to examine other contexts within which young children operate, such as the family context. Finally, investigations are needed that examine whether relationally aggressive behaviors predict future adjustment difficulties for young children.

MIDDLE CHILDHOOD

The majority of studies in which the adjustment correlates of relational aggression have been assessed have focused on samples of middle-childhood age. Similar to studies of preschoolers, studies of elementary-school-age children have shown that relational aggression is significantly associated with both concurrent and future rejection for both boys and girls during middle childhood (Crick, 1996; Crick & Grotpeter, 1995; Rys & Bear, 1997; Tomada & Schneider, 1997). For girls, but not for boys, this association remains significant even when physical aggression is first controlled statistically (i.e., relational aggression provides unique information in the prediction of peer rejection, beyond that accounted for by physical aggression). Additionally, relational aggression predicts changes in peer rejection (becoming more rejected) over the course of a school year for girls (Crick, 1996). These findings provide support for the importance of assessing relational aggression, in addition to physical aggression, particularly for understanding the social adjustment difficulties of girls.

The association between relational aggression and peer status has also been assessed in another way—through the identification of sociometric status groups (i.e., children whose status is classified as popular, average, neglected, rejected, or controversial). This research has demonstrated that controversial-status children (i.e., those who are both highly liked and highly disliked by peers) are significantly more relationally aggressive than all other status groups, and that rejected children (i.e., those who are highly disliked by peers) are more relationally aggressive than children of popular, average, and neglected status (Crick & Grotpeter, 1995; Tomada & Schneider, 1997). These results are consistent with those found in past studies of the sociometric classifications of physically aggressive children (for a review, see Coie, Dodge, & Kupersmidt, 1990). They indicate that some relationally aggressive children are well liked by some peers, a finding that echoes the earlier discussion of relational aggression and friendship (i.e., which showed that most relationally aggressive children have best friends; Grotpeter & Crick, 1996).

Relational aggression has also been shown to be related to internalizing problems (e.g., depression) during middle childhood for both boys and girls (Crick & Grotpeter, 1995). Research in which both relational and physical forms of aggression have been assessed, in addition to both internalizing and externalizing adjustment problems, has demonstrated that relational aggression was associated with both internalizing and externalizing difficulties, in contrast to physical aggression, which was shown to be related to externalizing problems only (Crick, 1997).

As discussed previously, investigators interested in understanding aggressive females, in addition to aggressive males, have begun to explore the possibility that a more gender-balanced assessment of adjustment outcomes is necessary than that generated in past research, which focused primarily on males. This approach, although limited in its scope thus far, has yielded promising results. One of the adjustment outcomes we have considered is borderline personality features. We selected this outcome type for two reasons: past research has shown that relationally aggressive children display a pattern of individual characteristics that appears similar to that of borderlines (e.g., dissatisfaction with relationships, hostile interpersonal attributions, negative affect); and similar to relational aggression, borderline personality has been found to be more typical of females than males (Crick & Grotpeter, 1995; Ludolph, Westen, & Misle, 1990). In a recent study of third-graders, we found that relationally aggressive children exhibited significantly higher levels of borderline personality features than did their peers (Crick, Werner, & Rockhill, 1997). In contrast, this relation was not obtained for physically aggressive children. In another sample, we investigated a second adjustment indicator known to be more typical of females than males, eating problems. Children with problematic eating behaviors were shown to be significantly more relationally aggressive (but not physically aggressive) than other children (Crick, Casas, & Werner, 1997). Results of these studies, together with those discussed previously, provide initial evidence that the adjustment trajectories of physically and relationally aggressive children should be considered as overlapping (e.g., both are predictive of peer rejection) but not necessarily the same in all respects. Future research is needed to identify additional adjustment outcomes that may be problematic for relationally aggressive children and to evaluate the specificity of the adjustment-aggression linkages studied previously.

One issue not addressed by the above studies concerns the relative adjustment of children who engage in gender-normative forms of aggression (e.g., physical aggression for boys and relational aggression for girls) versus those who engage in aggression that is relatively nonnormative within their gender groups (e.g., physical aggression for girls and relational aggression for boys). In a recent study we hypothesized that, due to the peer sanctions likely to be encountered during middle childhood for engaging in nonnormative behavior for their own gender (i.e., because same-sex interaction is the most common type during this age period; Maccoby,

1990), children who engage in such nonnormative forms of aggression would be at heightened risk for experiencing adjustment difficulties (Crick, 1997). Results supported this premise, demonstrating that, in addition to being more maladjusted than nonaggressive children, physically aggressive girls and relationally aggressive boys were significantly more maladjusted than physically aggressive boys and relationally aggressive girls, respectively. These findings highlight the importance of studying both boys and girls, in addition to both relational and physical forms of aggression, in the same investigation.

In addition to relationally aggressive children's risk of adjustment difficulties, such as depression and peer rejection, and in accordance with past research findings about physically aggressive peers (Cairns et al., 1989; Loeber, 1991; Olweus, 1979; Patterson, 1992), preliminary evidence indicates that relationally aggressive children are at risk for future aggressive behavior problems. Specifically, results of a short-term longitudinal study have shown the six-month stability of relational aggression to be quite high ($r = .60$) during middle childhood (Crick, 1996). Although firm conclusions await long-term longitudinal research, these findings indicate that relationally aggressive behavior problems may persist over time. If so, the adjustment difficulties of children who experience these behavior problems may also be cumulative. Further, these results highlight the importance of studying relational aggression in older samples (i.e., because relationally aggressive children may grow up to be relationally aggressive adolescents or even adults).

ADOLESCENCE AND ADULTHOOD

Only two studies to date have investigated the associations between relational aggression and adjustment after childhood, and both have focused on the adolescent period (MacDonald & O'Laughlin, 1997; Werner & Crick, in press). Consistent with prior research with children, Werner and Crick found in a sample of older adolescents that relational aggression was significantly associated with higher levels of peer rejection and lower levels of peer-rated prosocial behavior. Moreover, controversial-status adolescents in this study were more relationally aggressive than were adolescents of popular, neglected, and average status. These findings provide initial evidence suggesting that, despite the relative frequency of relational aggression in the peer groups of older adolescents (Crick, Werner, & Schellin, 1998), engagement in these behaviors may continue to have adverse consequences for peer status, as has been found in childhood.

Both Werner and Crick (in press) and MacDonald and O'Laughlin (1997) assessed links between relational aggression and internalizing difficulties. Consistent with studies with children, MacDonald and O'Laughlin reported that relational aggression was significantly correlated with depression in a sample of early adolescents. Werner and Crick, however, did not find that relational aggression predicted depressive features in late adolescence. It is important to note, however, that MacDonald and O'Laughlin obtained self-reports of both aggression and adjustment, whereas Werner and Crick utilized a peer-nomination instrument to assess aggressive behavior and self-reports to assess adjustment outcomes. These methodological differences may account, in part, for these divergent findings. However, given the significant links between relational aggression and depression found in preschool and childhood, it will be important to include depression as an outcome measure in longitudinal studies to determine if relational aggression does predict internalizing difficulties during later stages of development.

Relationally aggressive adolescents have also been found to engage in higher levels of externalizing behavior compared with nonrelationally aggressive adolescents. Specifically, relational aggression has been linked with aggressive and nonaggressive delinquency during mid-adolescence (MacDonald & O'Laughlin, 1997). In the Werner and Crick sample, relational aggression predicted some features of antisocial personality disorder (stimulus seeking, egocentricity) in both males and females, even after controlling statistically for the contribution of physical aggression. Further, another component of antisocial personality disorder, engagement in antisocial behaviors (e.g., destruction of property, lying, misbehaving in school; Morey, 1991), was found to be associated with relational aggression, but for females only. Together, these findings suggest, not only that relational aggression is an important indicator of serious externalizing behavior in adolescence, but that relational aggression may be a better predictor of these difficulties among females than is physical aggression, which has most often been linked with conduct problems and antisocial behavior in prior research.

Werner and Crick (in press) also examined the links between relational aggression, features of borderline personality disorder, and eating disorder symptomatology. With respect to borderline features, we found that relational aggression was significantly associated with affective instability, negative relationships, and engagement in self-harming behaviors among females but not males. Relational aggression was also shown to be correlated with bulimic eating patterns.

CONCLUSION

The findings reported here provide initial evidence for both similarity and dissimilarity in the adjustment difficulties associated with relational and physical aggression across development. During each of the developmental periods assessed thus far, rejection by peers has been found to be a robust correlate of relational aggression. Given what we know about the consequences of peer rejection for future adjustment (e.g., Parker & Asher, 1987), and in light of preliminary evidence of intra-individual stability in children's engagement in relational aggression (Crick, 1996), these findings highlight the importance of early identification of relationally aggressive, in addition to physically aggressive, children.

The studies reported in this section also demonstrate robust associations among relational aggression and externalizing behaviors during childhood and adolescence. Although externalizing problems were not assessed in our studies with preschoolers, young children who engage in relational aggression were found to engage in low levels of positive, prosocial behaviors toward peers (Casas & Crick, 1997). In middle childhood, teachers rated relationally aggressive children high on measures of impulsivity and oppositional behaviors (Crick, 1997), and in adolescence, more serious conduct problems such as delinquency and features of antisocial personality were linked with relational aggression (MacDonald & O'Laughlin, 1997; Werner & Crick, in press). These findings provide evidence that children and adolescents who engage in high levels of relational aggression are likely to suffer some of the same consequences as do physically aggressive individuals.

Although most relationally aggressive children participate in mutual friendships (Grotpeter & Crick, 1996), they may be at risk for the development of disturbances centered around close relationships, as suggested by the links found between relational aggression and borderline personality features (Crick, Werner, & Rockhill, 1997; Werner & Crick, in press). It may be that early experiences of rejection from family or from peers lead some children to develop a hypersensitivity to perceived rejection or hostility, or heightened distress or concern with relationship issues, characteristics that have been found in both relationally aggressive children and adolescent and adult borderlines (e.g., Crick, 1995; Ludolph et al., 1990). That the association between relational aggression and borderline features was significant for adolescent females only in the Werner and Crick study is highly consistent with reported gender differences in both engagement in relational aggression and in the prevalence of borderline personality disorder in clinical populations. Further, the aggression-adjustment specificity demonstrated by these findings suggests that there may be different trajectories, not only for relationally versus physically aggressive children, but also for relationally aggressive males versus females.

Finally, it appears that relationally aggressive children and young adolescents are also at risk for concurrent internalizing problems, including loneliness and depression (Casas & Crick, 1997; Crick, 1997; Crick & Grotpeter, 1995; MacDonald & O'Laughlin, 1997). These links have been found to be particularly true for relationally aggressive girls, suggesting once again that the outcomes associated with aggression may be different for females versus males. Longitudinal research is needed to determine if relational aggression leads to the development of internalizing problems in childhood, difficulties that may continue into adolescence and adulthood.

General Conclusion

Although research on relational aggression is still in its infancy, the available evidence thus far provides compelling support for the importance of this construct. Further, this evidence demonstrates that, although a more gender-balanced assessment of aggressive behavior can greatly enhance our understanding of aggressive girls (i.e., through the assessment of relational aggression in addition to physical aggression), this strategy alone is not sufficient. That is, it may be necessary to reconsider past theoretical and empirical models of both the antecedents and the consequences of aggression to account for unique factors in the etiology and development of relational versus physical forms of aggression for boys versus girls.

NOTE

1. Because of ethical considerations, we were unable to measure parental physical aggression directed toward the child.

REFERENCES

Abramovitch, R., Corter, C., & Lando, B. (1979). Sibling interaction in the home. *Child Development, 50*, 997–1003.

Achenbach, T. M., McConaughy, S. H., & Howell, C. T. (1987). Child/adolescent behavioral and emotional problems: Implications of cross-informant correlations for situational specificity. *Psychological Bulletin, 101*, 213–232.

Aronson, E. (1988). *The social animal* (5th ed.). New York: W. H. Freeman.

Asher, S. R., & Coie, J. D. (1990). *Peer rejection in childhood*. New York: Cambridge University Press.

Bandura, A. (1973). *Aggression: A social learning theory analysis*. Englewood Cliffs NJ: Prentice Hall.

Bandura, A. (1977). *Social learning theory*. Englewood Cliffs NJ: Prentice Hall.

Bandura, A. (1986). *Social foundations of thought and action*. Englewood Cliffs NJ: Prentice Hall.

Bandura, A., & Walters, R. H. (1959). *Adolescent aggression*. New York: Ronald Press.

Bandura, A., & Walters, R. H. (1963). *Social learning and personality development*. New York: Holt, Rinehart, & Winston.

Beardsall, L. (1987). *Sibling conflict in middle childhood*. Unpublished doctoral dissertation, Cambridge University.

Berkowitz, L. (1993). *Aggression: Its causes, consequences, and control*. New York: Academic Press.

Berndt, T. J., & Bulleit, T. N. (1985). Effects of sibling relationships on preschoolers' behavior at home and at school. *Developmental Psychology, 21*, 761–767.

Bierman, K. L. (1986). Process of change during social skills training with preadolescents and its relation to treatment outcome. *Child Development, 57*, 230–240.

Bjorkqvist, K., Lagerspetz, K. M. J., & Kaukiainen, A. (1992). Do girls manipulate and boys fight? Developmental trends in regard to direct and indirect aggression. *Aggressive Behavior, 18,* 117–127.

Bjorkvist, K., & Niemela, P. (1992). New trends in the study of female aggression. In K. Bjorkvist & P. Niemela (Eds.), *Of mice and women: Aspects of female aggression* (pp. 1–15). San Diego CA: Academic Press.

Bjorkqvist, K., Osterman, K., & Kaukiainen, A. (1992). The development of direct and indirect aggressive strategies in males and females. In K. Bjorkqvist & P. Niemela (Eds.), *Of mice and women: Aspects of female aggression* (pp. 51–64). San Diego CA: Academic Press.

Bjorkqvist, K., Osterman, K., & Lagerspetz, K. M. J. (1994a, June). *Patterns of aggression among adolescents of three age groups: A cross cultural comparison.* Paper presented at the 13th biennial meeting of the International Society for the Study of Behavioral Development, Amsterdam, Netherlands.

Bjorkqvist, K., Osterman, K., & Lagerspetz, K. M. J. (1994b). Sex differences in covert aggression among adults. *Aggressive Behavior, 20,* 27–33.

Block, J. H. (1983). Differential premises arising from differential socialization of the sexes: Some conjectures. *Child Development, 54,* 1335–1354.

Brehm, S. S., & Kassin, S. M. (1990). *Social psychology.* Boston: Houghton Mifflin.

Brody, G., Stoneman, Z., & Burke, M. (1987). Child temperaments, maternal differential behavior, and sibling relationships. *Developmental Psychology, 23,* 354–362.

Bronfenbrenner, U. (1970). *Two worlds of childhood: U.S. and U.S.S.R.* New York: Russell Sage Foundation.

Brown, B. B., Clasen, D. R., & Eicher, S. A. (1986). Perceptions of peer pressure, peer conformity dispositions, and self-reported behavior among adolescents. *Developmental Psychology, 22,* 521–530.

Buhrmester, D. (1990). The developmental courses of sibling and peer relationships. In F. Boer & J. Dunn (Eds.), *Children's sibling relationships: Developmental and clinical issues* (pp. 19–39). Hillsdale NJ: Lawrence Erlbaum.

Buhrmester, D. (1996). Need fulfillment, interpersonal competence, and the developmental contexts of early adolescent friendship. In W. M. Bukowski, A. F. Newcomb, & W. W. Hartup (Eds.), *The company they keep: Friendship in childhood and adolescence.* New York: Cambridge University Press.

Buhrmester, D., & Prager, K. (1995). Patterns and functions of self-disclosure during childhood and adolescence. In K. J. Rotenberg (Ed.), *Disclosure processed in children and adolescents.* New York: Cambridge University Press.

Bukowski, W. M., & Hoza, B. (1989). Popularity and friendship: Issues in theory, measurement, and outcome. In T. J. Berndt and G. W. Ladd (Eds.), *Peer relationships in child development.* New York: John Wiley and Sons.

Buss, A. H. (1961). *The psychology of aggression.* New York: John Wiley.

Buss, A. H., & Perry, M. (1992). The aggression questionnaire. *Journal of Personality and Social Psychology, 63*, 452–459.

Cairns, R. B., & Cairns, B. D. (1994). *Lifelines and risks*. New York: Cambridge University Press.

Cairns, R. B., Cairns, B. D., Neckerman, H. J., Ferguson, L. L., & Gariepy, J. L. (1989). Growth and aggression: 1. Childhood to early adolescence. *Developmental Psychology, 25*, 320–330.

Casas, J. F., & Crick, N. R. (1997). Social information-processing and relational aggression in preschool. Manuscript forthcoming.

Coie, J. D., Dodge, K. A., & Kupersmidt, J. (1990). Peer group behavior and social status. In S. R. Asher & J. D. Coie (Eds.), *Peer rejection in childhood*. New York: Cambridge University Press.

Crick, N. R. (1995). Relational aggression: The role of intent attributions, feelings of distress, and provocation type. *Development and Psychopathology, 7*, 313–322.

Crick, N. R. (1996). The role of overt aggression, relational aggression, and prosocial behavior in children's future social adjustment. *Child Development, 67*, 2317–2327.

Crick, N. R. (1997). Engagement in gender normative versus non-normative forms of aggression: Links to social-psychological adjustment. *Developmental Psychology, 33*, 610–617.

Crick, N. R., & Bigbee, M. A. (1998). Relational and overt forms of peer victimization: A multi-informant approach. *Journal of Consulting and Clinical Psychology, 66*, 337–347.

Crick, N. R., Bigbee, M. A., & Howes, C. (1996). Gender differences in children's normative beliefs about aggression: How do I hurt thee? Let me count the ways. *Child Development, 67*, 1003–1014.

Crick, N. R., Casas, J. F., & Ku, H. (in press). Physical and relational peer victimization in preschool. *Developmental Psychology*.

Crick, N. R., Casas, J. F., & Mosher, M. (1997). Relational and overt aggression in preschool. *Developmental Psychology, 33*, 579–588.

Crick, N. R., Casas, J. F., & Werner, N. E. (1997). *The social adjustment of children with eating problems*. Manuscript forthcoming.

Crick, N. R., & Dodge, K. A. (1994). A review and reformulation of social information-processing mechanisms in children's social adjustment. *Psychological Bulletin, 115*, 74–101.

Crick, N. R., & Dodge, K. A. (1996). Social information-processing mechanisms in reactive and proactive aggression. *Child Development, 67*, 993–1002.

Crick, N. R., & Grotpeter, J. K. (1995). Relational aggression, gender, and social-psychological adjustment. *Child Development, 66*, 710–722.

Crick, N. R., & Grotpeter, J. K. (1996). Children's treatment by peers: Victims of relational and overt aggression. *Development and Psychopathology, 8*, 367–380.

Crick, N. R., Grotpeter, J. K., & Bigbee, M. A. (1998). *Relationally and physically aggressive children's intent attributions and feelings of distress for rela-*

tional and instrumental peer provocations. Manuscript submitted for publication.

Crick, N. R., & Werner, N. E. (in press). Response decision processes in relational and overt aggression. *Child Development*.

Crick, N. R., Werner, N. E., & Rockhill, C. M. (1997). *A gender-balanced approach to the study of aggression and its consequences*. Manuscript forthcoming.

Crick, N. R., Werner, N. E., & Schellin, H. (1998). *Aggression among college students: The role of gender of aggressor, gender of target, and form of aggression*. Manuscript forthcoming.

Crouter, A., & McHale, S. (1989, April). *Childrearing in dual- and single-earner families: Implications for the development of school-age children*. Paper presented at the biennial meeting of the Society for Research in Child Development, Kansas City.

Cummings, E. M., & Cummings, J. L. (1988). A process-oriented approach to children's coping with adults' angry behavior. *Developmental Review, 8*, 296–321.

Davies, P. T., & Cummings, E. M. (1994). Marital conflict and child adjustment: An emotional security hypothesis. *Psychological Bulletin, 116*, 387–411.

Dishion, T. J. (1990). The peer context of troublesome child and adolescent behavior. In P. Leone (Ed.), *Understanding troubled and troublesome youth* (pp. 128–153). Newbury Park CA: Sage.

Dishion, T. J., Andrews, D. W., & Crosby, L. (1995). Anti-social boys and their friends in early adolescence: Relationship characteristics, quality, and interactional processes. *Child Development, 66*, 139–151.

Dishion, T. J., Patterson, G. R., & Griesler, P. C. (1994). Peer adaptations in the development of antisocial behavior: A confluence model. In L. R. Huesmann (Ed.), *Current perspectives on aggressive behavior* (pp. 61–95). New York: Plenum.

Dodge, K. A. (1980). Social cognition and children's aggressive behavior. *Child Development, 51*, 162–170.

Dodge, K. A. (1990). The structure and function of reactive and proactive aggression. In D. Pepler & K. H. Rubin (Eds.), *The development and treatment of childhood aggression* (pp. 210–218). Hillsdale NJ: Lawrence Erlbaum.

Dodge, K. A., Bates, J. E., & Pettit, G. S. (1990). *Science, 250*, 1678–1683.

Dodge, K. A., & Coie, J. D. (1987). Social information-processing factors in reactive and proactive aggression in children's playgroups. *Journal of Personality and Social Psychology, 53*, 1146–1158.

Dodge, K. A., & Crick, N. R. (1990). Social information-processing bases of aggressive behavior in children. *Personality and Social Psychology Bulletin, 16*, 2–22.

Dollard, J., Doob, C. W., Miller, N. E., Mowrer, O. H., & Sears, R. R. (1939). *Frustration and aggression*. New Haven CT: Yale University Press.

Dunn, J., & Kendrick, C. (1982). *Siblings: Love, envy, and understanding*. Cambridge: Harvard University Press.

Dunn, J., & McGuire, S. (1992). Sibling and peer relationship in childhood. *Journal of Child Psychology and Psychiatry, 33*, 67–105.

Dunn, J., & Munn, P. (1986). Sibling quarrels and maternal intervention: Individual differences in understanding and aggression. *Journal of Child Psychology and Psychiatry, 27*, 583–595.

Dunn, L. M., & Dunn, L. M. (1981). *Peabody Picture Vocabulary Test—Revised*. Circle Pines MN: American Guidance Service.

Easterbrooks, M. A., & Emde, R. N. (1988). Marital and parent-child relationships: The role of affect in the family system. In R. Hinde & J. Stevenson-Hine (Eds.), *Relationships within families: Mutual influences* (pp. 83–103). Oxford: Clarendon Press.

Emery, R. E. (1982). Interparental conflict and the children of discord and divorce. *Psychological Bulletin, 92*, 310–330.

Felson, R. B., & Russo, N. (1988). Children's evaluations of retaliatory aggression. *Child Development, 59*, 961–968.

Feshbach, N. D. (1969). Sex differences in children's modes of aggressive responses toward outsiders. *Merrill-Palmer Quarterly, 15*, 249–258.

Ford, M. E. (1982). Social cognition and social competence in adolescence. *Developmental Psychology, 18*, 323–340.

Ford, M. E., & Keating, D. P. (1981). Development and individual differences in long-term memory retrieval: Process and organization. *Child Development, 52*, 234–241.

Foster, S. L., DeLawyer, D. D., & Guevremont, D. C. (1986). A critical incidents analysis of liked and disliked peer behaviors and their situational parameters in childhood and adolescence. *Behavioral Assessment, 8*, 115–133.

Freud, S. (1930). *Civilization and its discontents*. London: Hogarth.

Galen, B. R., & Underwood, M. (1997). A developmental investigation of social aggression among girls. *Developmental Psychology, 33*, 589–599.

Gormly, A. V., & Brodzinsky, D. M. (1993). *Life-span human development*. Orlando FL: Holt, Rinehart, & Winston.

Grotpeter, J. K., & Crick, N. R. (1996). Relational aggression, overt aggression, and friendship. *Child Development 67*, 2328–2338.

Grotpeter, J. K., & Crick, N. R. (1997). *Relational aggression, physical aggression, and family relationships*. Manuscript forthcoming.

Grotpeter, J. K., Crick, N. R., & O'Brien, K. M. (1996, April). *Relationally and overtly aggressive children's relationships with their mothers*. Paper presented at the biennial meeting of the Conference on Human Development, Birmingham AL.

Grotpeter, J. K., Geiger, T., Nukulkij, P., & Crick, N. R. (1998). *Friendships of relationally and overt victimized children: With friends like this, who needs enemies?* Manuscript forthcoming.

Grych, J. H., & Fincham, F. D. (1990). Marital conflict and children's adjustment: A cognitive-contextual framework. *Psychological Bulletin, 108*, 267–290.

Grych, J. H., & Fincham, F. D. (1993). Children's appraisals of marital conflict. *Child Development, 64*, 215–230.

Grych, J. H., Seid, M., & Fincham, F. D. (1992). Assessing marital conflict from the child's perspective: The children's perception of interparental conflict scale. *Child Development, 63*, 558–572.

Guerra, N. G., & Slaby, R. G. (1989). Evaluative factors in social problem solving by aggressive boys. *Journal of Abnormal Child Psychology, 17*, 277–289.

Hall, J. A., & Rosenthal, R. (1991). Testing for moderator variables in a meta-analysis: Issues and methods. *Communication Monographs, 58*(4), 437–448.

Hart, C. H., Nelson, D. A., Robinson, C. C., Olsen, S. F., & McNeilly-Choque, M. K. (1998). Overt and relational aggression in Russian nursery-school-age children: Parenting style and marital linkages. *Developmental Psychology, 34*, 687–697.

Hart, C. H., Nelson, D. A., Robinson, C. C., Olsen, S. F., McNeilly-Choque, M. K., Porter, C. L., & McKee, T. R. (in press). Russian parenting styles and family processes: Linkages with subtypes of victimization and aggression. In K. A. Kerns, J. M. Contreras, & A. M. Neal-Barnett (Eds.), *Family and peers: Linking two social worlds.* Westport CT: Praeger.

Hart, C. H., Yang, C., Nelson, D. A., Jin, S., Bazarskaya, N., & Nelson, L. (1998). Peer contact patterns, parenting practices, and preschoolers' social competence in China, Russia, and the United States. In P. Slee & K. Rigby (Eds.), *Peer relations amongst children: Current issues and future directions* (pp. 3–30). London: Routledge.

Hart, C. H., Yang, C., Nelson, D. A., Jin, S., Robinson, C. C., Olsen, S. F., & McNeilly-Choque, M. K. (1998). *Subtypes of aggression and victimization in Chinese, Russian, and U.S. preschoolers: Sex and peer status linkages.* Manuscript under review.

Hartup, W. W. (1974). Aggression in childhood: Developmental perspectives. *American Psychologist, 29*, 336–341.

Hartup, W. W. (1983). Peer relations. In E. M. Hetherington (Ed.), *Handbook of child psychology: Vol. 4. Socialization, personality, and social development* (4th ed., pp. 103–196). New York: Wiley.

Hartup, W. W. (1996). The company they keep: Friendships and their developmental significance. *Child Development, 67*, 1–13.

Haselager, G. J. T., Hartup, W. W., Van Lieshout, C. F. M., & Riksen-Walraven, M. (1995). *Friendship similarity in middle childhood as a function of sex and sociometric status.* Unpublished manuscript, University of Nijmegen.

Ho, D. Y. F. (1986). Chinese patterns of socialization: A critical review. In M. H. Bond (Ed.), *The psychology of the Chinese people* (pp. 1–37). New York: Oxford University Press.

Hudley. C., & Graham, S. (1993). An attributional intervention to reduce peer-directed aggression among African-American boys. *Child Development, 64*, 124–138.

Jarvinen, D. W., & Nicholls, J. G. (1996). Adolescents' social goals, beliefs about the causes of social success, and satisfaction in peer relations. *Developmental Psychology, 32*, 435–441.

Kail, R. (1990). *The development of memory in children* (3rd ed.). New York: Freeman.

Keenan, K., & Shaw, D. (1997). Developmental and social influences on young girls' early problem behavior. *Psychological Bulletin, 121*, 95–113.

Ladd, G. W., & Mars, K. T. (1986). Reliability and validity of preschoolers' perceptions of peer behavior. *Journal of Clinical Child Psychology, 15*, 16–25.

Lagerspetz, K. M. J., & Bjorkqvist, K. (1994). Indirect aggression in girls and boys. In L. R. Huesmann (Ed.), *Aggressive behavior: Current perspectives* (pp. 131–150). New York: Plenum.

Lagerspetz, K. M. J., Bjorkqvist, K., & Peltonen, T. (1988). Is indirect aggression more typical of females? Gender differences in aggressiveness in 11–12-year-old children. *Aggressive Behavior, 14*, 403–414.

Levy-Schiff, R., & Hoffman, M. A. (1989). Social behavior as a predictor of adjustment among three-year-olds. *Journal of Clinical Child Psychology, 18*, 65–71.

Loeber, R. (1991). Antisocial behavior: More enduring than changeable? *Journal of the American Academy of Child and Adolescent Psychiatry, 30*, 393–397.

Loeber, R., & Dishion, T. J. (1983). Early predictors of male delinquency: A review. *Psychological Bulletin, 94*, 68–99.

Ludolph, P., Westen, D., & Misle, B. (1990). The borderline diagnosis in adolescents: Symptoms and developmental history. *American Journal of Psychiatry, 147*, 470–476.

Maccoby, E. (1990). Gender and relationships: A developmental account. *American Psychologist, 45*, 513–520.

MacDonald, C. D., & O'Laughlin, E. M. (1991, April). *Relational aggression and risk behaviors in middle school students.* Poster presented at the biennial meeting of the Society for Research in Child Development, Washington DC.

MacDonald, K., & Parke, R. (1984). Bridging the gap: Parent-child play interaction and peer interactive competence. *Child Development, 55*, 1265–1277.

McNeilly-Choque, M. K., Hart, C. H., Robinson, C. C., Nelson, L. J., & Olsen, S. F. (1996). Overt and relational aggression on the playground: Correspondence among different informants. *Journal of Research in Childhood Education, 11*, 47–67.

Morey, L. (1991). *The personality assessment inventory: Professional manual.* Lutz FL: Psychological Assessment Resources.

Mueller, E., & Lucas, T. (1975). A developmental analysis of peer interaction among toddlers. In M. Lewis & L. A. Rosenblum (Eds.), *Friendship and peer relations.* New York: Wiley.

Myers, D. G. (1990). *Social psychology.* New York: McGraw-Hill.

Neilsen, A., & Gerber, D. (1979). Psychosocial aspects of truancy in early adolescence. *Adolescence, 14*, 312–326.

Nelson, D. A., Hart, C. H., Robinson, C. C., & Olsen, S. F. (1998). *Measuring overt and relational aggression in Russian nursery schools.* Manuscript under review.

O'Brien, K., & Crick, N. R. (1997). *Relational and physical aggression in sibling relationships: From hitting and kicking to ignoring and excluding, siblings do it all.* Manuscript submitted for publication.

O'Brien, K., & Werner, N. E. (1997). *The characteristics of the friends of relationally aggressive children.* Unpublished data, University of Minnesota.

Olson, S. L., & Lifgren, K. (1988). Concurrent and longitudinal correlates of preschool peer sociometrics: Comparing rating scale and nomination measures. *Journal of Applied Developmental Psychology, 9,* 409–420.

Olweus, D. (1979). Stability of aggressive reaction patterns in males: A review. *Psychological Bulletin, 86,* 852–875.

Olweus, D. (1993). *Bullying at school: What we know and what we can do.* Oxford: Blackwell.

Owens, L. D. (1996). Sticks and stones and sugar and spice: Girls' and boys' aggression in schools. *Australian Journal of Guidance & Counselling, 6,* 45–55.

Paquette, J. A., & Underwood, M. K. (in press). Children's experience of peer victimization: Gender differences in accounts of social and physical aggression. *Merrill-Palmer Quarterly.*

Parke, R. D. (1992). Epilogue: Remaining issues and future trends in the study of family-peer relationships. In R. D. Parke & G. W. Ladd (Eds.), *Family-peer relationships: Modes of linkage.* Hillsdale NJ: Lawrence Erlbaum.

Parke, R. D., MacDonald, K., Beitel, A., & Bhavnagri, N. (1988). The role of family in the development of peer relations. In K. Kreppner & R. M. Lerner (Eds.), *Family systems and life-span development.* Hillsdale NJ: Lawrence Erlbaum.

Parke, R. D., & Slaby, R. G. (1983). The development of aggression. In E. M. Hetherington (Ed.), P. H. Mussen (Series Ed.), *Handbook of child psychology: Vol. 4. Socialization, personality, and social development* (pp. 547–642). New York: Wiley.

Parker, J. G., & Asher, S. R. (1987). Peer acceptance and later personal adjustment: Are low-accepted children "at risk"? *Psychological Bulletin, 102,* 357–389.

Parker, J. G., & Asher, S. R. (1993). Friendship and friendship quality in middle childhood: Links with peer group acceptance and feelings of loneliness and social dissatisfaction. *Developmental Psychology, 29,* 611–621.

Patterson, G. R. (1982). *Coercive family processes.* Eugene OR.

Patterson, G. R. (1986). The contribution of siblings to training for fighting: A microsocial analysis. In D. Olweus, J. Block, & M. Radke-Yarrow (Eds.), *Development of antisocial and prosocial behavior: Research, theories, and issues.* New York: Academic Press.

Patterson, G. R. (1992). Developmental changes in antisocial behavior. In R. D. Peters, R. J. McMahan, and V. L. Quinsey (Eds.), *Aggression and violence throughout the life span.* Newbury CA: Sage.

Patterson, G. R., DeBaryshe, B. D., & Ramsey, E. (1989). A developmental perspective on antisocial behavior. *American Psychologist, 44,* 329–335.

Patterson, G. R., & Dishion, T. J. (1988). Multilevel family process models: Traits, interactions, and relationships. In R. Hinde & J. Stevenson-Hinde (Eds.), *Relationships within families: Mutual influences* (pp. 283–310). Oxford: Clarendon Press.

Price, J. M., & Dodge, K. A. (1989). Reactive and proactive aggression in childhood: Relations to peer status and social context dimensions. *Journal of Abnormal Child Psychology, 17*, 455–471.

Putullaz, M. (1987). Maternal behavior and children's sociometric status. *Child Development, 54*, 417–426.

Rabiner, D. L., & Coie, J. D. (1989). The effect of expectancy inductions on rejected children's acceptance by unfamiliar peers. *Developmental Psychology, 25*, 450–457.

Robins, L. N. (1986). The consequences of conduct disorder in girls. In D. Olweus, J. Block, & M. Radke-Yarrow (Eds.), *Development of antisocial and prosocial behavior: Research, theories, and issues* (pp. 385–409). New York: Academic Press.

Rys, G. S., & Bear, G. G. (1997). Relational aggression and peer rejection: Gender and developmental issues. *Merrill-Palmer Quarterly, 43*, 87–106.

Sancilio, F. M., Plumert, J. M., & Hartup, W. W. (1989). Friendship and aggressiveness as predictors of conflict outcomes in middle childhood. *Developmental Psychology, 25*, 812–819.

Selman, R. L. (1976). Social-cognitive understanding: A guide to educational and clinical practice. In T. Likona (Ed.), *Moral development and behavior: Theory, research, and social issues* (pp. 299–316). New York: Holt, Rinehart, & Winston.

Snedecor, G. W., & Cochran, W. G. (1989). *Statistical methods.* Ames: Iowa State University Press.

Sullivan, H. S. (1953). *The interpersonal theory of psychiatry.* New York: Norton.

Sutton-Smith, B., & Rosenberg, B. (1968). Sibling consensus on power tactics. *Journal of Genetic Psychology, 112*, 63–72.

Thorne, B. (1986). Girls and boys together . . . but mostly apart: Gender arrangements in elementary schools. In W. W. Hartup & Z. Rubin (Eds.), *Relationships and development* (pp. 167–184). Hillsdale NJ: Lawrence Erlbaum.

Tomada, G., & Schneider, B. H. (1997). Relational aggression, gender, and peer acceptance: Invariance across culture, stability over time, and concordance among informants. *Developmental Psychology, 33*, 601–609.

Waas, G. A. (1988). Social attributional biases of peer-rejected and aggressive children. *Child Development, 59*, 969–992.

Wasik, B. H. (1987). Sociometric measures and peer descriptors of kindergarten children: A study of reliability and validity. *Journal of Clinical Child Psychology, 16*, 218–224.

Werner, N. E., & Crick, N. R. (in press). Relational aggression and social-psychological adjustment in a college sample. *Journal of Abnormal Psychology.*

Younger, A. J., Schwartzman, A. E., & Ledingham, J. E. (1985). Age-related changes in children's perceptions of aggression and withdrawal in their peers. *Developmental Psychology, 21,* 70–75.

Younger, A. J., Schwartzman, A. E., & Ledingham, J. E. (1986). Age-related changes in children's perceptions of social deviance: Changes in behavior or perspective. *Developmental Psychology, 22,* 531–542.

Zahn-Waxler, C. (1993). Warriors and worriers: Gender and psychopathology. *Development and Psychopathology, 5,* 79–89.

Challenging Sexual Naturalism, the Shibboleth of Sex Research and Popular Sexology

Leonore Tiefer

Albert Einstein College of Medicine and New York University School of Medicine

The Problem Is Not So Obvious

One of the primary, if not *the* primary, examples of gendered areas of motivation and behavior is sexuality, right? I mean, if you stopped five people on the street and asked them in what ways are men and women most different, would you not expect at least something about sexuality to be on everyone's list?

And, both reflecting and contributing to this belief, if you walked into any bookstore in the country, you would be confronted with piles of pop-psych books like *Mars and Venus in the Bedroom*, which begins, "He wants sex. She wants romance. Sometimes it seems as if our partners are from different planets. . . . In the bedroom, it is *obvious* that men and women are different, but we may not realize *just how different* we are" (Gray, 1995, p. 1, emphasis added).

Furthermore, it is not just ordinary people and psychobabblers who make this assumption. Sex and gender differences have been a major focus in psychological research and academic sex research since their beginnings about 100 years ago. A recent book of theories about human sexuality included 15 different scholarly approaches, from anthropology to physiology to phenomenology to developmental psychology (Geer and O'Donohue, 1987). The book's introduction presents its editors' search for common ground: "There are several issues that appear with some regularity across chapters. . . . The two most obvious repeated themes are (a) the relative contribution of biological versus experiential variables, and (b) the nature and source of sex differences" (p. 17).

In the face of this unanimity, it would seem straightforward for a talk on sexuality at a symposium on gender to begin with a discussion of sex differences in sexuality on the descriptive and theoretical level. What kinds of sex differences in sexuality have been studied? What are the causes and consequences of these sex differences in sexuality? Are we from different planets, and can we get better aligned?

Now, whereas I am interested in such empirical issues, and especially in identifying sex differences in the meaning of various sexual experiences—a topic beginning to be studied by the new qualitative research methods—today a strictly empirical approach to studying sex and gender can be a red herring. The more we compare men's and women's sexual behaviors and attitudes, the more comfortable we become viewing male and female as "natural" categories and sexuality as something "real" and "natural." When all of our research takes the form of questions about how often men and women masturbate or about the attitudes men and women have toward this or that sexual behavior, we are taking our concepts of men, women, and sexuality for granted. I believe that in this way we become part of the problem rather than part of the solution, if our goal is to really understand gender and sexuality.

Because I view sexuality and gender as constructed by and in social processes, as fluid ideas that change in relationship to important social trends, I am wary of research that fails to examine the categories of gender or sexuality and just takes them for granted. How we view these categories is part of their construction in the real world. Academic opinions carry expert weight, and professionals must be as careful about how we use language as we are about how we cite facts and research findings. They are all part of how sexuality and gender come to be viewed in the world.

Why Are We So Interested in Gender and Sexuality?

When we think of our own or other people's sexuality, we are actually considering the end product of social regulation of human potentials for procreation, imagination, and pleasure. It could be called the Jell-o model of sexuality—the thing gets shaped by the contours of the container. These human potentials have been developed and customized in many different ways around the world and throughout history; there is no "natural" gender or sexuality existing outside culture. That insight is the important first step to see how amazingly diverse sexual identities, relationships, preferences, and values can be.

The next revealing step is to ask about power—in whose interests are these variations set up? Along with Gerda Lerner (1986) and many feminist scholars over several decades, I observe that a limited set of overall principles govern all the diverse social arrangements, principles that permit men to hold power in important institutions of society and restrict women's access to that power. Gender and sexuality are inevitably constructed so as to comply with these arrangements of power in society, and as each of us individually learns and participates in the social arrangements, we replicate and reproduce particular versions of gender and sexuality. We recognize, sometimes through explicit instruction but more often just through taking in the world in which we grow up, privileges for certain kinds of gendered or erotic behavior and sanctions for others. Some people's attachment and love are celebrated; others' are discouraged. Some forms of erotic activity are encouraged; others are ridiculed. Some kinds of pleasure are available for everyone; other kinds of pleasure are restricted only to specially qualified people or are forbidden entirely. These norms and guidelines are the social signs of power, and as we learn to follow the rules, we also participate in the social construction of gender and sexuality.

That is, sexuality and gender are produced in and then by each of us in compliance with particular social arrangements that derive from unequal distributions of social power. We are rarely aware of these processes because sex and gender customs are largely justified and understood through the distorting rhetoric of naturalism, which alleges that sexuality and gender are the product of "nature," some universal, biologically based, "precultural," hard-wired source of influence.

That is why I titled this chapter "Challenging Sexual Natural-ism, the Shibboleth of Sex Research and Popular Sexology." A shib-boleth is a political or religious doctrine that is so fundamental to a society that every member of the group must embrace it on pain of death. Our sexual shibboleth says that sexuality is inexorably linked to natural, precultural categories of gender and reproduction. But the rhetoric of naturalistic sex and gender, as I hope I explain, is a smokescreen perpetuated by vested interests, which distracts us from understanding how social forces and social inequalities are at the heart of our gender and sexual arrangements.

Here is a political reading of the social regulation of sexuality from 1971, which emphasizes, in the take-no-prisoners language of that time, how unequal social power is maintained through both in-ternal and external means:

> In patriarchal cultures like the one we were all brought up in, sexuality is a crucial issue. Beyond all the symbolic aspects of the sexual act . . . it assumes an overwhelming practical im-portance. . . . The only way a man can be absolutely sure that he is the one to have contributed sperm to [a particular off-spring] is to control the sexuality of the woman. . . . He may keep her separate from any other man as in a harem, he may threaten her with violence if she strays, he may devise a me-chanical method of preventing intercourse like a chastity belt, he may remove her clitoris to decrease her erotic impulses, or he may convince her that sex is the same thing as love and if she has sexual relations with anyone else, she is violating the sacred ethics of love. (Marval, 1971, quoted in Hrdy, 1997, p. 7)

This makes it sound like individual men are doing this regulating, but of course it is more complex than that. Gender itself is produced as both men and women learn to conform in body and mind to a so-ciety's expectations—expectations that result in giving to men more options, control, and pleasure, that is, more power, than the share given to women.

Gender, Sexuality, and Power

In a recent telephone survey conducted by sociologists Emily Kane and Mimi Schippers (1996), participants were asked two questions to indicate their beliefs about sexual drive: "In general who do you think tends to have a stronger sex drive: men or women?" and "Thinking of differences in men's and women's sex drives, do you think these differences are natural, or do you think our society teaches men and women to have different sex drives?" About 70% of participants viewed men's sexual drives as greater than women's, with no gender difference in the responses. However, most men viewed the difference in drive as natural, whereas women were equally split between viewing the differences in drive as natural versus social.

Next, participants were asked two questions about their beliefs about gender and power in sexuality. "Some people think that men in our society have more power than women in terms of both how and when sexual relations take place, while others think that women have more power in these matters. Which comes closer to your opinion?" Again, the follow-up question asked about causes: "Thinking of differences that exist in men's and women's power in sexual relations, do you think these differences are natural, or do you think our society gives men and women unequal power in sexual relations?" Here, women respondents were much more likely to see men's sexual power as greater than their own, whereas men felt the two sexes had equal power. Again, women far more often viewed the differences in power as social, whereas men viewed them as natural.

The meaning of the term *sexual power* seemed quite different to the men and women participants, although the researchers did not probe into this complicated subject very deeply. Men seemed to see women's sexual power in terms of how women aroused men but then might or might not be available to satisfy that arousal. Women, by contrast, seemed to see men's sexual power as freedom from the double standard and also in terms of men's use of coercion to get sex.

Why are women more likely to feel sexuality is not all that natural? One important clue comes from women's greater experience of the connection between sexuality and the overt exercise of power. In a well-publicized national survey on sexual attitudes and behaviors (Laumann, Gagnon, Michael, & Michaels, 1994), these University of Chicago researchers asked their representative sample of 18- to 59-year-olds of all economic and ethnic backgrounds whether they had ever been forced to do something sexual that they did not want to do (p. 334). While fewer than 2% of men respondents reported this experience, about 22% of women respondents reported this experience.

Another survey question inquired about the first time respondents had participated in sexual intercourse: "was it something you wanted to happen at the time, something you went along with, but did not want to happen, or something that you were forced to do against your will?" (p. 328). About 8% of men respondents said it was not something they wanted to happen, but they did it generally out of curiosity and peer pressure. However, 29% of women responded that it was not something they wanted, but they did it out of affection for the partner and, to a lesser extent, out of peer pressure or curiosity. A much larger percentage of black women, 41%, reported not wanting their first experience of intercourse to happen when it did, compared to women of other racial and ethnic groups.

I think that women's direct experience of the "continuum of sexual violence" (Kelly, 1987), ranging from various forms of sexual harassment through various forms of sexual assault, gives them greater awareness of the complicated social arrangements around sexual activity and makes them less likely to subscribe to the shibboleth of naturalness.

Learning Gender and Sexuality

Sexuality does not just develop—that is too passive a formulation. It implies a teleological view of human behavior and biology that flies in the face of the vast human diversity in sexual norms, identities, and experiences. Sexuality as scripted behavior and interior experience is *produced*, along with gender, as people develop and are socialized by life experiences with bodies, behaviors, and feelings (Gagnon & Simon, 1973).

The fundamental insight into gender, I believe, is that it is a concept requiring comparison, difference, and hierarchy (Rhode, 1990). You cannot have one gender. Male and female people are constantly produced in comparison to each other and to the standards established for maleness and femaleness. Although the focus in this symposium is on gender, it is crucial to recognize that gender never exists apart from other hierarchical ideas about difference such as race and class. As philosopher Elizabeth Spelman (1988) notes, it is a form of "white middle-class privilege [to assume] that gender identity exists in isolation from race and class identity" (p. x). Spelman points out how, through history, the concepts of "masculinity" and "femininity" are, at the same moment, both gender and race ideas. We must try to keep this in mind as we further discuss sexuality and gender.

Everything about sexuality is learned within the larger context of gender (Tiefer & Kring, 1995). So, for example, in the earliest months of life, the tactile and kinesthetic experiences of babies develop in accordance with their assigned gender, as infants labeled girls are more often caressed and patted whereas infants labeled boys are more often tickled and rough-housed (Unger & Crawford, 1992). Everyone knows you are supposed to treat boy and girl babies differently, and they do.

Education about one's own genitals begins with early emotional and kinesthetic bathing and diapering experiences and continues into verbal learning as children are instructed about their own and others' penises and vaginas. No one, by the way, seems to be told much about those wrinkled flappy parts the nonpenised children have between their legs that seem to have no name (Lerner, 1976). The sense of disempowerment and lack of ease that both men and women have about women's genitals dates from these early experiences of instructional omission and awkwardness.

Sex and gender learning goes on, as children learn about prettiness and love and touching your weewee in public and how boys and girls are different and about sex abuse and what bodies and minds can do alone and together, and what is normal, and what makes people happy, and so on. Adolescence is an especially intense peer-governed time for learning about gender role behavior, about sexual identity, about scripts for sexual conduct.

By adulthood, for many people, *sexuality has become the "mainstay" of gender identity and gender role* (Person, 1980). That is, not only have sexual behavior and experience become organized in a deeply gendered way, but one's sense of one's own and other people's gender is deeply connected to the performance and experience of sexuality. It seems very difficult to imagine one's own sexuality apart from one's gender; it seems equally difficult to just think about how we experience and observe gender without a linkage to sexuality. Sexuality is gendered, and gender is sexualized.

Gender and sexuality continue to be linked in each of us through a lifetime of learning. The specific linkages—what does it mean in terms of sexuality to be a male person or a female person— have to do with the specific cultural context in which these aspects of life are shaped into being. Class, religion, ethnic subgroup, place of birth—these provide the specifics and determine the particular gender differences.

Let me offer one illustration from my clinical practice. A couple came to me for help with a very unsatisfying sexual life. It was the first marriage for both (of four years' duration); both were in their middle 30s and lower middle class; both were healthy and employed; he was Italian-American and she was Burmese-American.[1] One might assume that their sexual values would be very different since they came from different religious and cultural backgrounds. Yet because they were a man and a woman, had become attracted to each other, and had decided to marry, they had assumed sex would just happen "naturally." However, they couldn't get turned on together and conduct a sexual encounter without tears and frustration, and they had no idea why.

After a great deal of discussion and inquiry, we realized that cultural discrepancies in kissing compounded with the consequences of pronounced gender scripting were causing their problems. The wife, being Asian, shared her region's dislike of mouth-to-mouth kissing (Tiefer, 1995). Many Asian (and African and South American) groups regard mouth-to-mouth kissing as dirty, dangerous, and disgusting, something like sticking one's tongue in another's nose and wiggling it around. The husband, by comparison, had learned the European rules wherein deep kissing is highly intimate and highly erotic, and he felt rejected and discouraged by his wife's consistently negative reactions.

Their gender socialization compounded the difficulty. The couple had both learned that men are supposed to know all about and take the lead in sex and that women are supposed to be relatively modest and unassertive. Asian women are likely to avoid taking the role of sexual initiator and to feel uncomfortable articulating their physical likes and dislikes in the bedroom (Leong, 1996). Neither member of the couple realized that sexual conduct was the result of learning social rules, and even after we all "realized" what the difficulty was, it took them a long time to overcome deeply ingrained expectations and habits and to create a mutually agreeable sexual life together. He could not suddenly stop wanting to kiss any more easily than she could suddenly start wanting to; their sexual scripts were intimately connected to feelings of bodily comfort, safety, pride, and gender desirability. It took a lot of talking and a lot of practicing for them to create a new psycho-physical script and feel spontaneous in its enactment.

Beyond Naturalistic Thinking

Now, this idea that sexuality and gender are produced by learning experiences, and that they are ultimately the product of arrangements of social power, is the social-constructionist perspective. Looking at gender and sexuality this way can be—should be—very unsettling. It makes it less satisfying to ask whether men and women differ in masturbation or romantic values because the question seems too little, too late, too superficial. The important subjects seem to be how beliefs and experiences about gender and sexuality are taught and learned: how they include messages about entitlement and opportunity; how diapering and anatomical labeling produce feelings about one's body; how wearing brassieres or teasing the wearers of brassieres produces feelings about one's own sexuality; how dealing with menstruation or showering in groups affects people; how MTV produces gender and sexuality; how immigration experiences produce and alter gender and sexuality.

Thinking about social construction also directs our attention to the question of special interests. How do pharmaceutical ads for estrogen-replacement therapies or plastic surgeon ads for liposuction and hair implants affect gender self-image or feelings of sexual desirability? How do religious messages about sexual normalcy and desirability contribute to values and feelings about sex and gender? How does the availability of safe and legal abortion or of condoms affect one's sense of sexual opportunity? How do TV talk shows or movies focusing on sensational sexual subjects influence people's sense of what others' sexual lives and gender experiences are actually like?

Studying sex differences usually means dividing the world into two categories that are assumed to be straightforward, natural, and not overlapping and then comparing them with each other. But once one adopts the constructivist view, it is hard to go back. You can tabulate differences between men and women in masturbation, but you say to yourself, I am studying the caboose and I know nothing about the train that's pulling it.

Sexuality and ReproThink

Much conventional thinking about gender and sexuality persists because we suffer from ReproThink, the exaggeration of the relevance of reproduction to human behavior. It is as if we suffered from a mass posttraumatic stress disorder, unable to get beyond that moment when most of us first learned about sex. "You are telling me that the way you make a baby is that the daddy puts the thing between his legs into the mommy's thing between her legs?" Yikes![2] We seem permanently riveted on those things between our legs.

You would think the fact that we have babies in test tubes and sheep being cloned, transgendered gay bars and sex on the phone, penile prostheses and cybersex queers would allow us to wean ourselves from thinking that the main way to understand sex is to think a lot about matters relating to reproduction. *What are we, stupid?*

Naturalization of Sex Differences in Sexuality

No, we are not stupid. Or, rather, we *are* stupid, but it is not our fault. It is not that we were "traumatized" by learning how babies get born. It is more that we have been lobotomized by centuries of stereotyped thinking embedded in religion, custom, and codes of law, making us sexually insecure and gullible consumers of naturalistic myths.

It is ironic, actually. In the words of Alfred Kinsey, the Indiana University zoologist whose sex surveys inaugurated modern sex research, though we think we are so modern, we find ourselves using "scientific classifications. . . nearly identical with theologic classifications and with moral pronouncements of the English common law of the fifteenth century" (Kinsey, Pomeroy, and Martin, 1948, p. 202).

"The interpretation of gender relations as natural facts is extraordinarily widespread," according to Australian gender sociologist Bob Connell (1987, p. 245). It is widespread and remarkably adaptable, as Carol Tavris (1992; also see the first chapter in this volume) has shown time and again. When society needs men to be sexier than women, then women's sexual passivity is natural. When society needs men and women to be equally sexy, then equal drive and same orgasm are natural. When society needs children to be sexually curious, they are—or sexually innocent—hey, that is natural, too. Or what about old people? It used to be natural to be sexually disinterested after menopause (remember dirty old men?). Now, it is natural to want sexual intimacy with one foot in the grave. And which gender is thought to be more jealous? Which has more pleasure from sex? Who is capable of multiple orgasms? Well, it changes, but it is always natural.

So, it is not that we are stupid. As Connell (1987) points out, "Naturalization, then, is not a naive mistake. . . . At a collective level it is a highly motivated ideological practice. . . . Real practices are messy and complicated, ideological representations of them squeaky-clean" (p. 246). I want to unpack some naturalistic ideological distortion in this essay, as I have tried to do for over a decade (Tiefer, 1995).

Sex in the Nebraska Symposium in the Past

Just to show I am in good company, I should mention that previous sex experts in the Nebraska Symposium on Motivation have also begged audiences and readers to get away from naturalistic ReproThink.

Forty years ago, Frank Beach (1956), my major professor at Berkeley, presented his thoughts on "Characteristics of Masculine 'Sex Drive'" to this Nebraska Symposium. He discussed the physiology, motivation, and behavioral aspects of animal mating patterns, but you might be surprised at his remarks: "Sexual *appetite* has little or no relation to biological or physiological needs. . . . sexual appetite is a product of *experience*, actual or vicarious. . . . Sexual tendencies depend for their arousal upon *external stimuli*. . . . it is unlikely that in the absence of erotic stimuli, [the male animal] exists in a constant state of undischarged sexual tensions. *This would be equally true of the human male, were it not for the potent effects of symbolic stimuli*" (pp. 4–5; emphasis added). There it is—the potent effects of symbolic stimuli. People as thinkers, symbolizers, makers of meaning, not rutting animals.

Twenty years later here in Lincoln, sex sociologists William Simon and John Gagnon underscored even more sharply that understanding sexuality was hampered by ReproThink. Gagnon (1973) emphasized that people acquire sexuality through complicated learning processes involving body and mind. However, he said, we are unaware of much of the learning and forget the rest: "In the absence of a clear-cut contact with our earlier experiences, a simple reproductive or drive-based sexual teleology is substituted for the complexity of learning situations, making adult sexual experience the outcome of biological imperatives, independent of historical and cultural contexts" (p. 56). This certainly rings true when it comes to understanding my Italian-Burmese couple's difficulties. They had completely forgotten, if indeed they had ever been aware of, how much of their sexualities were the result of complex learning experiences.

As a skeptic from New York, however, I must add that I think there is more to it than *accidental* forgetting. I think we are confused about sexuality because there are pervasive social interests at work mystifying our understanding of sexuality. Some interested constituencies, like religious leaders and lawmakers, want to control people's sexuality "for their own good." Others with economic self-interests, like magazine editors, moviemakers, or pharmaceutical company representatives, want to influence people's sexuality so as to sell their products. Doctors and therapists are somewhere in between, I guess. They definitely peddle a particular sexual ideology, which they often promote as being in the public interest, but self-interest is certainly involved as well. The point is that all these interested groups disguise their influence and encourage people to believe that the desire for sex arises spontaneously out of "natural" sexual impulses derived from evolution.

Like Gagnon, Bill Simon also complained in 1973 that "we have seen the reproductive aspect of sexual behavior as something of an organizing principle, almost as if a powerful and direct commitment to species responsibility were programmed as an attribute of all individual actors" (Simon, 1973, p. 64). In an unforgettable passage, he also argued that a focus on the symbolic aspects of sexuality would better capture the diversity of human sexual experience and motivation:

> Imagine, if you will, a panel of matched penises entering an equal number of matched or randomized vaginas: the penises all thrust the identical number of thrusts, all simultaneously achieve orgasms of equal magnitude, and all withdraw at the same time, leaving all vaginas in an equal state of indifference. What can we possibly know about the character of any of these acts? Or any of the involved actors? Let me suggest, if I may, some reasonable candidates for this panel: (a) a lower-class male, having a mild sensual experience, though glowing with the anticipation of the homosocial acknowledgement he will receive as long as the vagina did not belong to his wife; (b) an upper-middle-class male crushed by his inability to bring his partner to orgasm; (c) a male achieving unusual orgasmic heights because his partner is a prostitute or someone else of equally degraded erotic status; . . . (e) a husband fulfilling his marital obligations while dreaming dreams of muscular young truck drivers; etc. (pp. 64–65)

Simon's penis-eye-view caricatures sex research that simply counts and compares sexual acts or self-reports, but his target is more than lazy quantitative research. He is after the overall naturalistic view of sexuality as self-evident, as some universal what-you-see-is-what-you-get drama rooted in human nature. Simon's penises are connected to human beings—to thinkers, makers of meaning, symbolizers. There is nothing any more "natural" about those penises than about the mouths and lips of my Burmese-Italian couple. They have all been given erotic and gender meanings during a lifetime of connection to socially situated human beings.

The Language of "Naturalism"

I thought for years that sex was a natural act, but now I realize that I never stopped to think what exactly I meant by that, or what my evidence was. Let us consider some typical uses of naturalism language about sexuality:

> The whole of sexual experience for both the human male and female is constituted in two . . . separate systems . . . that co-exist *naturally*. (Masters & Johnson, 1970, p. 219)

> Present-day legal determinations of sexual acts which are acceptable, or "*natural*," and those which are "contrary to *nature*," are not based on data obtained from biologists, nor from *nature* herself. (Kinsey et al., 1948, p. 202)

> It is an essential part of our conceptual apparatus that the sexes are a polarity, and a dichotomy in *nature*. (Greer, 1971, p. 15)

Raymond Williams (1976), the historian of culture, identifies three important uses of the term *nature* originating in 17th-century political debates to replace a moral order based on the divine right of kings with one based on a democratic world view. He begins his discussion, by the way, by saying that *nature* is "perhaps the most complex word in the language" (p. 219).

The first use of the term *nature* means *essential quality* of something, as seen in phrases like "the nature of the Nebraska motivation conference," that is, the essential quality of the thing. Nature here is a metaphor for what is bedrock, fundamental.

The second use is nature as *inherent force* directing the world. This can be seen in the legal use of the phrase "contrary to nature." This term, still in legal use, means that some sexual act is contrary to a higher force directing the world. Nature here is a stand-in for God. Do not fool with Mother Nature. We are talking about power.

The third use is nature as *material world*, particularly as *fixed material world*. This seems to be the most common usage. When Germaine Greer (1971) says that the sexes are a dichotomy in nature, she means a dichotomy in the "real," external, world. When people say that orgasm is natural, they are saying it is not like the tango, which is clearly a human invention of a particular culture and class, not expected to be present everywhere and in all times; they are saying orgasm exists out there in the world, outside of human construction.

You can begin to see why the term *nature* carries so much weight. Its special rhetorical power seems to rely on the validity of nature *by contrast with culture*, as if anything human-made can be artificial and arbitrary, but that something prior to and outside of human culture is real and solid. The laws of nature, for example, are thought to be above politics, whereas the laws of people are nothing but politics (Schiebinger, 1986).

Sexual nature, then, sounds solid and valid, not arbitrary or the result of culture. In a world where people do not teach you or show you how to be sexual and yet they tell you that being sexual is very, very important, it is no wonder people want to believe in some bedrock sexual nature. Keep in mind, though, that it is a belief, a paradigm, if you will, that people choose to believe because it suits their purposes. And do not forget that men seem more invested in this particular view of sexuality than women.

I believe that the term *nature* is used in sex research and in ordinary conversation about sex and gender to provide legitimacy for a particular point of view. We can understand why, in the heat of argument, an ordinary person would want to attack or defend a particular sexual practice or identity as *natural*. But why have sex researchers adhered so faithfully to the rhetoric of naturalism? I believe they felt they needed to do it, or there would have been no sex research at all.

A Brief Digression into the History of Sex Research

You may not realize how difficult it has been in this country to study sexuality. We forget so fast. Historians have identified repeated waves of sexual liberalism and sexual conservatism in the United States (D'Emilio & Freedman, 1988). Each time, the focus would be different—public information about contraception, unchaperoned dating, depictions of sexuality in paintings or theater or movies, coed education, abortion, sex education, depictions of sexuality on the Internet. But regardless of the topic, the shift is always back and forth between repression and permission.

You should know the name of Anthony Comstock, a tireless, 19th-century dry-goods salesman (1844–1915) who adopted as his life's work the task of eliminating sex in print, art, or even private correspondence (Money, 1985). Backed by others with conservative agendas, Comstock achieved his major political victory in 1873, when the U.S. Congress passed, without debate, "An act for the suppression of trade in and circulation of obscene literature and articles of immoral use." This revision of the postal law forbade the mailing of obscene, lewd, or indecent writing or advertisements, which basically included everything about sexuality or contraception. It was not until 1965 that a Supreme Court decision finally outlawed laws curtailing access to birth control information and devices.

Comstock is both a symptom and a cause of "the persistence of prudery," as sexologist John Money calls it. The enormous concern that openly talking about sex is indecent has inhibited both sex research and social intercourse even to the present moment. Investigating sex continues to be enormously difficult and controversial, and there are so many areas about sex that are still taboo. Many legislators (holding the purse strings of much social science and health research) justify their moralistic disapproval by claiming that sex research can harm people by legitimizing or encouraging disapproved practices (Laumann et al., 1994, p. xxvii). The controversies about pornography and the explicit depiction of sexual and erotic images suggest that the majority of people in this country may actually believe that people need to be protected from sexual information and images (Strossen, 1995).

Some legislators argue against sex research by saying that sex is private and will be diminished by being brought into the public light. It is hard to know what that means in a society where sexuality is the main topic of magazines, movies, comedians, and dozens of television talk shows every day. Perpetuating a spurious distinction between public and private topics forces ordinary people to gain most of their information (and misinformation) about sex from unreliable sources whose motivation is to sell products rather than to educate. This is so irrational, yet such a popular view, that I can only retreat back to my metaphor of a society that has been lobotomized.

In 1922, in the middle of "Comstockery," a Committee for Research in Problems of Sex was begun with financial support from the Rockefeller Foundation (Bullough, 1985). Rockefeller continued to fund the committee until 1953, when the public controversy surrounding Alfred Kinsey's survey on the sexual practices of American women caused Rockefeller to get cold feet (Pomeroy, 1972).

During those 30 years, about 585 investigators had received research support. "One result of such funding was the establishment of a kind of dominant group in sex research. . . . [a] 'sex establishment' " (Bullough, 1985, p. 118). It is important to realize that until Kinsey began his survey of human sexual practices in the late 1940s, this "sex establishment" mostly studied biological aspects of mating behavior in nonhuman species. Human sex research was just too controversial.

Our 1956 Nebraska sex expert, Frank Beach, repeatedly received this Rockefeller money to study mating patterns and biology in rodents and dogs. Along with the other researchers, Beach endorsed a naturalized perspective on sexuality to tie human behavior, which he was not studying but which provided the justification for the work, to the study of reproductive mating behaviors in rats and hamsters and dogs, which he was studying. As Beach began his 1951 book, *Patterns of Sexual Behavior,* "Although the phrase 'sexual behavior' is part of our common vocabulary, it is likely to mean different things to different people. As used in this book, the term refers exclusively to behavior involving stimulation and excitation of the sexual organs. Since heterosexual coitus, i.e., intercourse between a male and a female, is the means whereby the species is perpetuated, copulation between the sexes is taken as the core of our book" (Ford & Beach, 1951, p. 2).

The mammalian continuity theory required by the ban on human research ensured this naturalistic attitude, but it is important to see how Beach simultaneously acknowledges the variety of sexual behavior and causes this variety to disappear through the magic of introducing ReproThink into the study of heterosexual intercourse.

In the chapter "The Nature of Coitus," Beach states, "This chapter presents factual information concerning the nature of heterosexual intercourse. We deal here with the coital act as it is performed by mature males and females in different societies and by animals of different species. Forms of copulatory behavior vary from species to species and from one human society to another. But at the same time certain basic similarities that emerge from these comparisons give an essential unity to intercourse as it is practiced in all societies and through the scale of mammals" (p. 18).

Say, what? What essential unity? We are being hoodwinked again by language. Recall Simon's identical penises and identical vaginas. Whatever essential unity exists among those penises is a very minor aspect of the situation, but the Rockefeller-funded sex researchers had to define sexuality in such a way as to justify their ability to conduct any sex research, and the public and sexologists both are still struggling with this inheritance. This is how vested interests develop at one point and then become institutionalized. Gay and lesbian studies, which have recently contributed so much to our understanding of the social construction of human sexuality, are not indebted to this tradition of funding and therefore are not beholden to the naturalistic line of thinking that it required.

Popularized Sociobiology

This detour into the history of American sex research allows us to better understand how discussions about human sexuality became inextricable from naturalism-lubricated, simplistic extrapolations from laboratory and field studies of animal behavior or physiology. This type of rhetoric continues to flow most freely in "popularized sociobiology" or "evolutionary psychology," the primary contemporary forms of naturalistic mystification about sexuality.

Sociobiology, introduced in 1975 by Edward O. Wilson, was heralded by a page one article in the *New York Times* announcing that a new scientific discipline had been established that carried the revolutionary implication that much of human behavior is biologically based and genetically influenced.

Sociobiological thinking links gender and sexual behaviors to reproductive success, that is, to anything that helps one's genes get passed on to future generations. Twenty years after Wilson's (1975) first book, this kind of thinking has become widely accepted—for example, it "explains" such observed sex differences as male promiscuity or male preference for younger partners. The trouble with these claims is either that empirical data do not support them, or as Carol Tavris points out in her introduction, that the claims are generally phrased in ways that make them unfalsifiable. If one specific illustration is proven false, the specific terms are changed without the overall theory being challenged. It is kind of a Teflon theory. Here is an example of what happened to the claims about the evolutionary basis for male promiscuity. First, the theory: "Because sperm are plentiful (the male body manufactures millions per day), whereas the egg is comparatively rare (only one is produced per month), and therefore precious, it makes evolutionary sense for the male to inseminate many females but for the female to be careful about which genes are paired with hers in the rare egg" (Oliver & Hyde, 1993, p. 30).

However, in their meta-analysis of research on sex differences and sexuality, Oliver and Hyde found only small and inconsistent differences in men's and women's actual reports of numbers of sexual partners. Moreover, the more recent studies in their sample showed the least sex differences.

Oliver and Hyde argue: "The advent of highly effective contraceptives, dating from the introduction of the birth control pill in 1960, may well have *changed the nature of reproductive strategies for females.* When sexual activity does not involve reproduction, then . . . females can have as many partners as males without squandering precious eggs." Then they point out that their kind of reasoning challenges ReproThink: "This of course *assumes a cognitive approach to decisions about sexual behavior that is missing in sociobiology*" (p. 46; emphasis added).

Here is the claim and the data on another favorite sociobiological example, according to primatologist Sarah Hrdy's (1997) recent work:

> According to nineteenth-century social Darwinists like Herbert Spencer, it was the natural function of woman to be beautiful. . . . Privately practicing what he publicly preached, Spencer rejected a liaison with [the novelist George Eliot] on the grounds that she was more intelligent than she was beautiful. . . . Like Spencer, some contemporary evolutionary psychologists [like David Buss—see Buss & Malamuth, 1996] are convinced that they have discovered a "species-typical" universal male preference, insisting that "beautiful young women are sexually attractive to men because beauty and youth are closely linked with fertility and reproductive value." (p. 2)

However, Hrdy continues, "There is not a shred of evidence for any other primate that youth or neoteny ["baby-faced" features] affect male willingness to mate. Instead, for *every* monkey or ape species on which information on male preferences is available priority is given to fully adult females who have had one or more offspring" (p. 3).

The goal of sociobiology is to explain social behavior in terms of its evolutionary basis, that is, its contributions to adaptation, reproduction, and survival. But feminists have analyzed for two decades how the scientific part of sociobiology is deeply flawed, and how, therefore, its wide reception and popularity must be explained on political and ideological grounds (Birke & Silvertown, 1984). Sociobiology serves to "explain" current patterns of social behavior with biological arguments that justify existing social inequalities. The differences in accomplishments and actions of men and women, as well as people of different regional and ethnic groups, are justified when they are based in evolutionary biology. Such a basis makes it difficult if not impossible to change these arrangements, insofar as they have presumably been built into our DNA over the course of millennia.

To the scholar not mired in ReproThink, however, biological reductionism is not scientifically persuasive. I no longer believe, for example, that sex research on small biological units is the most "basic" research and that discoveries made at the molecular level will necessarily have useful theoretical or clinical consequences at the molar level (Tiefer, 1996). Sherif (1979) argues that physiology and biochemistry (and nowadays we would add molecular biology and the various genetics sciences) are defined as basic, "not because they can necessarily tell us more about a human individual than religious history or sociology, but because physiology and biochemistry are more prestigious" (p. 100) due to the successful promotion of reductionistic ideas and the power of technical language.

Naturalistic Sexuality: Universalizing and Biologizing

There are two primary elements of the rhetoric of naturalism that make it so appealing. The first is universalization. Buss's claims about the attractiveness of youth appear so significant because when he claims these preferences are natural, he seems to be saying something that applies to each and every one of us, something "universal." Of course, a universal claim can be undermined by a single exception, which is why Hrdy's data are so effective.

Secondly, the rhetoric of naturalism implies that there is some biological cause for the behavior, since what else in human life could be universal and presocial but some kind of specieswide biology? Now, of course, *everything* human is biological in the sense that there is no behavior without a body, no personality without a brain. But it is just descriptive and fairly uninteresting to talk about the biological "basis" of some behavior if one is only talking about the nerves, muscles, and organs that operate when the behavior is exhibited. By contrast, when a "natural" behavior is discussed, and biology is involved or implied, it is usually because somehow the biology is felt to "cause" the behavior, making it somehow beyond the person's control. Perhaps the biology is thought to operate in some automatic way, as with a "drive" or "instinct." Perhaps the biology is thought to set limits on what the person can perform or experience. My impression is that the general public, pumped up by extensive publicity about sociobiology and all sorts of new "breakthroughs" in biological research, is under the impression that there are all sorts of crucial areas of behavior, chief among them sexuality, where the biological body is in fact in control. Let us take a closer look.

The Human Sexual Response Cycle

Let me offer an extended example of how the idea of a "natural" sexuality comes about. It actually takes much work and sleight of hand to perpetuate a naturalized sexuality. This example concerns what some people feel is the most natural, the most essential, the most basic element in human sexuality—the physiology of sexual response (Tiefer, 1991).

Many people know that in 1966 William Masters and Virginia Johnson published their physiological study of observations and measurements of couples and individuals engaging in masturbation and intercourse. The goal of their research was to answer the question "What physical reactions develop as the human male and female respond to effective sexual stimulation?" (Masters and Johnson, 1966, p. 4).

They described their results as the "human sexual response cycle," which they said consisted of an invariant sequence of four phases of physical changes occurring throughout the body when a person was sexually aroused: excitement, plateau, orgasm, and resolution. This sexual response cycle has become the contemporary definition of normal sexual functioning and has profoundly influenced treatment of sexual problems, sex research, terminology for sexuality, popular thinking about sexuality, and professional education about sexuality. It has contributed to maintaining coitus, the reproductive act, as the centerpiece of adult heterosexual sexual activity, and it has normalized orgasm as a major sexual goal for both men and women.

Masters and Johnson claimed that their cycle was natural and universal. At no point do they talk of *a* human sexual response cycle, but only of *the* human sexual response cycle. Yet their research cannot in fact be generalized at all, much less to the whole planet, because of four profound limits of their method.

SUBJECT SELECTION BIASES: ORGASM WITH COITAL AND MASTURBATORY EXPERIENCE

In a passage buried four pages from the end of their text, Masters and Johnson revealed that for their research they had established "a *requirement* that there be a positive history of masturbatory and coital orgasmic experience before any study subject is accepted into the program" (p. 311; emphasis added). That is, they did not set out to discover what physiological changes occurred while people were being sexual; they were interested in only those people who reported sexual activities following a certain pattern. Half the people I know would not qualify—so much for universality.

SUBJECT SELECTION BIASES: CLASS DIFFERENCES

Similarly, Masters and Johnson indicated that their "sample was weighted purposely toward higher than average intelligence levels and socioeconomic backgrounds" (p. 12). They assumed that physiology is universal and that class differences would not affect behavior. In fact, Alfred Kinsey's survey data from the 1930s and 1940s as well as the 1994 University of Chicago study show wide differences among members of different socioeconomic classes with regard to masturbation, premarital sex, petting, sex with prostitutes, positions used in intercourse, oral-genital sex, and even men's nocturnal emissions, a presumably involuntary behavior.

EXPERIMENTER BIAS IN THE SEXUALITY LABORATORY

Masters and Johnson made no secret of the fact that subjects volunteering for their research underwent a period of training, or a "controlled orientation program," as they called it (p. 22), that helped subjects "gain confidence in their ability to respond successfully while subjected to a variety of recording devices" (p. 23). Moreover, they admit being sex therapists for their subjects: "When female orgasmic or male ejaculatory failures [*sic*] develop in the laboratory, the *situation is discussed* immediately. Once the individual has been *reassured*, *suggestions* are made for improvement of future performance" (p. 314, emphasis added).

It is not any kind of research I know when a study is interrupted so the participants can be coached on how to change their behavior. In addition to overt instruction and feedback, there were probably plenty of covert cues as well. Research has shown that volunteer subjects often are more sensitive to experimenters' covert cues than are nonvolunteers (Rosenthal & Rosnow, 1969). Masters and Johnson say their volunteers were characterized by a "desire for effective sexual performance" (Masters & Johnson, 1966, p. 315), suggesting that volunteers may well have looked for signs that they were performing as expected for the white-coated researchers.

THE BIAS OF "EFFECTIVE" SEXUAL STIMULATION

Recall that Masters and Johnson set out to answer the question "What physical reactions develop as the human male and female respond to effective sexual stimulation?" (p. 4). What is this "effective" sexual stimulation? In fact, I think this is a key question in stripping the veil of naturalism from the human sexual response cycle.

"It constantly should be borne in mind," claim Masters and Johnson, "that the primary research interest has been concentrated quite literally upon what men and women do in response to effective sexual stimulation" (p. 20). The *intended* emphasis in this sentence, I believe, is on the authors communicating that their "primary" interest is not in euphemism or vague generality but in the "literal" physical reactions people experience during sexual activity. However, I think the *actual* emphasis of the sentence communicates that the authors are interested in only one type of sexual response. It is akin to researchers of vision only being interested in optic system response to blue or historians of music only studying opera.

Although the phrase "effective stimulation" appears dozens of times in the text, it is not in the glossary or the index, and no definition or description can be found. The reader must infer the meaning of the phrase from observations such as the following, taken from the section on labia minora (those flappy wrinkled parts between women's legs do have a name after all, albeit a Latin one) in the "female external genitalia" chapter: "Many women have progressed well into plateau-phase levels of sexual response, had the effective stimulative techniques withdrawn, and been unable to achieve orgasmic-phase tension release" (p. 41).

Effective stimulation turns out to be that stimulation which facilitates "progress" from one stage of the human sexual response cycle to the next, on to orgasm. That's what matters—that's what sex is. Any stimulation that results in responses other than further physiological excitation and orgasm is considered "ineffective" and is not of interest.

This seems to me to be fundamental to sexual naturalism thinking. Masters and Johnson imply that their research has tapped *directly into the natural body*, into a sexuality presumably unlearned and without culture, and certainly having nothing to do with power or patriarchal social arrangements. Yet Masters and Johnson did not "discover" the human sexual response cycle; they designed and conducted research to examine a particular orgasm-oriented sexual pattern that they already assumed was normal and universal. Their research examined the physiology of arousal and orgasm that occurs with people highly experienced in and goal-oriented toward that response with intercourse and masturbation. Great! But "natural"? I don't think so.

Gender and Masturbation

Recall that Masters and Johnson required all their subjects to be orgasmic with both intercourse and masturbation. Let us look a little further into what masturbation can tell us about gender and sexuality.

First, the apparently identical performance requirements for their male and female research subjects masks the bias of real-world gender differences in masturbatory experience. Masters and Johnson began their physiological research in 1954. In 1953, the Kinsey group had reported in their broad survey research that only "58 per cent of the females in our sample were masturbating to orgasm at some time in their lives" (Kinsey, Pomeroy, Martin, & Gebhard, 1953, p. 143), whereas 92% of men reported masturbatory experience (Kinsey, Pomeroy, & Martin, 1948, p. 339). This is a substantial difference in real-world experience, but the data are from a half-century ago.

However, in Oliver and Hyde's 1993 meta-analysis of gender differences in sexuality, which looked at 21 different sexual attitudes and behaviors in 177 different studies, the incidence of masturbation was by far the biggest sex difference in behavior—in fact, it was the only behavioral sex difference about which the authors felt confident across the studies. It appears that this difference in sexual experience of men and women is persisting.

This gender difference was further echoed in the most recent data, the 1994 University of Chicago sex survey, which is considered to be based on a representative cross-section of the American population (Laumann et al., 1994). Whereas 27% of men reported masturbating at least once per week, only 8% of women reported the same frequency. More than half the women respondents (58%) reported not masturbating at all, whereas only 38% of men reported no masturbation activity. Repeating the Kinsey findings, the Chicago group showed that this persistent difference between men and women is profoundly related to all the social variables they measured: education, religion, ethnicity, and age. Respondents with more education masturbated more. Similarly, members of the dominant cultural group masturbated more than members of minority ethnic groups.

Naturalistic sexologists had speculated that frequency of masturbation reflected a compensatory notion of inborn sexual drive—the more you have one kind of sexual outlet, the less you "need" another, but in the Chicago study masturbation was not related to presence or absence of a sexual partner or in any simple way to frequency of partnered sexual activity. If we can wrench ourselves away from naturalistic thinking, we might usefully view masturbation as telling us about how people learn in a social context what kinds of bodily pleasure are available and permissible. We might say that learning about masturbation is learning about entitlement, empowerment, and access, in the same way as is learning about vacations or other forms of privileged pleasure and recreation. Masturbation is a sexual activity about which some people are privileged to learn and to be able to practice, whereas others are discouraged from learning about or practicing this activity in any pleasure-oriented way (e.g., without guilt or shame). Masturbation can teach us a lot about how sexuality relates to social power and the processes of social construction, and therefore about what gender differences in sexuality really mean.

There is beginning to be historical work that can shed some light on the social construction of masturbation. A recent collection of essays presents masturbation as a complex cultural phenomenon that illuminates how sexual identities have been developed in history (Bennett & Rosario, 1995). For most of the 18th and 19th centuries, for example, there was a greatly feared (sometimes fatal) disease called "masturbatory insanity," which affected people known as masturbators or *onanists*. Long before society had produced category names like *homosexuals* and *heterosexuals*, the category of *onanist* set the tone for characterizing, separating, defining, and stigmatizing or privileging people by their sexual interests.

We look back on these "masturbation insanity" times with amazement at the bizarre theories and the array of painful devices to punish and prevent genital touching. The new cultural theorists argue that the panic over masturbation may have represented social fears of the imagination going wild, fears stimulated by the development of the novel and photograph, by the growth of individualism and the self. The "solitary vice," it was said, opened the Pandora's box of the imagination, but fear of the imagination was really fear about social change. In the same way, people in the 21st or 22nd century may look back on our categories of *homosexual* or *heterosexual* as merely a way to enhance waning religious-based forms of social control during rapid technological and social change.

People of the future may come to see our era's emphasis on gender differences as the last gasp of a culture wherein such differences had actually been rendered obsolete by social and scientific change but wherein institutions, families, and people themselves were slow to embrace these developments. Many groups with economic and political interests, as I have discussed, are taking advantage of the public's social conservatism. From this perspective, research on sex differences is like fiddling while Rome burns, a form of distraction and denial that allows people to maintain belief that the world as they know it is not being pulled out from under their feet. The shibboleth of naturalism meets the needs of both these special interests and the public's general social conservatism well—it is no surprise it is so hard to dislodge.

Music as the Metaphor for Sex

My mother is a professional musician, and the metaphor of music seems more useful to me in terms of understanding sexuality than the metaphor of naturalism.

Open a textbook on sexuality, and 9 times out of 10 it will begin with chapters on anatomy and physiology. This sets the stage for the assumption that "the biological bedrock," as it is often called, must be understood before we can look at anything else, such as what people experience or how they get their ideas of what sex should be about. Furthermore, the biology presented in these texts, that old ReproThink, always dwells on the anatomy and physiology of the genital organs, never the physiology of the lips. So, it is not just biology that is being portrayed as fundamental, but a certain kind of biology.

Open a textbook on music, on the other hand, and you will not find chapters on the bones and muscles of the fingers (for playing the piano) or the mouth (for playing the flute). What about the physiology of hearing or of the sense of rhythm? Why do they not start with biology in music texts? Is biology not as fundamental to music as it is to sexuality?

It is, and it isn't. It depends on what you mean by "fundamental." If you mean that music requires human physiology to produce and experience it—of course, this is largely true. But if you mean that the physiological aspect is the most human, the most complex, the most interesting, or the most important—well, few musicians would agree. By privileging biology within the discourse of sexuality, and by privileging genital physiology over any other aspect of bodily experience, writings about sexuality draw our attention on the earliest pages to the physical differences between men and women and set us up for naturalized thinking that gender *differences* will be leading elements of sexuality.

There are other consequences. Insisting that "sex is a natural act" identifies as experts those social actors who know a lot about bodily organs, rather than those who understand learning, culture, and imagination. Doctors, then, rather than psychologists or novelists, become the appointed authorities, which is a big problem.

All human actions need a body, but only part of human sexuality has to do with actions, and even that part only requires a body in the way that playing the piano does. What is done, when, where, by whom, with whom, with what, and why—-these things are the result of cultural values and individual life experience. The less we subscribe to the shibboleth of naturalism, the more clearly we will able to begin to understand these definitive variables.

NOTES

1. Burma is now known as Myanmar. It is a large Southeast Asian country located between India and China.
2. Many kids are told this in technical terms: the daddy puts his "peepee" into the mommy's "weewee."

REFERENCES

Beach, F. A. (1956). Characteristics of masculine "sex drive." *Current Theory and Research in Motivation, 4*, 1–32.

Bennett, P., & Rosario, V. A. (Eds.). (1995). *Solitary pleasures: The historical, literary, and artistic discourses of eroticism*. New York: Routledge.

Birke, L., & Silvertown, J. (1984). *More than the parts: Biology and politics*. London: Pluto Press.

Bullough, V. (1985). The Rockefellers and sex research. *Journal of Sex Research, 21*, 113–125.

Buss, D. M., & Malamuth, N. M. (1996). *Sex, power, conflict: Evolutionary and feminist perspectives*. New York: Oxford University Press.

Connell, R. W. (1987). *Gender and power: Society, the person and sexual politics*. Cambridge UK: Polity Press.

D'Emilio, J., & Freedman, E. B. (1988). *Intimate matters: A history of sexuality in America*. New York: HarperCollins.

Ford, C. S., & Beach, F. A. (1951). *Patterns of sexual behavior*. New York: Harper & Row.

Gagnon, J. H. (1973). Scripts and the coordination of sexual conduct. *Current Theory and Research in Motivation, 21,* 27–60.

Gagnon, J. H., & Simon, W. (1973). *Sexual conduct: The social sources of human sexuality.* Chicago: Aldine.

Geer, J. H., & O'Donohue, W. T. (Eds.). (1987). *Theories of human sexuality.* New York: Plenum Press.

Gray, J. (1995). *Mars and Venus in the bedroom: A guide to lasting romance and passion.* New York: HarperCollins.

Greer, G. (1971). *The female eunuch.* New York: McGraw-Hill.

Hrdy, S. B. (1997). Raising Darwin's consciousness: Female sexuality and the prehominid origins of patriarchy. *Human Nature, 8,* 149.

Kane, E., & Schippers, M. (1996). Men's and women's beliefs about gender and sexuality. *Gender and Society, 10,* 650–665.

Kelly, L. (1987). The continuum of sexual violence. In J. Hanmer & M. Maynard (Eds.), *Women, violence, and social control* (pp. 46–60). Atlantic Highlands NJ: Humanities International Press.

Kinsey, A. C., Pomeroy, W. B., & Martin, C. E. (1948). *Sexual behavior in the human male.* Philadelphia: W. B. Saunders.

Kinsey, A. C., Pomeroy, W. B., Martin, C. E., & Gebhard, P. H. (1953). *Sexual behavior in the human female.* Philadelphia: W. B. Saunders.

Laumann, E. O., Gagnon, J. H., Michael, R. T., & Michaels, S. (1994). *The social organization of sexuality: Sexual practices in the United States.* Chicago: University of Chicago Press.

Leong, R. (Ed.) (1996). *Asian American sexualities: Dimensions of the gay and lesbian experience.* New York: Routledge.

Lerner, G. (1986). *The creation of patriarchy.* Oxford: Oxford University Press.

Lerner, H. (1976). Parental mislabeling of female genitals as a determinant of penis envy and learning inhibitions in women. *Journal of the American Psychoanalytical Association, 24,* 269–283.

Masters, W. H., & Johnson, V. E. (1966). *Human sexual response.* Boston: Little, Brown.

Money, J. (1985). *Destroying angel.* Buffalo NY: Prometheus Books.

Oliver, M. B., & Hyde, J. S. (1993). Gender differences in sexuality: A meta-analysis. *Psychological Bulletin, 114,* 29–51.

Person, E. S. (1980). Sexuality as the mainstay of identity: Psychoanalytic perspectives. *Signs, 5,* 605–630.

Pomeroy, W. B. (1972). *Dr. Kinsey and the Institute for Sex Research.* New York: Harper & Row.

Rhode, D. L. (Ed.) (1990). *Theoretical perspectives on sexual difference.* New Haven CT: Yale University Press.

Rosenthal, R., & Rosnow, R. L. (1969). The volunteer subject. In R. Rosenthal & R. L. Rosnow, (Eds.), *Artifact in Behavioral Research.* New York: Academic Press.

Schiebinger, L. (1986). Skeletons in the closet: The first illustrations of the female skeleton in 18th century anatomy. *Representations, 14,* 42–82.

Sherif, C. (1979). Bias in psychology. In J. A. Sherman & E. T. Beck (Eds.), *The prism of sex: Essays in the sociology of knowledge*. Madison: University of Wisconsin Press.

Simon, W. (1973). The social, the erotic, and the sensual: The complexities of sexual scripts. *Current Theory and Research in Motivation, 21*, 61–82.

Spelman, E. V. (1988). *Inessential woman: Problems of exclusion in feminist thought*. Boston: Beacon Press.

Strossen, N. (1995). *Defending pornography: Free speech, sex, and the fight for women's rights*. New York: Scribner.

Tavris, C. (1992). *The mismeasure of woman*. New York: Simon & Schuster.

Tiefer, L. (1991). Historical, scientific, clinical and feminist criticisms of "the human response cycle" model. *Annual Review of Sex Research, 2*, 1–23.

Tiefer, L. (1995). *Sex is not a natural act and other essays*. Boulder CO: Westview.

Tiefer, L. (1996). The medicalization of sexuality: Conceptual, normative, and professional issues. *Annual Review of Sex Research, 7*, 252–282.

Tiefer, L., & Kring, B. (1995). Gender and the organization of sexual behavior. *Psychiatric Clinics of North America, 18*, 25–37.

Unger, R., & Crawford, M. (1992). *Women and gender: A feminist psychology*. New York: McGraw-Hill.

Williams, R. (1983). *Keywords: A vocabulary of culture and society* (Rev. ed.). New York: Oxford University Press.

Wilson, E. O. (1975). *Sociobiology: The new synthesis*. Cambridge: Harvard University Press.

Gender and Competitive Motivation: From the Recreation Center to the Olympic Arena

Diane L. Gill

University of North Carolina at Greensboro

Within the overall theme of this symposium, Gender and Motivation, the main contribution of this chapter is to add sport to the mix. I have considered the mix of gender, motivation, and sport in chapters in other publications (e.g., Gill, 1992a, 1995), with a focus on gender scholarship in the psychology literature, but those chapters addressed sport psychology audiences who usually know sport well, have some understanding of psychology areas that have been more prominent in sport psychology (e.g., motivation), and have almost no understanding of gender scholarship. In this chapter I shift the focus to sport and how sport mixes with gender and motivation. Most readers know motivation well and know the gender scholarship in psychology (or can refer to Carol Tavris's excellent opening chapter in this volume), but they may not know specific sport psychology work and the context of sport psychology, which is the exercise and sport context. Sport psychology is applied and thus is context dependent. Moreover, the context of sport psychology extends far beyond competitive athletics to encompass diverse participants in all forms of physical activities, in varied exercise and sport settings.

The theme of this chapter is that gender and motivation in sport are much like gender in other domains, and social context is the key.

We "do" gender in sport as we do gender in society. We may do gender in sport a bit differently than we do gender in some areas, but those differences reflect circumstances rather than biological destiny. Sport does have a unique social-historical context, and much of this chapter is devoted to exploring that context.

The Context of Gender and Sport

First, let us consider the gender and sport context today. In a recent television advertisement several young women argued that they would be better physically (e.g., less risk of cancer and heart disease), mentally (less depression), and socially (better grades, less teenage pregnancy, greater career success) "if you let me play sports." The athletic company that developed the advertisement drew upon the literature that documents these claims and supports the many benefits of sport participation for women. The business world is not particularly altruistic or liberal on gender issues but sees females as athletes and as athletic consumers. Indeed, female athletic participation has exploded in the last generation. Still, the numbers of female and male participants are not equal. More important, even if the numbers were equal, female athletes are not the same as male athletes. The main point of this chapter is that gender makes a difference, but we must look beyond numbers, biological sex, simple dichotomous sex differences, and individual differences to the powerful, gendered psychosocial context of sport to understand the female athlete.

Most prominently, sport is a physical activity. We call attention to the physical and biological. *Citius, Altius, Fortius*—the Olympic motto—translates as "swifter, higher, stronger," which clearly highlights the physical. That motto also inherently implies that sport is competitive and hierarchical (clearly, sport is not a feminist dream). Sport seems a likely place to emphasize sex differences, and in some ways, gender in sport differs from gender in other domains. However, in this chapter I take a feminist, social dynamics approach and argue that gender is different in sport not because of the physical emphasis but because the social-historical context is different. The average male may be higher, faster, and stronger than the average female, but sport does not have to be higher, faster, stronger—sport might be fun, flair, and friendship. In the constructivist style, I note my biases—I am not high, fast, or strong, and I am one of the least competitive people I know—so that readers may recognize those biases in this chapter.

Gender is part of social context and social processes in sport. Although biological sex is part of the gender mix in sport, biology does not explain the mix; all the meanings, social roles, expectations, standards of appropriate behavior, beauty, power, and status are constructed in the sport culture. We are not born to wear high heels or high-top sneakers. Gender varies with other cultural categories. For example, in the United States field hockey is almost entirely a women's sport, whereas in India field hockey is largely a men's sport, and in Australia and New Zealand both women and men play it.

Before considering the research and professional literature on gender and sport, consider how gender affects interpretations, responses, and the possible approaches to the following athletes:

A soccer player who lacks control and is prone to angry outbursts on the field explains by stating, "I really get 'up' for the game, and sometimes I just lose it."

A basketball player who plays tentatively and lacks confidence explains, "I'm just not a leader, and I can't play the way the coach wants."

The coach thinks a 16-year-old figure skater may have an eating disorder, but the skater explains, "I'm working to keep that 'line,' make it to nationals, and get endorsements."

Does gender influence your responses? Did you identify athletes as male or female? Do you think a coach, sport psychologist, trainer, or parent would behave the same with a female athlete as with a male athlete? If you try to be nonsexist, treat everyone the same, and assume that gender does not matter, you will probably have difficulty. Gender does matter, and it is not biological gender that makes the big difference. Imagine each case with a female athlete, and then go back and imagine the same scenario with a male athlete. Trying to treat everyone the same does a disservice to the athletes.

From the time we are born, our world is shaped by gender. Our parents, teachers, peers, and coaches react to us as girls or boys. Gender is such a pervasive influence in society that it is impossible to pinpoint that influence. Sport is no exception, but the sport world does have unique characteristics.

The Historical Context of Gender and Sport Psychology

To understand gender and motivation in sport, we must first understand the social and historical context. Specifically, I focus on placing women in the history of sport psychology. As Bohan (1992) notes in her history of women in psychology, the task is more correctly described as re-placing women. Women have always been present; women have been invisible, have been neglected, have faced exclusionary practices, have been misrepresented and trivialized—but women have not been absent.

Early roots of sport psychology may be found in both psychology and physical education, and both of these areas have their beginnings in the late 1800s. We can find women and gender issues in both histories, but the histories are quite different. In psychology we find women pioneers facing discriminatory practices and attitudes but persisting to make a place in the academic discipline of psychology, much as women have made a place in many scholarly fields. In physical education we find a legacy of strong women leaders who developed women's physical education as an alternative, separate from men's physical education programs. These two separate roots of women's place in sport psychology seldom crossed or interacted. Sport psychology has drawn from psychology theories and research since its emergence in the 1960s, but we have not drawn upon scholarship on the psychology of women, and the psychologists (mostly women) working on gender issues have largely ignored sport and physical activity. Women and gender issues in sport psychology today have roots in women's physical education and some parallels in psychology, but we have few direct ties and must do some searching to find those roots.

PSYCHOLOGY ROOTS

Within the last decade, women's early contributions to psychology have been rediscovered, and women's issues, such as violence toward women, have become prominent. Some scholars looked at the history of psychology and discovered early women pioneers. Denmark and Fernandez (1993) cite Mary Putnam Jacobi's (1877) book, *The Question of Rest for Women during Menstruation,* which argued against the belief that women should refrain from physical activity during menstruation, and Mary Bissell's arguments against the "fragility" of women and her advocacy of outdoor play and physical as well as intellectual development for women. These studies stand out not only as neglected psychology works but also as works that have particular relevance for sport and exercise psychology.

Several women who did research in psychology around the turn of the century are now recognized as pioneers: Mary Calkins, Christine Ladd-Franklin, Margaret Washburn, Helen Thompson Woolley, and Leta Hollingworth (Furumoto & Scarborough, 1985; Denmark & Fernandez, 1993). These women completed important work despite formidable obstacles. Both Calkins at Harvard and Ladd-Franklin at Johns Hopkins completed all Ph.D. requirements but did not receive degrees because of the prohibition against women. The others eventually obtained degrees, but only after confronting and finding ways around similar obstacles, and all met resistance in the academic and professional world. Women scholars typically found employment at women's colleges, if anywhere, and married women were barred from many institutions. For example, Calkins taught at Wellesley, Washburn at Wells and Vassar, and Ladd-Franklin never had a regular faculty position.

Still, these pioneers conducted research, published, and were active in psychology organizations. They were recognized for their contributions, and their writings foreshadow more current feminist views. Most of these women took on topics that now fall within the realm of psychology of women or gender issues, and generally their findings and interpretations rejected Social Darwinism by emphasizing sociocultural influences and refuting myths of male superiority. Thompson's (1903) studies of sex differences in mental ability stressed the similarity of the sexes and environmental influences, and Hollingworth's (1914) study on mental and motor abilities refuted myths about sex differences with logic and empirical evidence.

Psychology of women came on strong in the 1970s. Bardwick's book, *The Psychology of Women,* appeared in 1970, and Sherman's influential handbook, *On the Psychology of Women,* followed in 1971. *Sex*

Roles and *Signs* began publication in 1975, and the *Psychology of Women Quarterly* first appeared in 1976. In response to challenges posed by the independent Association for Women in Psychology, Division 35 (psychology of women) officially formed in 1973 and remains an influential part of the American Psychological Association (APA). Three Division 35 fellows have been APA presidents: Florence Denmark in 1980, Janet Spence in 1984, and Bonnie Strickland in 1987.

Although psychology of women scholars have not embraced the topics of sport or physical activity, some have made important contributions to our field. Janet Spence's work has been as influential in sport psychology as in the larger field of psychology. Her early work on anxiety is cited in our competitive anxiety literature, and her work in and measures of instrumentality-expressiveness and achievement orientation have influenced many sport psychologists. Spence has given major addresses at sport psychology conferences and has reviewed for our journals. Bonnie Strickland's influential clinical and health psychology work has not been directly adopted in sport psychology, but with increasing attention to exercise and health, we may find her woman-oriented approach relevant in sport and exercise psychology work. Also, Strickland has a physical education background and presented the first Coleman Griffith lecture at the first conference of the Association for the Advancement of Applied Sport Psychology (AAASP) in 1986.

Many sport psychologists have used the work of Spence, Denmark, and other psychology of women scholars, but Carolyn Sherif is the woman psychologist with the greatest influence. Sherif, who has constantly emphasized broader questions and sociocultural context in all her work, posed an early, persuasive feminist challenge that helped turn psychology away from the delimiting internal focus identified by Weisstein (1971) to a more social and woman-oriented perspective. Sherif's legacy is evident in psychology (e.g., Sherif, 1982), and she often contributed directly to sport psychology (e.g., Sherif, 1976). Sherif was a speaker at the 1972 research conference on women and sport organized by Dorothy Harris, and her insightful paper on females in the competition process appears in those proceedings (Sherif, 1972). Sherif also gave major addresses at sport psychology conferences, invited addresses at university sport psychology graduate programs, and reviewed for our journals. Fortunately, I heard Carolyn Sherif speak both formally and informally, and her early and persistent advocacy of social psychology, as well as women's issues, has had considerable influence on my thoughts and work, as it has on several others in our field.

PHYSICAL EDUCATION ROOTS

Just as women had a place in the formation of the psychology discipline in the late 1800s, women had a place in the early days of physical education. Indeed, women had a highly visible presence. Women's colleges, which offered academic homes to women psychologists, typically promoted physical activity as part of women's education and development. Moreover, physical education for women was considered separate from men's physical training, and women specialists in women's physical training were needed to plan and conduct such programs. Women's physical education, organized by and for women, provided a women-oriented environment that promoted women's development and achievement long before the women's movement of the 1970s began to encourage such programs.

The Boston Normal School of Gymnastics (BNSG) and its director, Amy Morris Homans, were particularly influential in developing early women leaders (Spears, 1979). Boston philanthropist Mrs. Mary Hemenway established the BNSG in 1889 and named Homans as director. The BNSG later became part of Wellesley College, which was also the academic home of psychology pioneer Mary Calkins. When the prestigious American Academy of Physical Education elected its 100th member in 1952, 9 of the 33 women in the academy were from that one program, including Homans, a charter member, and Mabel Lee. As a side note, my count of the 1993 Academy membership list reveals that 28 of the 100 currently active fellows are women, a drop in percentage, perhaps suggesting that today's women scholars have not regained the academic status of those early leaders in the first half of the 20th century. By all accounts, Homans was a strict mentor in a tightly controlled program who personally placed her students in their academic positions. Indeed, the field of women's physical education through the first half of the 20th century seems a close-knit profession with its own "politically correct" code of conduct for the women in the field.

The legacy of the early women physical educators includes some elements that seem to be models for today's sport psychologists and other elements that present some conflicts. No doubt the active, successful women leaders served as role models to encourage talented women to enter the field. The professional writings of early women leaders are prominent in the overall field and familiar to anyone who has delved into the history or philosophy of physical education. For example, Ruth Glassow's (1932) *Fundamentals of Physical Education* and Mabel Lee's (1937) *The Conduct of Physical Education*, which includes a chapter on healthy personality, were widely used texts with considerable influence on physical education practice. Anna Espenschade's research and publications (e.g., Espenschade, 1940) are classics continually cited in the motor development literature.

Early women physical educators focused more on philosophical issues and professional practice than on the science of sport and exercise. Those professional and philosophical works were highly influential in their time, and some foreshadow current debates, but the tradition of women's physical education did not encourage scientific research, and many women had difficulty maintaining a place in the field with the emergence of the subdisciplines (including sport psychology) and the research emphasis in the 1960s.

One other aspect of early women's physical education that seems at odds with today's sport psychology is the approach to competition and athletics. Both men's and women's physical education of the late 1800s started with an emphasis on physical training as part of healthy development and education. As men's programs turned more to competitive athletics, women's physical education turned in other directions. The April 1923 Conference on Athletics and Physical Recreation for Girls and Women presided over by Mrs. Herbert Hoover and attended by key physical education leaders of the day (e.g., Helen Hazelton, Mabel Lee, Frederick Rand Rogers, Blanche Trilling, Agnes Wayman, Jesse Feiring Williams) is a benchmark for this anticompetition movement. The guidelines developed by this conference included putting athletes first, preventing exploitation, downplaying competition while emphasizing enjoyment and sportsmanship, promoting activity for all rather than an elite few, and women serving as leaders for girls' and women's sports. In a clarifying statement, the Women's Division of the National Amateur Athletic Federation (1930) stated that they *did* believe in competition but disapproved of *highly intense, specialized competition*. The evil in competition was the emphasis on winning rather than participation, and that statement concluded with the classic line "A game for every girl and every girl in a game."

Some women were not listening to the experts, for women were competing in the early 1900s. Gertrude Ederle swam the English Channel in 1925, Mildred (Babe) Didrikson set three track and field records in the 1932 Olympics, communities and companies sponsored team sport programs, and women golfers and tennis players received public acclaim. When researching women's physical education history, I discovered the *Sportswoman*, a magazine that began publication in 1924 with Constance Applebee as editor and ceased (at least in our library) in 1936. The first issue noted that women's interest and participation in physical education and athletics had increased a hundredfold in the last 25 years, and the opening editorial (September 1924, p. 1) stated: "After a long and laborious struggle, mainly on the part of schools and colleges, and recently on the part of the United States Field Hockey Association, women's athletics are at last coming into their own. We feel therefore that it is a propitious moment for the SPORTSWOMAN to enter the arena, confident that a woman's magazine, published by women, devoted to all forms of sports in which women take part, linking together the interests of all players and keeping them in touch with each other's achievements, will supply a real need."

SPORT PSYCHOLOGY ROOTS

In the late 1960s a more research-oriented discipline of exercise and sport science, including such scientific specializations as exercise physiology, motor behavior, and sport psychology, emerged from the more professionally oriented physical education field. Women in physical education maintained an emphasis on professional issues and seemed more reluctant to move away from teaching and service to research. Records of early meetings, conferences, and organizations reveal that sport psychology was heavily male dominated, like other subdisciplines within exercise and sport science. A few women were active in the formation of the subdiscipline, and these early contributions should be noted.

Dorothy V. Harris was exceptional in adopting a research approach in a subdisciplinary specialty, claiming her place in the emerging sport psychology of the late 1960s and maintaining that place through the 1970s and 1980s. As Deb Feltz (1992) writes, Harris's death on 4 January 1991 brought to a close a distinguished 25-year academic career in sport psychology and women's issues in sport and physical activity. Harris started the nation's first graduate sport psychology specialization, at Pennsylvania State University, and organized the influential Research Conference on Women in Sport in 1972. Dorothy Harris published many influential research articles on a range of sport psychology topics including stress, gender roles, and imagery. Like Harris, Carole Oglesby was, and continues to be, an active gender and sport scholar. In 1978 she edited and published *Women and Sport*, probably the first book on women and sport with a clearly feminist perspective. That book included sport psychology issues in Oglesby's chapter on masculinity and femininity and Duquin's chapter on androgyny.

The formation of professional organizations marked the emergence of sport psychology in the late 1960s and early 1970s. The International Society of Sport Psychology (ISSP) meeting in Washington DC in 1968 served as a catalyst for North American sport psychologists to begin forming their own organization. The proceedings of that conference (Kenyon & Grogg, 1970) indicated that Ema Geron of Bulgaria (now of Israel) was the only woman on the ISSP Executive Council. The proceedings included a total of 101 invited addresses and reports, primarily presented by men.

The North American Society for the Psychology of Sport and Physical Activity (NASPSPA) formed in the late 1960s and held its first separate meeting at Allerton, Illinois, in 1973. No women were on the program at the first NASPSPA meetings from 1967 to 1970 (Loy, 1974), but the 1971 meeting included a panel discussion on "Women in Sport: Needed Research and Future Directions," and the proceedings (Wade & Martens, 1974) included papers by Dorothy Harris on body image, Dorothy Allen on self-concept, and Tara Scanlan on antecedents of competitiveness.

Several women (including this author) have been president of the NASPSPA, and the AAASP, which formed in 1985 with a more applied orientation than the NASPSPA, elected its first woman president in 1993–94. The ISSP has had no women as president since its founding in 1965. Division 47 (Exercise and Sport) of the APA has had 6 men presidents since its formation in 1986, with this author becoming its first woman president in 1999.

Journal editorships provide another indicator of the status of women in the field. The *Journal of Sport and Exercise Psychology* began as the *Journal of Sport Psychology* in 1979 and is the oldest sport psychology research journal. *The Sport Psychologist* began publication in 1987 with a more applied orientation, and the *Journal of Applied Sport Psychology*, published by the AAASP, started in 1989. Although all began with men editors, women have subsequently become editors. Many women have contributed to sport and exercise psychology through their research, teaching, and service roles, but as in most fields, women have not attained formal leadership positions in proportion to their numbers.

THE COMPETITIVE ATHLETICS CONTEXT

Competitive athletics today is a vastly different athletic world than we might have experienced 25, 15, or even 5 years ago. In 1967 Kathy Switzer created a stir when she defied the rules barring women and sneaked into the Boston Marathon; today, after much prodding, we have an Olympic marathon for women. I grew up as an avid backyard baseball player but was left with few options when most of my teammates moved into Little League; today two girls are the star players on my nephew's soccer team. The landmark beginning for this turnaround in women's sports was the 1972 passage of Title IX of the Educational Amendments Act.

Title IX emerged from the civil rights and women's movements, when larger discrimination issues were highlighted by actions such as those of Switzer and several other young women who tried to break into all-male athletic programs. Title IX is not an athletics regulation but a broader ban on sex discrimination in all educational programs receiving federal assistance, including educational sports programs. Most educational programs quickly moved to eliminate discrimination, but athletic programs took a defensive posture. Discrimination persists and Title IX challenges continue today, but women and girls have taken giant steps into the sport world. The number of girls in interscholastic athletics and women in intercollegiate athletic programs has increased about 6- to 10-fold from pre–Title IX days.

In the United States, the civil rights and women's movements of the 1970s helped women gain a place in sport, and women now constitute about one-third of the high school, college, and Olympic athletes in the country. However, one-third is not one-half, and in other ways women have lost ground. The world of competitive sport is hierarchical, and women are clustered at the bottom. The glass ceiling is lower and more impervious than in other domains, and women have not become coaches, administrators, sports writers, or sports medicine personnel in significant numbers. Before Title IX (1972) nearly all women's athletic teams (over 90%) were coached by women and had a woman athletic director. Today less than half of the women's teams are coached by women, and only 16% have a woman director (Carpenter & Acosta, 1993; Gill, 1992a, 1995; Nelson, 1991; Uhlir, 1987).

While women have moved into previously all-male competitive athletics, other programs with more emphasis on participation, skill development, and recreation have been lost to both men and women. Even a cursory review of sport psychology conferences, journals, and organizations reveals that males dominate sport psychology research and practice as well as competitive athletics. Safrit (1984) noted declining numbers of women in university physical education and exercise science departments, particularly in research-oriented programs, and a continuing low percentage of women as authors and editors in the professional literature. Duda (1991) specifically noted that from 1979 to 1986 most articles in the *Journal of Sport and Exercise Psychology*, our main research journal, were by male authors, on male athletes, and focused on competitive sports. During my editorial term, 1985–1990 (Gill, 1992b), most samples included both males and females, and although we had more male than female authors, proportions were closer to equal. Still, my observations of conferences, journals, and organizations suggest that males (definitely white males) dominate research and professional practice in sport psychology as well as competitive athletics. Thus, sport is male dominated with a clear hierarchical structure that is widely accepted and communicated in so many ways that we seldom notice.

Gender Scholarship in Sport Psychology

Given the social and historical context of women's sport, it is not surprising that our limited gender scholarship did not develop within sport science. Instead, gender scholarship in sport psychology largely follows gender scholarship within psychology, which has generally progressed from sex differences (males and females are opposites) to an emphasis on gender role as personality (males = females, if treated alike) to more current social psychology models that emphasize social context and processes (gender is complex; there is no easy answer).

SEX DIFFERENCES

The early sex difference work, exemplified by Maccoby and Jacklin's (1974) review, assumed dichotomous biology-based psychological differences—male and female are opposites. In practice, dichotomous sex differences typically are translated to mean that we should treat males one way and females the other way. Today, consensus holds that psychological characteristics associated with females and males are neither dichotomous nor biology based (e.g., Bem, 1993; Deaux, 1984; Eagley, 1987; Gill, 1992a, 1995; Hyde & Linn, 1986).

Ashmore (1990) summarized the meta-analyses and research on sex differences and concluded that sex differences are relatively large for certain physical abilities (i.e., throwing velocity) and body use or posturing, more modest for other abilities and social behaviors (e.g., math, aggression), and negligible for all other domains (e.g., leadership, attitudes, some physical abilities such as reaction time and balance). Even the larger sex differences are confounded with nonbiological influences. Ashmore, as well as Maccoby (1990) and Jacklin (1989), advocates abandoning sex differences approaches for more multifaceted and social approaches. Most biological factors are not dichotomously divided but are normally distributed within both females and males. For example, the average male basketball center is taller than the average female center, but the average female center is taller than most men. For social psychological characteristics such as aggressiveness or confidence, even average differences are elusive, and the evidence does not support biological, dichotomous sex-linked connections. With criticisms of the sex differences approach and its failure to shed light on gender-related behavior, psychologists turned to personality.

PERSONALITY AND GENDER ROLE ORIENTATION

Psychologists have focused on gender role orientation as the relevant personality construct—specifically, Bem's (1974, 1978) work and the Bem Sex Role Inventory (BSRI). Personality is not a function of biology. Instead, both males and females can have masculine or feminine personalities, and androgyny is best. Advocates of androgyny argue that practitioners should treat everyone the same and encourage both masculine and feminine personalities. The masculine and feminine categories and measures have been widely criticized, and even Bem (1993) has progressed to a more encompassing gender perspective, but most sport psychology gender research is based on her early work.

Helmreich and Spence (1977) sampled intercollegiate athletes using their Personality Attributes Questionnaire (PAQ) and reported that most female athletes were either androgynous or masculine in personality, in contrast to their nonathlete college female samples, who were most often classified as feminine. Several subsequent studies with female athletes yielded similar findings. Harris and Jennings (1977) surveyed female distance runners and reported that most were androgynous or masculine. Both Del Rey and Sheppard (1981) and Colker and Widom (1980) found that most intercollegiate athletes were classified as androgynous or masculine. Myers and Lips (1978) reported that most female racquetball players were androgynous, whereas most males were masculine. Many more studies have surveyed women athletes using the BSRI or PAQ, but listing more findings would not tell us much about women's sport and exercise behavior.

Overall, this research suggests that female athletes possess more masculine personality characteristics than do female nonathletes (Gill, 1992a, 1995). This is not particularly enlightening. Sport, especially competitive athletics, demands instrumental, assertive behaviors. Both the BSRI and PAQ include "competitive" as a masculine item, and the higher masculine scores of female athletes probably reflect an overlap with competitiveness. Competitive orientation can be measured directly (e.g., Gill & Deeter, 1988; Gill & Dzewaltowski, 1988), and we do not need to invoke more indirect, controversial measures that do not add any information.

More important, athlete-nonathlete status is an indirect and nonspecific measure of behavior. If instrumental and expressive personality characteristics predict instrumental and expressive behaviors, then we should examine those behaviors in sport. Even within highly competitive sports, expressive behaviors may be advantageous. Creative, expressive actions may be the key to success for a gymnast; supportive behaviors of teammates may be critical on a soccer team; and sensitivity to others may help an Olympic coach or a sport psychologist communicate with each athlete. Today, most psychologists recognize the limits of earlier sex difference and gender role approaches and look beyond the male-female and masculine-feminine dichotomies to socialization and social cognitive models for explanations.

GENDER AND SPORT ACHIEVEMENT

Most sport and exercise activities involve achievement behavior, particularly competitive achievement. In the early achievement studies (McClelland, Atkinson, Clark, & Lowell, 1953) researchers simply took male behavior as the norm until Matina Horner's (1972) doctoral work focused attention on gender. Horner's work on fear of success (FOS) was widely publicized but quickly dismissed by critics (e.g., Condry & Dyer, 1976; Tresemer, 1977). McElroy and Willis (1979), who specifically considered women's achievement conflicts in sport contexts, concluded that no evidence supports a FOS in female athletes and that achievement attitudes of female athletes are similar to those of male athletes.

We have replaced global achievement motives with multidimensional constructs and an emphasis on achievement cognitions. Spence and Helmreich (1978, 1983) developed a multidimensional measure with separate dimensions of mastery, work, and competitiveness and found that males score higher than females do on mastery and competitiveness, whereas females score higher than males do on work. Gender differences on mastery and work diminish for athletes, but males remain higher than females on competitiveness. Also, masculinity scores relate positively to all three achievement dimensions, whereas femininity scores relate slightly positively to work and negatively to competitiveness. Generally, gender influence is strongest and most consistent for competitiveness.

Research on Competitive Sport Orientation

My work (Gill, 1988, 1993) on competitive sport orientation also suggests that gender influences vary across dimensions. Several years ago, with the help of graduate students and colleagues, I developed a sport-specific, multidimensional measure of competitive orientation, the Sport Orientation Questionnaire (soq; Gill & Deeter, 1988), that assesses competitiveness (an achievement orientation to enter and strive for success in competitive sport), win orientation (a desire to win and avoid losing), and goal orientation (an emphasis on achieving personal goals). We began a line of research focusing on the relationship of competitiveness and achievement orientation to athletic participation across a wide range of samples.

Athlete Comparisons With several samples, athletes were more competitive on all soq measures, and the competitiveness score was the primary discriminator between athletes and nonathletes. We further explored the nature of competitiveness with other measures that force a choice between win and goal (outcome and performance) and found that athletes are more likely than nonathletes to endorse performance goals and less likely to emphasize winning outcomes. That particular finding, which was surprising to many, confirms current sport psychology practice, which emphasizes a mastery orientation and focus on performance goals.

Gender Comparisons Although gender was not our initial focus, we did consider gender throughout our research, and that aspect of the work is especially relevant to this symposium. From our first study, and through most of our samples, we found gender differences. Males typically score higher than females do on competitiveness

Table 1. *Sport Orientation Questionnaire Competitiveness Scores for Males and Females in University and High School Samples, by Gender*

Sample	Males M	Females M	Combined M (SD)
University	52.8	43.7	48.3 (10.9)
High School	52.2	43.8	47.8 (11.6)

and win orientation, whereas females typically score slightly higher than males do on goal orientation. Also, with our original university and high school samples, we not only used the soq but also assessed participation in competitive sport, in noncompetitive sport, and in nonsport achievement activities. Overall, males consistently scored higher than females on soq competitiveness and win orientation, and males also reported more competitive sport activity and experience. However, females were just as high as males, and sometimes higher, on soq goal orientation and general achievement. Also, females were just as likely as males to participate in noncompetitive sport and nonsport achievement activities.

Variations within Sport After developing the soq with our initial university and high school samples, we used the soq with several varied athlete samples. We often found differences among athlete groups on competitive orientations, and many were stronger than the gender differences. At the University of Iowa we sampled several highly competitive women's and men's teams and found that teams varied in competitiveness and especially in win-goal orientation. Moreover, the variation was not simply a gender difference but was related to sport demands. With a sample of international and university athletes and nonathletes from Taiwan, we found strong differences between athletes and nonathletes but minimal gender differences. With one unique sample of ultramarathoners competing in a selective event, we found low win orientations but very high goal orientations, and we did not find gender differences as with other samples.

Tables 1 and 2, which show the soq competitiveness scores from several of our samples, help put the gender "differences" of our research into perspective. Generally, in line with the overall theme of this symposium, we see that, *on average*, males are more competitive than females. However, overlap and similarity is the rule. More-

Table 2. *Sport Orientation Questionnaire Competitiveness Scores for Male and Female Athletes and Nonathletes*

Iowa								
		Athletes		Nonathletes			Combined	
		Male	Female	Male	Female		Male	Female
		59.1	57.1	49.4	43.5		54.9	49.4

Taiwan									
	International		University		Nonathletes		Combined		
	Male	Female	Male	Female	Male	Female	Male	Female	
	56.6	53.3	50.6	49.9	48.2	42.8	50.7	46.9	

Ultramarathoners		
	Male	Female
	47.5	50.3

over, gender is not the key differentiating factor; differences between athletes and nonathletes, and within athlete samples, typically are stronger than gender differences.

Table 1 shows that gender differences exist in our early university and high school samples and that gender difference was statistically significant (see Gill, 1988, for details). However, note that the difference in means is less than 1 standard deviation, suggesting considerable overlap in the range of female and male competitiveness scores. We have found standard deviations of approximately 10 for SOQ competitiveness consistently in all our samples, and this helps put differences in perspective.

Table 2 specifically depicts gender differences (or lack of differences) for athlete and nonathlete samples (see Gill, 1993, for a more detailed review of these studies). First, the overall sample of athletes and nonathletes from Iowa at the top of Table 2 did yield a gender difference similar to that of the earlier samples. However, examination of the separate athlete and nonathlete scores indicates the gender difference is not consistent. Female athletes do not differ significantly from male athletes, and, moreover, the mean for female athletes is identical to the mean for male nonathletes.

The middle section of Table 2 depicts competitiveness scores from a study (Kang, Gill, Acevedo, & Deeter, 1990) comparing international athletes, university athletes, and nonathletes in Taiwan. Overall, females were slightly (but not significantly) lower than males on competitiveness scores. Again, athlete-nonathlete differences were much stronger than gender differences, and the pattern is similar to the Iowa sample; female international athletes are more competitive than male university athletes, and female university athletes are more competitive than male nonathletes.

Finally, the bottom section of Table 2 depicts the competitiveness scores of our sample of ultramarathoners. Not only is the gender difference nonsignificant, but females were slightly higher than males. Also, note that the ultramarathoners are similar in competitiveness scores to the earlier university samples. (Note that they were much higher than other nonathlete and athlete samples on goal orientation.)

Overall, gender differences in competitiveness are limited and do not seem to reflect either general achievement orientation or interest in sport and exercise activities per se. Instead, competitiveness seems to reflect opportunity and experience in competitive sport, and gender is related to an emphasis on social comparison and winning within sport.

Other researchers report similar gender influences on reactions to competitive sport. When McNally and Orlick (1975) introduced a cooperative broomball game to children in urban Canada and in the northern territories, they found girls were more receptive to the cooperative rules than were boys. They also noted cultural differences, with northern Inuit children being more receptive than those in urban areas, but the gender influence held in both cultures. Duda (1986) similarly reported both gender and cultural influences on competitiveness with white and Navajo children in the southwestern United States. White male children were the most win oriented and placed the most emphasis on athletic ability. Weinberg and Jackson (1979) found that males were more affected by success or failure than were females, and in a related study, Weinberg and Ragan (1979) reported that males were more interested in competitive activities whereas females preferred noncompetitive activities.

Although several lines of research suggest gender influences on competitive sport achievement, the research does not point to any unique gender-related personality construct as an explanation. Instead, most investigators are turning to socialization, societal influences, and social cognitive models for explanations.

Jacquelynne Eccles's (1985, 1987; Eccles et al., 1983) expectancy-value model incorporates such sociocultural factors along with achievement cognitions. Eccles recognizes that both expectations and importance or value determine achievement choices and behaviors. Gender differences in expectations are common, and gender also influences the value of sport achievement. Eccles further notes that gender differences in expectations and value develop over time and are influenced by gender role socialization, stereotyped expectations of others, and sociocultural norms, as well as individual characteristics and experiences. Recently, Eccles and Harold (1991) summarized existing work and provided new evidence showing that her expectancy-value model holds for sport achievement, that gender influences children's sport achievement perceptions and behaviors at a very young age, and that these gender differences seem to be the product of gender role socialization.

Physical Activity and Self-Perceptions Before moving away from personality and individual differences, I want to consider the role of sport and exercise in influencing self-perceptions, particularly body image and self-esteem. Females often lack confidence in their sport and exercise capabilities. Thus, sport has a tremendous potential to enhance women's sense of competence and control. Many women who begin activity programs report such enhanced self-esteem and a sense of physical competence that often carries over into other aspects of their lives. A few studies add some support to these testimonials. Holloway, Beuter, and Duda (1988), Brown and Harrison (1986), and Trujillo (1983) all report that exercise programs, particularly weight and strength training, enhance the self-concepts of women participants.

As well as developing feelings of physical strength and confidence, sport offers the opportunity to strive for excellence, the chance to accomplish a goal through effort and training, and the psychological challenge of testing oneself in competition. Diana Nyad, the marathon swimmer, expressed these feelings about her sport: "When asked why, I say that marathon swimming is the most difficult physical, intellectual, and emotional battleground I have encountered, and each time I win, each time I reach the other shore, I feel worthy of any other challenge life has to offer" (Nyad, 1978, p. 152).

Sport psychologists should take particular note of the work on gender and body image within sport and exercise settings. (For reviews, see *The Bodywise Woman* by the Melpomene Institute, 1990; Rodin, Silberstein, and Striegel-Moore, 1985.) First, the information clearly points to a strong sociocultural influence on body image. Our images of the ideal body, and particularly the ideal female body, have changed through history and across social contexts. Certainly today's ideal is a slender, lean female body. Just as clearly, most women recognize and strive for that ideal, which is much less than ideal in terms of physical and mental health. Boys and men also have concerns about body image, but the literature indicates that girls and women are much more negative about their bodies. Moreover, the concerns are gender related. Girls are particularly concerned with physical beauty and maintaining the ideal thin shape, whereas boys are more concerned with size, strength, and power. Society shapes body image, and this societal pressure for a body image that is not particularly healthy nor attainable for many women likely has a negative influence on self-esteem and psychological well-being, as well as on physical health and well-being.

Concerns about body image affect all women, and athletes are just as susceptible as other women to the general societal pressure toward unrealistic, unhealthy thinness and eating disorders. Pressures toward thinness and, thus, unhealthy eating behaviors are of most concern in the "thin body" sports, such as gymnastics, dance, and running. Coaches in such sports should be especially sensitive to what they communicate about ideal and realistic body shapes to their athletes. For example, one athlete reported, "At age 14 my cycling coach told me I was 'fat' in front of my entire team. . . . At 5'5", 124 pounds, I was not fat, but my self-esteem was so low that I simply believed him. After all, he was the coach" (Melpomene Institute, 1990, p. 36). Pressuring an athlete, who already has tremendous societal pressure to lose weight, is not a desirable approach. Most enlightened coaches and instructors follow nutritional guidelines and emphasize healthy eating rather than weight standards.

GENDER AND SPORT: SOCIAL PERSPECTIVES

In the 1980s gender research moved away from the sex differences and personality approaches to a more social approach, emphasizing gender beliefs and stereotypes. How people think males and females differ is more important than how they actually differ. Although actual differences between females and males on such characteristics as independence or competitiveness are small and inconsistent, we maintain our stereotypes (e.g., Bem, 1985; Deaux, 1984; Deaux & Kite, 1987, 1993; Deaux & Major, 1987; Spence & Helmreich, 1978). These gender stereotypes are pervasive. We exaggerate minimal differences into larger perceived differences through social processes. These perceptions exert a strong influence that may elicit further gender differences. This cycle reflects the feminist position that gender is socially constructed.

Gender stereotypes and gender bias in evaluations certainly exist within sport. Eleanor Metheny (1965) identified gender stereotypes in her classic analysis of the social acceptability of various sports. She concluded that it is *not appropriate* for women to engage in contests in which

the resistance of the *opponent* is overcome by bodily contact,
the resistance of a *heavy object* is overcome by direct application of bodily force, or
the body is projected into or through space over long distances or for extended periods of time.

According to Metheny, acceptable sports for women (e.g., gymnastics, swimming, tennis) emphasize aesthetic qualities and often are individual activities in contrast to direct competition and team sports. Although Metheny offered her analysis over 25 years ago, our gender stereotypes have not faded away with the implementation of Title IX. Gender stereotypes persist, and they seem more persistent in sport than in other social contexts. For example, Kane and Snyder (1989) recently confirmed gender stereotyping of sports, as suggested by Metheny, and more explicitly identified physicality and the emphasis on males' physical muscularity, strength, and power as the key features.

Matteo (1986, 1988) and Csizma, Wittig, and Schurr (1988) confirmed that sports are indeed sex-typed (mostly as masculine). Matteo further reported that sex-typing influenced sport choice and that sex-typed individuals did not participate in gender-inappropriate sports.

Considerable research suggests a gender bias in the evaluation of female and male performance. Goldberg (1968) reported a bias favoring male authors when women judged articles that were equivalent except for sex of author. Subsequent studies confirmed a male bias but suggest that the bias varies with information and situational characteristics (e.g., Pheterson, Kiesler, & Goldberg, 1971; Wallston

& O'Leary, 1981). A series of studies that adopted the Goldberg approach to examine gender bias in attitudes toward hypothetical female and male coaches (Parkhouse & Williams, 1986; Weinberg, Reveles, & Jackson, 1984; Williams & Parkhouse, 1988) revealed a bias favoring male coaches. However, Williams and Parkhouse reported that female basketball players coached by a successful female did not exhibit this male bias, suggesting more complex influences on gender stereotypes and evaluations.

Gender beliefs and stereotypes are found everywhere. Socialization pressures are pervasive and strong, and they begin early. Parents, teachers, peers, and societal institutions treat girls and boys differently from birth (e.g., American Association of University Women, 1992; Geis, 1993; Sadker, Sadker, & Klein, 1991; Unger & Crawford, 1992). Overall, differential treatment is consistent with producing independence and efficacy in boys and emotional sensitivity, nurturance, and helplessness in girls.

Media One prominent source of differential treatment for sport is the media. Investigations of television, newspaper, and popular magazine coverage of female and male athletes reveal clear gender bias (e.g., Kane, 1989; Kane & Parks, 1992; Messner, Duncan, & Jensen, 1993). First, females receive little coverage (less than 10%), whether considering TV air time, newspaper space, feature articles, or photographs. Moreover, female and male athletes receive different coverage that reflects gender hierarchy. Generally, athletic ability and accomplishments are emphasized for men, but femininity and physical attractiveness are emphasized for female athletes. Kane (1989) describes one graphic example with the 1987–88 Northwest Louisiana State women's basketball media guide cover showing the team members in Playboy bunny ears and tails captioned, "These girls can Play, boy!" Gender bias in the sport media usually occurs in more subtle ways. Eitzen and Baca Zinn (1993) report that a majority of colleges had sexist nicknames or symbols (e.g., adding *-elle*, *-ette*, or *Lady*) that gender-marked the women athletes as different from and less than the men athletes.

In a study of 1989 NCAA basketball tournaments and U.S. Open tennis coverage, Messner et al. (1993) noted less stereotyping than in previous studies but still found considerable gender marking (e.g., *"women's* final four" but "final four" for men) and gendered hierarchy of naming (e.g., females referred to as "girls," "young ladies," or "young women"; men never referred to as "boys"). Gender marking may be appropriate when it's symmetrical or similar for women and men, as it was for most of the tennis coverage, but asymmetrical marking labels females as "other" than the norm for real sports. Gendered language was also apparent in comments about success/failure and strength/weakness. Comments about strength and weakness were ambivalent for women but were clearly about strength for men, and emotional reasons for failure (e.g., nerves, lack of confidence) were cited more often for women. Messner et al. noted that "dominants" in society typically are referred to by last names and subordinates by first names. They found first names used over 50% of the time to refer to females but only 10% of the time to refer to males. Also, the few male athletes referred to by first names were black male basketball players. No race differences were observed for females, and gender seemed to be the more powerful feature.

My own observations of recent Olympic and NCAA tournaments suggest improvement with less stereotyping and trivialization of female athletes, but institutional change is slow, and the sport media does not reflect current female sport participation. Overall, gendered beliefs seem alive and well in the sport world. Sport activities are gender stereotyped, and the sex-typing of sport activities seems linked with other gender beliefs (e.g., physicality). Gender beliefs influence social processes, and the research on gender bias in evaluation of coaches suggests that influence is at least as likely in sport as in other social interactions. Overt discrimination is unlikely, and participants may not recognize the influence of gendered beliefs in themselves or others. For example, many sport administrators and participants fail to recognize gender beliefs operating when athletic programs developed by and for men, stressing male-linked values and characteristics, are opened to girls and women.

The social aspect of gender is more than perceptions and stereotypes; it is the whole context. In *The Female World*, Jesse Bernard (1981) proposed that the social worlds for females and males are different, even when they appear similar. In earlier times we created actual separate sport worlds for females and males with segregated physical education and sport programs. Although we now have coed activities, the separate worlds have not disappeared. The social world differs for female and male university basketball players, for male and female joggers, and for the girl and boy in a youth soccer game.

Stereotypes are of concern because we act on them; we exaggerate minimal gender differences and restrict opportunities for both females and males. Gender beliefs keep many women out of sport, and gender beliefs restrict the behaviors of both men and women in sport. Both girls and boys can participate in youth gymnastics or baseball, and at early ages physical capabilities are similar. Yet, children see female gymnasts and male baseball players as role models, peers gravitate to sex-segregated activities, and most parents, teachers, and coaches support gender-appropriate activities of children.

Confidence To illustrate the role of social context, consider sport confidence. Considerable earlier research suggested females display lower confidence than males across varied settings. Lenney (1977) concluded that the social situation was the primary source of gender differences. Specifically, gender differences emerged with masculine tasks, in competitive settings, when clear, unambiguous feedback was missing. Several studies by Corbin and colleagues within sport psychology (e.g., Corbin, 1981; Corbin & Nix, 1979; Corbin, Stewart, & Blair, 1981; Corbin, Landers, Feltz, & Senior, 1983) confirmed Lenney's propositions. However, these studies were experimental studies with novel motor tasks rather than sport skills, conducted in controlled lab settings that purposely strip away social context. We cannot ignore social context in the real world of sport. Sport tasks are typically seen as masculine, competition is the norm, and males and females develop their confidence along with their sport skills through radically different experiences and opportunities.

Gender and Sexuality in Sport We should consider gender within the wider context of social diversity, but sport psychologists have not done that. Gender is just as prominent in youth sport, recreational settings, and exercise classes as in competitive athletics. Moreover, sport is not only male, but white, young, middle-class, heterosexual male, and gender stereotypes and beliefs affect men as well as women in sport.

As discussed by Michael Messner (1992), sport is a powerful force that socializes boys and men into a restricted masculine identity. He cites the two major forces in sport as competitive hierarchical structure with conditional self-worth that enforces the "must win" style, and homophobia. According to Messner, the extent of homophobia in sport is staggering, and homophobia leads all boys and men (gay or straight) to conform to a narrow definition of masculinity. Real men compete and above all avoid anything feminine that might lead one to be branded a sissy. One of the successful elite athletes interviewed by Messner noted that he was interested in dance as a child but instead threw himself into athletics as a football and track jock. He reflected that he probably would have been a dancer but wanted the macho image of the athlete. Messner ties this masculine identity to sport violence because using violence to achieve a goal is acceptable and encouraged within this identity. Notably, female athletes are less comfortable with aggression in sport. He further notes that homophobia in athletics is closely linked with misogyny; sport bonds men together as superior to women.

Messner's linking of homophobia and misogyny reflects Lenskyj's (1987, 1991) analysis citing compulsory heterosexuality as the root of sexist sport practices and Bem's (1993) contention that sexism, heterosexism, and homophobia are all related consequences of the same gender lenses in society. We expect to see men dominate women, and we are uncomfortable with bigger, stronger women who take active, dominant roles (just what we expect in athletes).

Homophobia in sport has been discussed most often as a problem for lesbians, with good reason. Nelson (1991), in her chapter "A Silence So Loud, It Screams," illustrates restrictions and barriers for lesbians by describing one LPGA tour player who remains closeted to protect her status with friends, family, sponsors, tour personnel, and the general public (in the pre–Muffin Spencer-Devlin days). Not surprisingly, those involved with women's athletics often go to extremes to avoid any appearance of lesbianism, like the golfer in Nelson's chapter, or deny a lesbian presence in sport. Pat Griffin, who has written and conducted workshops on homophobia in sport and physical education, describes the women's sport world as a giant closet with everyone "tip-toeing around the huge lavender elephant sleeping in the locker room" (1987, p. 3). As Griffin notes

(1987, 1992), lesbians are not the problem; homophobia is the problem. Homophobia manifests itself in women's sports as silence, denial, apology, promotion of a heterosexy image, attacks on lesbians, and preference for male coaches. We stereotypically assume that sport attracts lesbians, but of course not gay men. However, there is no inherent relationship between sexual orientation and sport (no gay gene will turn you into a softball player or figure skater). No doubt, homophobia has kept more heterosexual women than lesbians from sport participation, and homophobia restricts the behavior of all women in sport. Moreover, as the analyses of Messner (1992) and Ponger (1990) suggest, homophobia probably restricts men in sport even more than it restricts women.

So, the literature does not support dichotomous sex differences; males and females are not opposites. But women and men are not the same, and we cannot ignore gender. Gender is part of a complex, dynamic, ever-changing social network, and a particularly salient, powerful part within sport. Clearly, recognition of gender and diversity is critical to effective sport psychology practice. As I have continually tried to take a more social perspective in my own work, I have developed a stronger commitment to putting research into practice.

From Gender Scholarship to Feminist Practice in Sport Psychology

Following Kurt Lewin's lead and direction, my approach to putting scholarship into practice might be termed "practical theory"—integrating sources to find the bottom-line messages for application. Translating gender scholarship into sport and exercise practice is a challenge, but the expanding literature on feminist practice in psychology and sociocultural sport studies provides some guidance.

To translate gender scholarship into feminist practice we must first avoid sexist assumptions, standards, and practices. Then, we might follow the lead of psychologists who have moved beyond nonsexist practices to more actively feminist approaches. Feminist practice (Worell & Remer, 1992) incorporates gender scholarship, emphasizes neglected women's experiences (e.g., sexual harassment), and takes a more nonhierarchical, empowering, process-oriented approach that shifts emphasis from personal change to social change.

Sport psychology consultants and others who work with athletes might consider gender influences on interactions with athletes. For example, although we stereotype females as more talkative, research (e.g., Hall, 1987) indicates that men talk more, interrupt more, and take more space and dominant postures. If women and men have different communication styles, that suggests special concern for cross-sex interactions. Moreover, when a male sport psychology consultant is working with female athletes, we have the typical gender hierarchy of society raising further barriers. Training in communication and interpersonal skills, as well as familiarity with gender scholarship, may help. Still, the larger world is different for female and male athletes, and we can go beyond the immediate consultant-athlete setting to more social, egalitarian practice.

To take a more active feminist approach, we might consider going beyond gender awareness in our research issues, methods, and professional practice. For example, an aggressive soccer player could be male or female, but a male soccer player is more likely to grow up in a world that reinforces aggressive behavior, and a male athlete is more likely to continue to have such behaviors reinforced. The less aggressive, more tentative approach is more typical of female athletes. Even talented, competitive female athletes are socialized to keep quiet, be good, and let others take the lead. Moreover, most female athletes have a male coach, trainer, athletic director, and professors, and deal with males in most other power positions.

Overly aggressive, uncontrolled behavior is not exclusively male, nor are tentative styles exclusively female. Still, we will work more effectively if we recognize gender influences in the athlete's background and situation. Anger control or confidence building has a different context and likely requires different strategies for female and male athletes. For example, a consultant might examine the media and public relations for the women's team as well as the status of women's sports in general. How does sport fit into the player's life? How do others (coach, teammates, family, spectators, friends) react to the player? Behavior is not just within the athlete but is within a particular sport context and within a larger social context, and both the immediate situation and larger context are gender related.

A figure skater with a potential eating disorder could involve clinical psychologists as well as other professionals (e.g., physicians, nutrition specialists), but we focus on the sport psychology aspects here. Gender influences psychological disorders and diagnoses (e.g., Russo & Green, 1993; Travis, 1988). For example, women are more likely to present major depression and simple phobias, whereas men are more likely to present antisocial personality disorder or alcohol abuse. In the United States, the largest gender gap, by far, is for eating disorders. Although the overall incidence is lower than for other psychological disorders, females are nine times as likely as males to exhibit anorexia or bulimia. Moreover, the incidence is increasing, it is more prominent in adolescence and early adulthood, and participants in certain activities including dance and sport may be at higher risk. The figure skater with the potential eating disorder is much more likely to be female than male (as well as white, upper-middle class, and adolescent). But, personality and gender are not the only considerations; eating disorders are social phenomena, and body image plays a major role (e.g., Rodin et al., 1985).

Females in certain sports may have exaggerated body image concerns related to appearance and performance. Judges do look for a "line," and appearance does affect endorsements. For such cases an educational approach stressing proper nutrition, without discounting the athlete's understandable concern for body image, might be effective. Feminist practitioners might move still further to social action—educate others and try to change the system that leads athletes to pursue an unhealthy body image.

Summary

Gender makes a difference; we do gender in sport. Gender is a pervasive social force in society, and the sport world reflects society's gender hierarchy in the extreme. Gender is so ingrained in our sport structure and practice that we cannot simply treat all athletes the same. Nor can we assume that male and female athletes are dichotomous opposites, and treat all males one way and all females another way. Biology is part of the mix, but biology is not destiny. Gender is a dynamic, social influence that varies with the individual, situation, and time.

REFERENCES

American Association of University Women. (1992). *The AAUW report: How schools shortchange girls*. Executive summary. Washington DC: American Association of University Women Educational Foundation.

Ashmore, R. D. (1990). Sex, gender, and the individual. In L. A. Pervin (Ed.), *Handbook of personality theory and research* (pp. 486–526). New York: Guilford.

Bardwick, J. (1970). *The psychology of women: A study of bio-cultural conflicts*. New York: Harper & Row.

Bem, S. L. (1974). The measurement of psychological androgyny. *Journal of Consulting and Clinical Psychology, 42*, 155–162.

Bem, S. L. (1978). Beyond androgyny: Some presumptuous prescriptions for a liberated sexual identity. In J. Sherman & F. Denmark (Eds.), *Psychology of women: Future directions for research* (pp. 1–23). New York: Psychological Dimensions.

Bem, S. L. (1985). Androgyny and gender schema theory: A conceptual and empirical integration. In T. B. Sonderegger (Ed.), *Nebraska Symposium on Motivation, 1984: Psychology and gender* (pp. 179–226). Lincoln: University of Nebraska Press.

Bem, S. L. (1993). *The lenses of gender*. New Haven CT: Yale University Press.

Bernard, J. (1981). *The female world*. New York: Free Press.

Bohan, J. S. (1992). *Seldom seen, rarely heard: Women's place in psychology*. Boulder CO: Westview.

Brown, R. D., & Harrison, J. M. (1986). The effects of a strength training program on the strength and self-concept of two female age groups. *Research Quarterly for Exercise and Sport, 57*, 315–320.

Carpenter, L. J, & Acosta, R. V. (1993). Back to the future: Reform with a woman's voice. In D. S. Eitzen (Ed.), *Sport in contemporary society: An anthology* (4th ed., 388–398). New York: St. Martin's Press.

Colker, R., & Widom, C. S. (1980). Correlates of female athletic participation. *Sex Roles, 6*, 47–53.

Condry, J., & Dyer, S. (1976). Fear of success: Attribution of cause to the victim. *Journal of Social Issues, 32*, 63–83.

Corbin, C. B. (1981). Sex of subject, sex of opponent, and opponent ability as factors affecting self-confidence in a competitive situation. *Journal of Sport Psychology, 3*, 265–270.

Corbin, C. B., Landers, D. M., Feltz, D. L., & Senior, K. (1983). Sex differences in performance estimates: Female lack of confidence vs. male boastfulness. *Research Quarterly for Exercise and Sport, 54*, 407–410.

Corbin, C. B., & Nix, C. (1979). Sex-typing of physical activities and success predictions of children before and after cross-sex competition. *Journal of Sport Psychology, 1*, 43–52.

Corbin, C. B., Stewart, M. J., & Blair, W. O. (1981). Self-confidence and motor performance of preadolescent boys and girls in different feedback situations. *Journal of Sport Psychology, 3*, 30–34.

Csizma, K. A., Wittig, A. F., & Schurr, K. T. (1988). Sport stereotypes and gender. *Journal of Sport & Exercise Psychology, 10*, 62–74.

Deaux, K. (1984). From individual differences to social categories: Analysis of a decade's research on gender. *American Psychologist, 39*, 105–116.

Deaux, K., & Kite, M. E. (1987). Thinking about gender. In B. B. Hess & M. M. Ferree (Eds.), *Analyzing gender* (pp. 92–117). Beverly Hills CA: Sage.

Deaux, K. & Kite, M. E. (1993). Gender stereotypes. In F. L. Denmark & M. A. Paludi (Eds.), *Psychology of women: A handbook of issues and theories* (pp. 107–139). Westport CT: Greenwood Press.

Deaux, K., & Lewis, L. L. (1984). The structure of gender stereotypes: Interrelationships among components and gender label. *Journal of Personality and Social Psychology, 46*, 991–1004.

Deaux, K., & Major, B. (1987). Putting gender into context: An interactive model of gender-related behavior. *Psychological Review, 94*, 369–389.

Del Rey, P., & Sheppard, S. (1981). Relationship of psychological androgyny in female athletes to self-esteem. *International Journal of Sport Psychology, 12*, 165–175.

Denmark, F. L., & Fernandez, L. C. (1993). Historical development of the psychology of women. In F. L. Denmark & M. A. Paludi (Eds.), *Psychology of women: A handbook of issues and theories* (pp. 3–22). Westport CT: Greenwood Press.

Duda, J. L. (1986). A cross-cultural analysis of achievement motivation in sport and the classroom. In L. VanderVelden & J. Humphrey (Eds.), *Current selected research in the psychology and sociology of sport* (pp. 115–132). New York: AMS Press.

Duda, J. L. (1991). Editorial comment: Perspectives on gender roles in physical activity. *Journal of Applied Sport Psychology, 3*, 1–6.

Eagley, A. H. (1987). Sex differences in social behavior: A social-role interpretation. Hillsdale NJ: Erlbaum.

Eccles, J. S. (1985). Sex differences in achievement patterns. In T. Sonderegger (Ed.), *Nebraska Symposium of Motivation, 1984: Psychology and gender* (pp. 97–132). Lincoln: University of Nebraska Press.

Eccles, J. S. (1987). Gender roles and women's achievement-related decisions. *Psychology of Women Quarterly, 11*, 135–172.

Eccles, J. S., Adler, T. F., Futterman, R., Goff, S. B., Kaczala, C. M., Meece, J. L., & Midgley, C. (1983). Expectations, values and academic behaviors. In J. Spence (Ed.), *Achievement and achievement motives* (pp. 75–146). San Francisco: W. H. Freeman.

Eccles, J. S., & Harold, R. D. (1991). Gender differences in sport involvement: Applying the Eccles expectancy-value model. *Journal of Applied Sport Psychology, 3*, 7–35.

Eitzen, D. S., & Baca Zinn, M. (1993). The de-athleticization of women: The naming and gender marking of collegiate sports teams. In D. S. Eitzen (Ed.), *Sport in contemporary society: An anthology* (4th ed., pp. 396–405). New York: St. Martin's Press.

Espenschade, A. (1940). Motor performance in adolescence. *Monographs of the Society for Research in Child Development, 5*(1).

Feltz, D. L. (1992). Psychosocial perspectives on girls and women in sport and physical activity: A tribute to Dorothy V. Harris. *Quest, 44*, 135–137.

Furumoto, L., & Scarborough, E. (1985). Placing women in the history of psychology: The first women psychologists. *American Psychologist, 41*, 35–42.

Geis, F. L. (1993). Self-fulfilling prophecies: A social psychological view of gender. In A. E. Beall & R. J. Sternberg (Eds.), *The psychology of gender* (pp. 9–54). New York: Guilford.

Gill, D. L. (1988). Gender differences in competitive orientation and sport participation. *International Journal of Sport Psychology, 19*, 145–159.

Gill, D. L. (1992a). Gender and sport behavior. In T.S. Horn (Ed.), *Advances in sport psychology* (pp. 143–160). Champaign IL: Human Kinetics.

Gill, D. L. (1992b). Status of the *Journal of Sport & Exercise Psychology*, 1985–1990. *Journal of Sport & Exercise Psychology, 14*, 1–12.

Gill, D. L. (1993). Competitiveness and competitive orientation in sport. In R. N. Singer, M. Murphey, & L. K. Tennant (Eds.), *Handbook on research in sport psychology* (pp. 314–327). New York: Macmillan.

Gill, D. L. (1995). Gender issues: A social-educational perspective. In S. M. Murphy (Ed.), *Sport psychology interventions* (pp. 205–234). Champaign IL: Human Kinetics.

Gill, D. L., & Deeter, T. E. (1988). Development of the Sport Orientation Questionnaire. *Research Quarterly for Exercise and Sport, 59*, 191–202.

Gill, D. L., & Dzewaltowski, D. A. (1988). Competitive orientations among intercollegiate athletes: Is winning the only thing? *Sport Psychologist, 2*, 212–221.

Glassow, R. (1932). *Fundamentals of physical education*. Philadelphia: Lea & Febiger.

Goldberg, P. (1968). Are women prejudiced against women? *Transaction, 5*, 28–30.

Griffin, P. S. (1987, August). *Homophobia, lesbians, and women's sports: An exploratory analysis*. Paper presented at the convention of the American Psychological Association, New York.

Griffin, P. S. (1992). Changing the game: Homophobia, sexism, and lesbians in sport. *Quest, 44*, 251–265.

Hall, J. A. (1987). On explaining sex differences: The case of nonverbal communication. In P. Shaver & C. Hendrick (Eds.), *Sex and gender* (pp. 177–200). Newbury Park CA: Sage.

Harris, D. V., & Jennings, S. E. (1977). Self-perceptions of female distance runners. *Annals of the New York Academy of Sciences, 301*, 808–815.

Helmreich, R. L., & Spence, J. T. (1977). Sex roles and achievement. In R. W. Christina & D. M. Landers (Eds.), *Psychology of motor behavior and sport—1976* (Vol. 2, pp. 33–46). Champaign IL: Human Kinetics.

Hollingworth, L. S (1914). Functional periodicity: An experimental study of the mental and motor abilities of women during menstruation. *Teachers College Contributions to Education, 69*.

Holloway, J. B., Beuter, A., & Duda, J. L. (1988). Self-efficacy and training for strength in adolescent girls. *Journal of Applied Social Psychology, 18,* 699–719.

Horner, M. S. (1972). Toward an understanding of achievement-related conflicts in women. *Journal of Social Issues, 28,* 157–176.

Hyde, J. S., & Linn, M. C. (Eds.). (1986). *The psychology of gender: Advances through meta-analysis.* Baltimore: Johns Hopkins University Press.

Jacklin, C. N. (1989). Female and male: Issues of gender. *American Psychologist, 44,* 127–133.

Jacobi, M. (1877). *The question of rest for women during menstruation.* New York: G. P. Putnam & Sons.

Kane, M. J. (1989, March). The post–Title IX female athlete in the media. *Journal of Physical Education, Recreation and Dance, 60,* 58–62.

Kane, M. J., & Parks, J. B. (1992). The social construction of gender difference and hierarchy in sport journalism—Few new twists on very old themes. *Women in Sport and Physical Activity Journal, 1,* 49–83.

Kane, M. J., & Snyder, E. (1989). Sport typing: The social "containment" of women. *Arena Review, 13,* 77–96.

Kang, L., Gill, D. L., Acevedo, E. O., & Deeter, T. E. (1990). Competitive orientations among athletes and nonathletes in Taiwan. *International Journal of Sport Psychology, 21,* 146–157.

Kenyon, G. S., & Grogg, T. M. (1970). *Contemporary psychology of sport.* Chicago: Athletic Institute.

Lee, M. (1937). *The conduct of physical education.* New York: A. S. Barnes.

Lenney, E. (1977). Women's self-confidence in achievement settings. *Psychological Bulletin, 84,* 1–13.

Lenskyj, H. (1987). *Out of bounds: Women, sport and sexuality.* Toronto: Women's Press.

Lenskyj, H. (1991). Combatting homophobia in sport and physical education. *Sociology of Sport Journal, 8,* 61–69.

Loy, J. W. (1974). A brief history of the North American Society for the Psychology of Sport and Physical Activity. In M. G. Wade & R. Martens (Eds.), *Psychology of motor behavior and sport* (pp. 2–11). Champaign IL: Human Kinetics.

Maccoby, E. E. (1990). Gender and relationships. *American Psychologist, 45,* 513–520.

Maccoby, E. E., & Jacklin, C. (1974). *The psychology of sex differences.* Stanford CA: Stanford University Press.

Matteo, S. (1986). The effect of sex and gender-schematic processing on sport participation. *Sex Roles, 15,* 417–432.

Matteo, S. (1988). The effect of gender-schematic processing on decisions about sex-inappropriate sport behavior. *Sex Roles, 18,* 41–58.

McClelland, D. C., Atkinson, J. W., Clark, R. A., & Lowell, E. C. (1953). *The achievement motive.* New York: Appleton-Century-Crofts.

McElroy, M. A., & Willis, J. D. (1979). Women and the achievement conflict in sport: A preliminary study. *Journal of Sport Psychology, 1,* 241–247.

McNally, J., & Orlick, T. (1975). Cooperative sport structures: A preliminary analysis. *Movement, 7*, 267–271.

Melpomene Institute (1990). *The bodywise woman*. Champaign IL: Human Kinetics.

Messner, M. A. (1992). *Power at play: Sports and the problem of masculinity*. Boston: Beacon Press.

Messner, M. A., Duncan, M. C., & Jensen, K. (1993). Separating the men from the girls: The gendered language of televised sports. In D. S. Eitzen (Ed.), *Sport in contemporary society: An anthology* (4th ed., pp. 219–233). New York: St. Martin's Press.

Metheny, E. (1965). Symbolic forms of movement: The feminine image in sports. In E. Metheny, *Connotations of movement in sport and dance* (pp. 43–56). Dubuque IA: W. C. Brown.

Myers, A. E., & Lips, H. M. (1978). Participation in competitive amateur sports as a function of psychological androgyny. *Sex Roles, 4*, 571–578.

National Amateur Athletic Federation. Women's Division (Comp. and Ed.) (1930). *Women and athletics*. New York: A. S. Barnes.

Nelson, M. B. (1991). *Are we winning yet? How women are changing sports and sports are changing women*. New York: Random House.

Nyad, D. (1978). *Other shores*. New York: Random House.

Oglesby, C. (1978). *Women and sport: From myth to reality*. Philadelphia: Lea & Febiger.

Parkhouse, B. L., & Williams, J. M. (1986). Differential effects of sex and status on evaluation of coaching ability. *Research Quarterly for Exercise and Sport, 57*, 53–59.

Peterson, G. I., Kiesler, S. B., & Goldberg, P. A. (1971). Evaluation of the performance of women as a function of their sex, achievement, and personal history. *Journal of Personality and Social Psychology, 19*, 114–118.

Ponger, B. (1990). Gay jocks: A phenomenology of gay men in athletics. In M. A. Messner & D. F. Sabo (Eds.), *Sport, men and the gender order* (pp. 141–152). Champaign IL: Human Kinetics.

Rodin, J., Silberstein, L., & Streigel-Moore, R. (1985). Women and weight: A normative discontent. In T. B. Sonderegger (Ed.), *Nebraska Symposium on Motivation, 1984: Psychology and gender* (Vol. 32, pp. 267–307).

Russo, N. F., & Green, B. L. (1993). Women and mental health. In F. L. Denmark & M. A. Paludi (Eds.), *Psychology of women: A handbook of issues and theories* (pp. 379–436). Westport CT: Greenwood Press.

Sadker, M., Sadker, D., & Klein, S. (1991). The issue of gender in elementary and secondary education. *Review of research in education* (pp. 269–334). Washington DC: American Educational Research Association.

Safrit, M. J. (1984). Women in research in physical education: A 1984 update. *Quest, 36*, 104–114.

Sherif, C. W. (1972). Females in the competitive process. In D. V. Harris (Ed.), *Women in sport: A national research conference* (pp. 115–139). University Park: Pennsylvania State University.

Sherif, C. W. (1976). The social context of competition. In D. Landers (Ed.), *Social problems in athletics* (pp. 18–36). Champaign IL: Human Kinetics.

Sherif, C. W. (1982). Needed concepts in the study of gender identity. *Psychology of Women Quarterly, 6*, 375–398.

Sherman, J. (1971). *On the psychology of women.* Springfield IL: Charles C. Thomas.

Spears, B. (1979). Success, women, and physical education. In M. G. Scott & M. J. Hoferek (Eds.), *Women as leaders in physical education and sports* (pp. 5–19). Iowa City: University of Iowa.

Spence, J. T., & Helmreich, R. L. (1978). *Masculinity and femininity.* Austin: University of Texas Press.

Spence, J. T., & Helmreich, R. L. (1983). Achievement-related motives and behaviors. In J. T. Spence (Ed.), *Achievement and achievement motives: Psychological and sociological approaches* (pp. 7–74). San Francisco: W. H. Freeman.

Thompson, H. (1903). *The mental traits of sex.* Chicago: University of Chicago Press.

Travis, C. B. (1988). *Women and health psychology: Mental health issues.* Hillsdale NJ: Erlbaum.

Tresemer, D. W. (1977). *Fear of success.* New York: Plenum.

Trujillo, C. (1983). The effect of weight training and running exercise intervention on the self-esteem of college women. *International Journal of Sport Psychology, 14*, 162–173.

Uhlir, G. A. (1987). Athletics and the university: The post-women's era. *Academe, 73*, 25–29.

Unger, R., & Crawford, M. (1992). *Women and gender: A feminist psychology.* New York: McGraw-Hill.

Wade, M. G., & Martens, R. (1974). *Psychology of motor behavior and sport.* Champaign IL: Human Kinetics.

Wallston, B. S., & O'Leary, V. E. (1981). Sex and gender make a difference: The differential perceptions of women and men. *Review of Personality and Social Psychology, 2*, 9–41.

Weinberg, R. S., & Jackson, A. (1979). Competition and extrinsic rewards: Effect on intrinsic motivation. *Research Quarterly, 50*, 494–502.

Weinberg, R. S., & Ragan, J. (1979). Effects of competition, success/failure, and sex on intrinsic motivation. *Research Quarterly, 50*, 503–510.

Weinberg, R., Reveles, M., & Jackson, A. (1984). Attitudes of male and female athletes toward male and female coaches. *Journal of Sport Psychology, 6*, 448–453.

Weisstein, N. (1971). Psychology constructs the female, or the fantasy life of the male psychologist (with some attention to the fantasies of his friends the male biologist and the male anthropologist). *Social Education, 35*, 362–373.

Williams, J. M., & Parkhouse, B. L. (1988). Social learning theory as a foundation for examining sex bias in evaluation of coaches. *Journal of Sport and Exercise Psychology, 10*, 322–333.

Worell, J., & Remer, P. (1992). *Feminist perspectives in therapy: An empowerment model for women.* New York: John Wiley.

Subject Index

Page numbers in italics refer to figures or tables.

achievement behavior in sport, gender and, 187–188

adolescence, relational aggression in, 92–95
  gender differences, 98–101
  internalizing difficulties and, 129, 131
  social-psychological adjustment and, 128–130

adulthood, relational aggression in, 92–95
  gender differences, 98–101
  social-psychological adjustment and, 128–130

Affect Intensity Measure (AIM), 32

aggression
  childhood. *See* physical aggression; relational aggression
  forms of, 76, 77–78
  limitations of past research on, 76
  male/female overlap in, vii, 6

American Academy of Physical Education, 179

anger
  gender differences in
    expression of, 12
    at workplace, 47–48

Applebee, Constance, 181

approach-withdrawal pattern, in emotional communication, 56–57

Association for the Advancement of Applied Sport Psychology (AAASP), 178

Association for Women in Psychology, 178

attribution of essential group differences
  and influence on readers' perceptions, xix–xxi;
  research considerations for, viii–xi;
  visual/verbal representations of differences, xi–xlx.
  See also essentialist approach

Australia, childhood aggression research in, 104

Beck Depression Inventory, 10
Bem Sex Role Inventory (BSRI), 186
biology
    emotions and, 27–29
    sexual naturalism and, 162–163
    social constructionism and, 12–15
Bissell, Mary, 177
body image, sport and, 192–193, 201
The Bodywise Woman (Melpomene
    Institute), 192
borderline personality features, re-
    lational aggression and, 127,
    130, 131
Boston Normal School of Gymnas-
    tics (BNSG), 179
boys' emotions. See emotions
brain research, emotions and, 28

Calkins, Mary, 177, 179
childhood aggression. See physical
    aggression; relational aggres-
    sion
Children's Peer Relations Scale, 83
China, childhood aggression re-
    search in, 101–102
Civilization and Its Discontents
    (Freud), 5
coercion theory, childhood aggres-
    sion and
    in parent-child relationships, 111–
    112
    in sibling relationships, 114–115
Committee for Research in Prob-
    lems of Sex, 158
communication. See emotional
    communication
competition
    among girls/women, 52
    gender overlap in, vii
    sport and, 180–181, 183–185, 188–
    193
competitive individualism
    boy-boy interactions and, 50–51
    men's emotionality and, 47–50
competitive sport orientation re-
    search, 188–193
    athletic comparisons, 188

gender comparisons, 188–189,
    189, 190
physical activity and self-percep-
    tions, 192–193
social perspectives, 193–199
    gender stereotypes/beliefs,
    193–195
    media coverage, 195–197
    sport confidence, 197
variations within sport, 189–192
The Conduct of Physical Education
    (Lee), 180
confidence, sport psychology re-
    search on, 197
cross-gender relations, in relational
    aggression, 93–94
cultural stereotypes. See gender ste-
    reotypes

daily interactions, emotional dispo-
    sitions and, 35–38, 40–45
depression, relational aggression
    and, 129, 131
Didrikson, Mildred (Babe), 181

eating disorders
    relational aggression and, 127,
    130
    sport and, 200–201
Ederle, Gertrude, 181
emotional communication, gender
    differences in, 55–57
emotional cues, female sensitivity
    to, 55–56
emotional transmission
    between husband and wife, 57–
    59
    between work and home, 59–63
emotion culture, 46–47
    male and female, interaction of,
    63–64
emotions
    as biological programs, 27–29
    brain research and, 28
    daily rates
        of adolescent boys/girls, 35–38,
        36, 37, 42–45, 43, 44

in interpersonal *vs.* impersonal
contexts, 42–45
of married couples, 33–35, *34,
41*, 41–42
in public *vs.* home spheres, 41–
42
dispositions to experience, 28–29
gender-as-process perspective
for, 40
physiological findings, 39
politics of, in male-female family
interactions, 53–64
relational aggression and, 108
as sociocultural scripts, 29–31
top-down factor and, 26, 30–31,
38–40
essentialist approach, 5, 6
limitations of, 7–12, 18
false universalizations, 8–9
sex conflated with circumstances, 11–12
snapshots for blueprints, 7–8
stereotypic thinking, 9–11
reasons for popularity of, 15–18
vested interests and, 17, 146
See also social constructionist approach
evolutionary biology/psychology,
160–162
Experience Sampling Method
(ESM), 33–35
externalizing behavior, relational
aggression and, 129–130

fathers
interpretations of family role by,
53–55
The Female World (Bernard), 196
Finland, childhood aggression research in, 102–103
Friendship Qualities Questionnaire
(FQQ), 119
friendships, childhood aggression
and, 118–122
friendship quality, 120–121
friends' identity, 121–122
gender differences, 119–120

social status, 122
Fundamentals of Physical Education
(Glassow), 180

gender
learned nature of, 148–151
as performance, 6
power and, 145–148
ReproThink and, 152
social constructionist approach
to, 145–146, 151–152
See also emotions; relational aggression; sexuality; sexual naturalism; sport
gender-as-process perspective, 26,
40, 45–46
gender differences
diminishing, evidence for, 3–4
greatest periods of, 4
inherent, popularity of belief in,
2–3
reasons for, 15–18
See also specific differences
gender gap, 8
gender identity disorder, 13–14
gender research
essentialist approach, 5, 6
social constructionist critique
of, 7–12
science and politics of, 1–18
social constructionist approach,
5–7, 145–146, 151–152
See also specific research topics
gender role orientation, sport psychology and, 186–187
gender stereotypes, x–xi
cultural feminism and, 17
essentialism and, 9–11
sport and, 193–95
genes, emotion programs and, 28,
29
Geron, Ema, 182
girls' emotions. *See* emotions

Harris, Dorothy V., 178, 182
Hazelton, Helen, 180
Hemenway, Mary, 179

Homans, Amy Morris, 179
home sphere
    politics of emotion in, 53–64
    public sphere *vs.*, patterns of
        emotion in, *41*, 41–42
homophobia in sport, 198–199
homosexuality, biological research
    and, 13–14
human sexual response cycle
    in Masters and Johnson study,
        163–164
    limitations of, 164–166

Ifaluk of Micronesia, 30, 31
immediate reports of emotion, 32–
    33
    by adolescent boys/girls, 35–38,
        42–45
    by men and women, 33–35
indirect aggression, 77–78, 104
infancy
    emotional dispositions in, 39
    relational aggression in, 88–89
interparental relationships, child-
    hood aggression and, 108–113
interpersonal *vs.* impersonal con-
    texts, patterns of emotion in,
    42–45, *43*
intuition, gender differences and, 11
Italy, childhood aggression re-
    search in, 103–104

Journal of Applied Sport Psychology,
    183
*The Journal of Sport and Exercise Psy-
    chology*, 183, 184

Korean adolescents, patterns of
    emotional experience, *37*, 37–
    38
Kristol, Irving, 8

laboratory studies, limitations of,
    32
Ladd-Franklin, Christine, 177
lesbians in sport, homophobia and,
    198–199

The Longest War (Tavris & Wade), 1

male emotionality
    fathers' interpretation of family
        role, 53–55
    with friends, 50–51
    male emotion culture and, 51–53
    male-male interactions and
        with friends, 50–51
        at work, 46–50
    stonewalling and, 56
    See also emotions; gender differ-
        ences
marital conflict, childhood aggres-
    sion and, 110–111
Mars and Venus in the Bedroom
    (Gray), 2, 143
masturbation
    gender difference in incidence of,
        167
    Masters and Johnson study of,
        166–167
    social construction of, 168–169
"masturbatory insanity," 168
media, gender bias in sport cover-
    age by, 195–197
*Men Are from Mars, Women Are from
    Venus* (Gray), 2
middle childhood, relational ag-
    gression in, 87, 90–92
    cross-cultural studies, 101–105
    gender differences, 96–98
    internalizing problems, 126
    social-psychological adjustment,
        125–128
moral decisions, male-female differ-
    ences and, 11–12
motivation, sport and, 173–174
music, as metaphor for sexuality,
    169–170

naturalism. *See* sexual naturalism
nature, rhetorical power of, 156–157
Nebraska Symposium on Motiva-
    tion,
    naturalistic ReproThink and,
        153–155

onanists, 168
On the Psychology of Women (Sherman), 177

parent-child relationships, childhood aggression and, 108–113
Patterns of Sexual Behavior (Beach), 159
Peabody Picture Vocabulary Test—Revised, 90
peer reports, relational aggression and, 81–82
peer status, 130
   adolescence, 128
   middle childhood, 126
   preschool years, 124
Personality Attributes Questionnaire (PAQ), 186
physical aggression
   defined, 77
   gender differences, *99*, 99–101, *100*
   relational aggression and. *See* relational aggression
   subtypes of, 78–79
physical education, women/gender issues in, 176, 179–181
power. *See* sexual power
preschool years, relational aggression in, 89–90
   cross-cultural studies, 101–105
   gender differences, 95–96
   peer status and, 124
   social-psychological adjustment and, 122–131
proactive relational aggression, 79
psychology
   sport and, women's contribution to, 178–179
   of women, 177–178
   women's early contributions to, 176–177
The Psychology of Women (Bardwick), 177
Psychology of Women Quarterly (journal), 178

public *vs.* home spheres, patterns of emotion in, *41*, 41–42

The Question of Rest for Women during Menstruation (Jacobi), 177

reactive relational aggression, 79
relational aggression, 76, 77–78
   assessment of, 81–84
      naturalistic observation, 83–84
      peer reports, 81–82
      self-reports, 83
      teacher/parent reports, 82–83
   cross-cultural studies, 101–105
      future work in, 104
      middle childhood, 102–104
      preschool years, 101–102
   cross-gender relations in, 93–94
   defined, 77
   developmental manifestations of, 88–95
      adolescence/adulthood, 92–95
      infancy/toddlerhood/preschool years, 88–90
      middle childhood, 90–92
   externalizing behavior and, 129–130
   factors contributing to, 105–122
      emotion, 108
      friendships, 117–122
      parent-child/interparental relationships, 108–113
      sibling relationships, 113–117
      social information processing (SIP), 105–108
   gender differences, 107, 116, 119, 120, 131–132
      adolescence/adulthood, 98–99, 129–130
      borderline personality features, 131
      middle childhood, 96–98, 125–126
      preschool years, 95–96
      social-psychological adjustment, 122–123
   harmful nature of, 79–81

persistence of, 128
physical aggression and, 84–88,
100
social-psychological adjustment
and, 122–131
subtypes of, 78–79
ReproThink
defined, 152
heterosexual intercourse and, 159
as organizing principle, 154–155
Rogers, Frederick Rand, 180
The Rules (Fein & Schneider), 15
Russia, childhood aggression research in, 101–102

self-reports
limitations of, 32, 38
relational aggression and, 83
sex differences, sport psychology
research on, 185–186
sex research in U.S., history of,
157–160
Sex Roles (journal), 177–178
sexuality
gender and, in sport, 197–199
learned nature of, 148–151
male-female overlap in, vii
music as metaphor for, 169–170
ReproThink and, 152, 154, 159
sex differences in, 144
social constructionist approach
to, 145–146, 151–152
sexual naturalism, 145
gender differences regarding,
146–148
history of sex research and, 157–
160
human sexual response cycle
and, 163–166
language of, 155–157
masturbation and, 166–169
Nebraska Symposium and, 153–
155
sex differences in sexuality and,
152–155
sociobiology and, 160–162
universalizing aspect of, 162–163

vested interests and, 17, 146, 154
sexual power, 145–148
beliefs about, gender differences
in, 147–148
sibling relationships, childhood aggression and, 113–117
coercion theory, 114–115
relational aggression, 115
social learning theory, 114–115
unique features of sibling relationships, 115–117
Signs (journal), 178
social aggression, defined, 77, 78
social constructionist approach, 18
biology and, 12–15
body image and, 192–193
emotions and, 29–31
gender research and, 5–7
human sexual response cycle
and, 163–166
masturbation and, 168–169
questions asked by, 6–7, 14
sexuality/gender and, 151–152
social information processing (SIP),
childhood aggression and,
105–108
social learning theory, childhood
aggression and
interparental relationships, 109–
110
parent-child relationships, 110
sibling relationships, 114–115
social-psychological adjustment,
relational aggression and, 122–
131
in adolescence, 128–130
in adulthood, 128–130
in middle childhood, 125–128
preschool years, 123–125
social roles, 35
social status, relational aggression
and, 122
sociobiology, 160–162
sociocultural scripts, emotions as,
29–31
speech, male-female differences in,
11

sport
   competitive athletics context,
      183–184
   gender in, 174–176
      historical context, 176–183
   homophobia in, 198–199
   male domination in, 184
   social constructionist approach
      to, 174–176
Sport Orientation Questionnaire, 188
The Sport Psychologist (journal), 183
sport psychology, 173
   competitive athletics context for,
      183–184
   gender scholarship in
      applied, 185–188, 199–201
         achievement behavior, 187–
            188
         personality/gender role ori-
            entation, 186–187
         sex differences, 185–186
      historical context for, 176–184
         physical education roots, 179–
            181
         psychology roots, 176–179
         sport psychology roots, 181–183
      research/practice, male domina-
         tion of, 184

women's contribution to, 178–179
   See also competitive sport orienta-
      tion research
Sportswoman (magazine), 181
standing patterns
   of behavior, 46
   of emotion, 46
stonewalling, by men, 56
Strickland, Bonnie, 178
Switzer, Kathy, 183

Taylor, Frederick, 48
temperament, emotional dispositions and, 28–29
Title IX, Educational Amendments
   Act, 183–184
toddlerhood, relational aggression
   in, 88–89
top-down factor for emotional dispositions, 26, 30–31, 38–40
Trilling, Blanche, 180

verbal aggression, defined, 77

Washburn, Margaret, 177
Wayman, Agnes, 180
Williams, Jesse Feiring, 180

Author Index

Abramovitch, R., 114, 132
Abu-Lughod, L., 30, 40, 67
Acevedo, E. O., 190, 205
Achenbach, T. M., 87, 132
Acosta, R. V., 184, 202
Adler, T. F., 203
Allison, D. B., 14, 19
American Association of University Women, 195, 202
American Psychiatric Association, 19
Andrews, D. W., 118, 135
Archer, J., 40, 67
Aronson, E., 80, 132
Asher, S. R., 117, 118, 119, 124, 130, 132, 139
Ashmore, R. D., 185, 202
Asmussen, L., 44, 70
Atkinson, J. W., 187, 205
Averill, J. R., 30, 67

Baca Zinn, M., 195, 203
Bailey, J. M., 13, 19
Balswick, J., 26, 56, 67
Banaji, M., 26, 32, 38, 39, 45, 56, 70

Bandura, A., 75, 79, 105, 109, 114, 132
Bardwick, J., 177, 202
Barker, R. G., 46, 67
Barnett, R. C., 3–4, 19
Bates, J. E., 105, 135
Baumeister, R. F., 10, 19
Bazarskaya, N., 109, 137
Beach, F. A., 153–154, 159, 170
Bear, G. G., 82, 84, 97, 125, 140
Beardsall, L., 114, 132
Beaton, A. M., 3, 23
Beitel, A., 114, 139
Belenky, M. F., 3, 19
Bem, S. L., 185, 186, 194, 198, 202
Bennett, M. E., 52, 72
Bennett, P., 168, 170
Berkowitz, L., 79, 80, 105, 108, 132
Bernard, J., 196, 202
Berndt, T. J., 116, 132
Berscheid, E., 26, 39, 67
Bettencourt, B. A., 6, 19
Beuter, A., 192, 205
Bhavnagri, N., 114, 139
Bierman, K. L., 105, 132

Bigbee, M. A., 77, 81, 91, 97, 106, 108, 115, 134
Birke, L., 162, 170
Bjorkqvist, K., 76, 90, 92, 94, 98, 100, 102, 103, 104, 133, 138
Blair, W. O., 197, 202
Block, J. H., 107, 133
Blood, R. O., 56, 67
Bohan, J. S., 3–4, 5, 20, 176, 202
Bolger, N., 58, 60, 61, 67, 73
Bond, M. H., xx, xxiii
Bouchard, C., 14, 20
Brannon, R., 25, 68
Brehm, S. S., 77, 133
Brewer, M., 19, 20
Brickman, P., 28, 68
Brody, G., 114, 133
Brody, L. R., 31, 38, 39, 68
Brodzinsky, D. M., 77, 136
Bronfenbrenner, U., 101, 133
Brown, B. B., 52, 68, 121, 133
Brown, R., 3, 23
Brown, R. D., 192, 202
Buhman, D. C., xxi, xxiii
Buhrmester, D., 94, 116, 119, 133
Bukowski, W. M., 91, 133
Bulleit, T. N., 116, 132
Bullough, V., 158, 159, 170
Burke, M., 114, 133
Burke, P., 13, 20
Buss, A. H., 39, 68, 77, 78, 133, 134, 161
Buss, D. M., 170
Butler, J. P., 40, 68
Byne, W., 9, 20

Cacioppo, J. T., 59, 69
Cairns, B. D., 76, 121, 134
Cairns, R. B., 76, 78, 118, 121, 128, 134
Campbell, A., 9, 20
Cancian, F. M., 10, 20
Canetto, S. S., 10, 20
Carli, L. L., 11, 20
Carpenter, L. J., 184, 202
Casas, J. F., 81, 82, 89, 95, 102, 124, 125, 127, 131, 134
Catalano, R., 55, 59, 72

Celentano, E., 71
Chipuer, H., 28, 72
Chodorow, N., 3, 5, 20
Christensen, A., 56, 68
Church, R. B., 35, 71
Clark, R. A., 187, 205
Clasen, D. R., 121, 133
Clinchy, B. M., 3, 19
Clopton, N. A., 1220
Coates, D., 28, 68
Cochran, W. G., 84, 140
Cohn, L. D., 4, 11, 20
Coie, J. D., 78–79, 80, 105, 124, 126, 132, 134, 135, 140
Colker, R., 186, 202
Collins, W. A., 54, 68
Condry, J., 187, 202
Connell, R. W., 153, 170
Constantian, C. A., 35, 71
Coontz, S., 3, 20
Corbin, C. B., 197, 202
Corter, C., 114, 132
Cozza, T. M., 71
Crane, R. S., 35, 73
Crawford, D. W., 60, 68
Crawford, M., 5, 17, 20, 149, 172, 195, 207
Crick, N. R., xx, xxi, 9, 14–15, 20, 50, 76, 77, 79–80, 81, 82, 83, 84, 87, 89, 91, 92, 93, 94, 95, 97, 98, 102, 103, 105, 106, 107, 108, 109, 110, 111, 112, 113, 115, 117, 118, 119, 120, 122, 124–125, 126, 127, 128, 129, 130, 131, 134, 135, 136, 139, 140
Crosby, L., 118, 135
Crouter, A. C., 53, 60, 68, 72, 114, 135
Csikszentmihalyi, M., 33, 68, 70
Csizma, K. A., 194, 203
Cummings, E. M., 109, 110, 135
Cummings, J. L., 109, 110, 135

Davidson, R. J., 28, 68
Davies, P. T., 109, 135
Deaux, K., 6, 7, 20, 185, 194, 203
DeBaryshe, B. D., 112, 139
Deeter, T. E., 187, 188, 190, 204, 205
DeFries, J. C., 13, 22

de Lacoste-Utamsing, C., 9, 20
DeLawyer, D. D., 80, 136
DeLongis, A., 58, 67
Del Ray, P., 186, 203
D'Emilio, J., 157, 170
Denmark, F. L., 177, 203
Despres, J. P., 14, 20
DeVault, M. L., 59, 68
de Vries, B., 12, 23
Diamond, M. C., 8, 20
Diener, C., 29, 68
Diener, E., 29, 32, 68, 69, 73
Dishion, T. J., 109, 111, 118, 121, 135, 138, 140
Dodge, K. A., 76, 78–79, 90, 105, 106, 107, 126, 134, 135, 140
Doherty, R. W., 58, 69
Dollard, J., 79, 108, 135
Doob, C. W., 79, 135
Dooley, D., 55, 59, 72
Duda, J. L., 184, 192, 203, 205
Duncan, M. C., 195, 206
Dunn, J., 90, 113, 114, 135, 136
Dunn, L. M., 90, 136
Dyer, S., 187, 202
Dzewaltowski, D. A., 187, 204

Eagley, A. H., 185, 203
Easterbrooks, M. A., 109, 136
Eccles, J. S., 191–192, 203
Eicher, S. A., 121, 133
Eisenberg, N., 55, 69
Eitzen, D. S., 195, 203
Elshtain, J. B., 9, 20
Emde, R. N., 109, 136
Emery, R. E., 110, 136
Espenschade, A., 180, 203

Fausto-Sterling, A., 8, 17, 20
Fein, E., 15, 20
Feingold, A., 4, 21
Felson, R. B., 117, 136
Feltz, D. L., 182, 197, 202, 204
Ferguson, L. L., 76, 134
Fernandez, L. C., 177, 203
Ferree, M., 40, 69
Feshbach, N. D., 76, 77, 136

Fincham, F. D., 105, 109, 110, 111, 136, 137
Fischer, A. H., 10, 21
Fiske, S. T., 11, 21
Flowers, J., xxi, xxiii
Ford, C. S., 159, 170
Ford, M. E., 91, 94, 136
Foster, S. L., 80, 136
Franz, E., 61, 69
Freedman, E. B., 157, 170
Freud, S., 5, 21, 75, 136
Friedman, B., 12, 21
Friedman, W., 12, 21
Fujita, F., 32, 69
Furumoto, L., 177, 204
Futterman, R., 203

Gagnon, J. H., 147–148, 154, 171
Galen, B. R., 76, 78, 80, 136
Gariepy, J. L., 76, 134
Gebhard, P. H., 167, 171
Geer, J. H., 144, 171
Geiger, T., 81, 136
Geis, F. L., 195, 204
Gelles, R. J., 9, 21
Gerber, D., 114, 138
Gergen, K. J., 5, 21
Gerson, K., 3, 21
Gibbons, J. L., xi–xix, xxiii
Gilbert, D. C., 38, 69
Gill, D. L., xxii, 9, 15, 173, 184, 185, 186, 187, 188, 190, 204, 205
Gilligan, C., 3, 5, 11, 21
Gilmore, D. D., 9, 21
Glassow, R., 180, 204
Goff, S. B., 203
Gold, D. P., 61, 69
Goldberg, P. A., 194, 204, 206
Goldberger, N. R., 3, 19
Goldsmith, H. H., 28, 69
Goldstein, H., 66, 69
Gormly, A. V., 77, 136
Gorsuch, R. L., 73
Gottman, J. M., 58, 69, 70
Gould, S. J., 12–13, 21
Graham, S., 105, 137
Gray, J., 2, 143, 171

Green, B. L., 201, 206
Greene, A. L., 36, 69
Greer, G., 156, 171
Griesler, P. C., 118, 135
Griffen, P. S., 198–199, 204
Grogg, T. M., 182, 205
Grossman, M., 10, 21
Grotpeter, J. K., 9, 20, 76, 77, 81, 83,
    84, 87, 94, 97, 98, 103, 106, 108,
    109, 110, 111, 112, 113, 118, 119, 120,
    122, 125, 126, 127, 131, 134, 136
Grych, J. H., 105, 109, 110, 111, 136,
    137
Guerra, N. G., 105, 137
Guevremont, D. D., 80, 136
Gutherie, D. M., 58, 69

Hall, J. A., 11, 21, 50–51, 55, 69, 86,
    137, 200, 204
Hallahan, M., 16, 22
Halpern, D., 7, 21
Hamer, D. H., 29, 69
Hare-Mustin, R. T., 5, 21
Harold, R. D., 192, 203
Harré, R., 29, 30, 69
Harris, D. V., 182, 186, 204
Harris, M., 14, 21
Harrison, J. M., 192, 202
Hart, C. H., 79, 101, 102, 109, 137, 138
Hartup, W. W., 79, 91, 106, 118, 120,
    121, 137, 140
Haselager, G. J. T., 121, 137
Hatfield, E., 10, 21, 59, 69
Hauer, T. A., xxi, xxiii
Haviland, J. M., 10, 23, 38, 73
Hazan, C., 10, 22
Heavey, C. L., 56, 68
Hebb, J., 59, 69
Hedricks, C., 35, 71
Heelas, P., 30, 69
Helmreich, R. L., 186, 187, 194, 204,
    207
Henley, N., 11, 21
Herzog, T., 16, 22
Heshka, S., 14, 19
Hill, S., 71
Hirsch, L. S., 71

Ho, D. Y. F., 101, 137
Hoffman, M. A., 88, 138
Hollingworth, L. S., 204
Holloway, J. B., 192, 205
Holloway, R. L., 9, 20
Holloway, W., 40, 69
Hood, J., 40, 55, 69
Horner, M. S., 187, 205
Howell, C. T., 87, 132
Howes, C., 77, 91, 97, 115, 134
Hoza, B., 91, 133
Hrdy, S. B., 146, 161, 171
Hudley, C., 105, 137
Huston, T. L., 60, 68
Hyde, J. S., 161, 167, 171, 185, 205

Jacklin, C. N., 185, 205
Jackson, A., 191, 195, 207
Jacobi, M., 177, 205
Jacobs, G., 35, 73
Jacobson, N., 56, 70
Janoff-Bulman, R., 28, 68
Jarvinen, D. W., 94, 137
Jenkins, J. M., 10, 22
Jennings, S. E., 186, 204
Jensen, K., 195, 206
Jin, S., 109, 137
Johnson, J. S., 58, 71
Johnson, V. E., 156, 163, 164, 165–
    166, 171
Joly, S., 3, 23

Kaczala, C. M., 203
Kahn, A., 17, 23
Kail, R., 91, 138
Kane, E., 146–147, 171
Kane, M. J., 194, 195, 205
Kang, L., 190, 205
Kanter, R., 11, 21
Kassin, S. M., 77, 133
Katz, L., 58, 70
Kaukiainen, A., 90, 98, 103, 133
Keating, D. P., 91, 136
Keenan, K., 90, 138
Kellerman, H., 29, 72
Kelly, L., 148, 171
Kemper, T. D., 30, 70

Kendrick, C., 114, 135
Kenyon, G. S., 182, 205
Kessler, R. C., 10, 21, 26, 45, 58, 67, 70
Keyes, C. L. M., 18, 22
Kiesler, S. B., 194, 206
Kinsey, A. C., 152–153, 156, 158, 164, 167, 171
Kite, M. E., 194, 203
Klein, S., 195, 206
Kolb, B., 8, 22
Kramer, L., 58, 70
Krebs, D., 12, 23
Kring, B., 149, 172
Krokoff, L. J., 58, 72
Ku, H., 81, 134
Kupersmidt, J., 126, 134

Ladd, G. W., 88, 138
LaFrance, M., 26, 32, 38, 39, 45, 56, 70
Lagerspetz, K. M. J., 76, 77, 92, 98, 102, 103, 104, 133, 138
Lakoff, R. T., 11, 22
Lamb, M. E., 54, 70
Landers, D. M., 197, 202
Lando, B., 114, 132
Larsen, R. J., 32, 68
Larson, R., xx, xxi, 14, 25, 32–33, 34, 35, 36, 42, 44, 49, 50, 51, 54, 57, 60, 68, 69, 70
Laumann, E. O., 147–148, 158, 167, 171
Ledingham, J. E., 86, 141
Lee, F., 16, 22, 37
Lee, M., 71, 180, 205
LeFevre, J., 35, 71
Lenney, E., 197, 205
Lennon, R., 55, 69
Lenskyj, H., 198, 205
Leong, R., 150, 171
Lerner, G., 145, 171
Lerner, H., 149, 171
Levant, R. F., 25, 71
Levenson, R. W., 27, 71
Levy-Schiff, R., 88, 138
Lewin, K., 31, 71

Lewis, L. L., 203
Lifgren, K., 88, 139
Lightdale, J. R., 6, 22
Lin, Y., 72
Linn, M. C., 185, 205
Lips, H. M., 186, 206
Loeber, R., 111, 128, 138
Lott, B., 22
Lowell, E. C., 187, 205
Loy, J. W., 182, 205
Lucas, T., 88, 138
Ludolph, P., 127, 131, 138
Lushene, R., 73
Lutz, C. A., 29, 30, 31, 40, 67, 71
Lykken, D. T, 14, 19, 28, 71
Lytton, H., 5, 22

Maccoby, E. E., 4, 22, 50, 71, 80, 91, 93, 119, 138, 185, 205
MacDonald, K., 83, 92, 98, 114, 128, 129, 130, 131, 138, 139
MacEachern, M., 71
Major, B., 6, 7, 20, 194, 203
Malamuth, N. M., 161, 170
Marecek, J., 5, 17, 20, 21, 40, 71
Mars, K. T., 88, 138
Martens, R., 182, 207
Martin, C. E., 153, 167, 171
Marty, N., 71
Masters, W. H., 156, 163, 164, 165–166, 171
Matteo, S., 194, 205
McAdams, D. P., 35, 71
McClearn, G. E., 13, 22
McClelland, D. C., 187, 205
McClintock, M., 35, 71
McConaughy, S. H., 87, 132
McElroy, M. A., 187, 205
McGonagle, K. A., 10, 21
McGuinness, D., 7, 22
McGuire, S., 113, 136
McHale, S., 114, 135
McKee, T. R., 137
McLeod, J. D., 45, 70
McNally, J., 191, 206
McNaughton, N., 29, 71

McNeilly-Choque, M. K., 79, 82, 83, 84, 89, 96, 101, 102, 118–119, 124, 137, 138
McRae, J., 26, 70
Mednick, M., 17, 22
Meece, J. L., 203
Melpomene Institute, 192, 193, 206
Messner, M. A., 195, 196, 198, 199, 206
Metheny, E., 194, 206
Michael, R. T., 147–148, 171
Michaels, S., 147–148, 171
Miller, J. G., 16, 22
Miller, N., 6, 19
Miller, N. E., 79, 135
Miller, W. I., 30, 71
Mirowsky, J., 30, 71
Misle, B., 127, 138
Money, J., 157, 158, 171
Morey, L., 129, 138
Morris, M. W., 16, 22
Mosher, M., 81, 82, 89, 95, 102, 124, 125, 134
Mowrer, O. H., 79, 135
Mueller, E., 88, 138
Munn, P., 114, 136
Myers, A. E., 186, 206
Myers, D. G., 76, 80, 138

Nadeau, A., 14, 20
National Amateur Athletic Federation, Women's Division, 180–181, 206
National Center for Health Statistics, 71, 73
Neale, M. C., 14, 19
Neckerman, H. J., 76, 134
Neiderhiser, J., 28, 72
Neilsen, A., 114, 138
Nelson, C. B., 10, 21–22
Nelson, D. A., 101, 102, 109, 124, 137, 138
Nelson, L. J., 79, 109, 137, 138
Nelson, M. B., 184, 198, 206
Nezlek, J. B., 51, 72, 74
Nicholls, J. G., 94, 137
Niemala, P., 76, 100, 133

Nix, C., 197, 202
Nolen-Hoeksma, S., 10, 22, 44, 71
Noller, P., 58, 69
Notarius, C. I., 58, 71
Nukulkij, P., 81, 136
Nyad, D., 192, 206

Oatley, K., 10, 22
O'Barr, W. M., 11, 22
O'Brien, K. M., 80, 113, 115, 117, 122, 136, 139
O'Donohue, W. T., 144, 171
Oglesby, C., 182, 206
O'Laughlin, E. M., 83, 92, 98, 128, 129, 130, 131, 138
O'Leary, V. E., 195, 207
Oliver, M. B., 161, 167, 171
Olsen, S. F., 79, 101, 137, 138
Olson, S. L., 88, 139
Olweus, D., 116, 128, 139
Orimoto, L., 58–59, 69
Orlick, T., 191, 206
Osterman, K., 90, 92, 98, 104, 133
Owens, L. D., 76, 92, 98, 104, 139

Panksepp, J., 28, 72
Paquette, J. A., 81, 139
Parke, R. D., 76, 105, 114, 138, 139
Parker, J. G., 117, 118, 119, 124, 130, 139
Parkhouse, B. L., 195, 206, 207
Parks, J. B., 195, 205
Patterson, G. R., 105, 109, 111, 112, 114, 118, 128, 135, 139, 140
Peltonen, T., 76, 102, 138
Peng, K., 16, 22
Perry, M., 78, 134
Perry-Jenkins, M., 42, 53, 60, 68, 70, 72
Person, E. S., 149, 171
Pettit, G. S., 105, 135
Pheterson, G. I., 194, 206
Pleck, J. H., 25, 54, 64, 72, 73
Plomin, R., 13, 22, 28, 72
Plumert, J. M., 106, 140
Plutchik, R., 29, 72
Pollak, R., 13, 22

Pomeroy, W. B., 153, 158, 167, 171
Ponger, B., 199, 206
Porter, C. L., 137
Prager, K., 119, 133
Prentice, D. A., 6, 22
Presser, H. B., 64, 72
Price, J. M., 79, 80, 140
Putullaz, M., 114, 140

Rabiner, D. L., 105, 140
Ragan, J., 191, 207
Ramsey, E., 112, 139
Rapson, R. L., 10, 21, 59, 69
Real, T., 61, 72
Reis, H. T., 51, 52, 72, 74
Reis, M., 61, 69
Remer, P., 199, 207
Repetti, R. L., 60, 61, 72
Reveles, M., 207
Rhode, D. L., 148, 171
Richards, M. H., 33, 34, 35, 42, 49,
    50, 51, 54, 57, 60, 70
Richter, R. R., xi–xix, xxiii
Rieser-Danner, L. A., 28, 69
Riessman, C. K., 10, 22
Riksen-Walraven, M., 121, 137
Rivers, 3, 4, 19
Roberts, L. J., 58, 72
Robins, L. N., 76, 140
Robinson, A., 12, 21
Robinson, C. C., 79, 101, 137, 138
Rockhill, C. M., 127, 131, 135
Rodin, J., 192, 201, 206
Romney, D. M., 5, 22
Rook, K., 55, 59, 72
Rosaldo, M. Z., 41, 73
Rosaldo, R., 30, 73
Rosario, V. A., 168, 170
Rosenberg, B., 117, 140
Rosenthal, R., 86, 137, 165, 171
Rosnow, R. L., 165, 171
Ross, C. E., 30, 71
Rothbart, M. K., 39, 73
Rotundo, A. E., 47, 73
Russell, G., 54, 68
Russell, S., 35, 73
Russo, N., 117, 136

Russo, N. F., 201, 206
Rutter, M., 13, 22
Ryff, C. D., 18, 22
Rys, G. S., 82, 84, 97, 125, 140

Sadker, D., 195, 206
Sadker, M., 195, 206
Safrit, M. J., 184, 206
Sampson, E. E., 40, 73
Sancilio, F. M., 106, 140
Sandvik, E., 32, 68, 69
Sattel, J. W., 56, 73
Scarborough, E., 177, 204
Schellin, H., 80, 93, 94, 98, 129, 135
Schiebinger, L., 157, 171
Schippers, M., 146–147, 171
Schnedeker, J., 71
Schneider, B. H., 82, 103, 125, 140
Schneider, S., 15, 20
Schurr, K. T., 194, 203
Schwartzman, A. E., 86, 141
Sears, R. R., 79, 135
Seid, M., 111, 137
Selman, R. L., 91, 140
Senchak, M., 51, 72
Senior, K., 197, 202
Senneville, C., 61, 69
Shaver, P. R., 10, 22
Shaw, D., 90, 138
Sheppard, S., 186, 203
Sherif, C. W., 162, 172, 178, 206, 207
Sherman, J., 177, 207
Shields, S. A., 10, 12, 23, 25, 26, 73
Shweder, R. A., 30, 73
Silberstein, L., 192, 206
Silvertown, J., 162, 170
Simon, W., 148, 154, 155, 171, 172
Singelis, T. M., 69
Slaby, R. G., 105, 137, 139
Smith, P. B., xx, xxiii
Snedecor, G. W., 84, 140
Snodgrass, S. E., 11, 23
Snyder, E., 194, 205
Solomon, B., 51, 72
Sorell, G. T., 12, 20
Spears, B., 179, 207
Spelman, E. V., 149, 172

Spence, J. T., 186, 187, 194, 204, 207
Spielberger, C. D., 35, 73
Stacey, J., 3, 4, 23
Staines, G., 64, 72
Stapley, J. C., 10, 23, 38, 73
Stearns, P. N., 47, 48, 73
Stewart, M. J., 197, 202
Stiles, D. A., xi–xix, xxiii
Stillwell, A. M., 1019
Stoneman, Z., 114, 133
Straus, M. A., 9, 21
Striegel-Moore, R., 192, 206
Strossen, N., 158, 172
Sullivan, H. S., 113, 140
Sutton-Smith, B., 117, 140

Tarule, J. M., 3, 19
Tavris, C., xxi, 1, 9, 11, 13, 23, 153, 172
Tellegen, A., 28, 71
Thoma, S. J., 12, 23
Thomas, D. L., 32, 73
Thomas-Knowles, C., 30, 67
Thompson, A. T., 58, 73
Thompson, E. H., Jr., 25, 73
Thompson, E. P., 47, 73
Thompson, H., 207
Thompson, L., 61, 73
Thorne, B., 40, 50, 64, 73, 91, 140
Tiefer, L., xxi, 12, 15, 17, 23, 143, 149,
    150, 153, 162, 163, 172
Tomada, G., 82, 103, 125, 140
Tougas, F., 3, 23
Travis, C. B., 201, 207
Tremblay, A., 14, 20
Tresemer, D., 187, 207
Trevethan, S. D., 12, 23
Triandis, H. C., 16, 23
Trujillo, C., 192, 207
Turnage, K. D., xxi, xxiii
Turner, R., 60, 73
Twenge, J. M., 3, 23

Uhlir, G. a., 184, 207
Underwood, M. K., 76, 78, 80, 81,
    136, 139
Unger, R., 5, 23, 149, 172, 195, 207

Vagg, P. R., 73
Valenstein, E. S., 17, 23
Van Brakel, J., 30, 73
Van Heck, G. L., 73
Van Lieshout, C. F. M., 121, 137

Waas, G. A., 106, 140
Wade, C., 13, 23
Wade, M. G., 182, 207
Walker, L. J., 12, 23
Wallston, B. S., 194–195, 207
Walters, R. H., 75, 132
Wark, G. R., 12, 23
Wasik, B. H., 88, 140
Weinberg, R. S., 191, 207
Weiss, R. S., 49, 53, 73
Weisstein, N., 178, 207
Werner, N. E., 80, 81, 92, 93, 94, 98,
    107, 119, 122, 127, 128, 129, 130,
    131, 134, 135, 139, 140
West, C., 6, 23
Westen, D., 127, 138
Wethington, E., 58, 67
Wheeler, L., 51, 74
White, G. M., 29, 73
Widom, C. S., 186, 202
Wiley, D. C., xi–xix, xxiii
Williams, J. M., 195, 206, 207
Williams, R., 156, 172
Willis, J. D., 187, 205
Wilson, E. O., 160, 172
Wittig, A. F., 194, 203
Wolfe, D. M., 56, 67
Wood, W., 10, 21
Woodworth, R. S., ix–x, xx, xxiii
Worell, J., 199, 207
Wotman, S. R., 10, 19

Yang, C., 102, 109, 137
Yoder, J., 17, 23
Younger, A. J., 86, 141

Zahn-Waxler, C., 122–123, 141
Zhao, S., 10, 21
Zimmerman, D. H., 6, 23